Uncle Leroy's

CARTER FAMILY SCRAPBOOK

Ye ole Dinosaur

Patricia Carter

Heritage Books
2025

HERITAGE BOOKS
AN IMPRINT OF HERITAGE BOOKS, INC.

Books, CDs, and more—Worldwide

For our listing of thousands of titles see our website
at
www.HeritageBooks.com

Published 2025 by
HERITAGE BOOKS, INC.
Publishing Division
5810 Ruatan Street
Berwyn Heights, MD 20740

International Standard Book Number
Paperbound: 978-0-7884-4707-5

Special Thank You to

Mark Carter

&

Douglas Moore

For generously sharing research, photos and family stories.

I greatly appreciate your contributions.

Table of Contents

Leroy Carter Family

Back row: Julina Isabella (Issy), Thomas Alfred (Dick), Marion Columbus (Lum), James Walter (Jim), Harriet Athelene (Athey)
Front row: Nancy Corine (Corny), James Gilbert Leroy Carter, Mary Means Cooley Carter, Ardora Florence (Dora)

Family photo published in the Carthage Press newspaper on November 4, 2007

Carter Family Timeline

Norman invasion of Yorkshire England in the 11th century
Cartar family of blacksmiths at Easingwold, Yorkshire
Anglicization of southern Wales

William Cartar moved to London
Howell Griffith becomes a quaker preacher
1675 – William Cartar married Catherine Lash

1682 - Begin quaker migration to the new Province of Pennsylvania
Cartars settle in Bucks County
1684 - Howell Griffith imprisoned @ Haverfordwest Jail in Wales - released & migrated to Chester, PA

1696 - John Griffith moves from Chester to Bucks Co.
1702 - James Cartar, son of William & Catherine marries Susannah Griffith, daughter of John & Catherine

1732 - John Cartar, second son of James & Susannah marries Alice Nelson, daughter of Henry Nelson and his first wife Alice Hayhurst

1742 - Widow Alice Nelson Cartar marries widower Joseph Yates
1746 – Cartar / Yates family moves to western Loudoun County, Virginia Colony

1756 - James Carter the third son of John Cartar & Alice marries Hannah Eblen, eldest daughter of John & Mary Warner Eblen

1811 - James Carter 2nd the youngest child of James & Hannah marries Sarah Jane Myers and moves to Hampshire County, Virginia

1817 – James Carter 2nd family moves to Franklin County, Ohio – severe flooding & crop failures

1830 – James Carter 2nd family moves to Marion County, Indiana
1839 – sons Lemuel and Salathiel convicted of arson based on circumstantial evidence
1839 – Lemuel purchases 40 acres in Jasper County, Missouri, rest of family moves to Missouri

1848 – Lemuel, Salathiel, Washington & Alfred were early participants in California Gold Rush

1849 – Leroy marries Mary Means Cooley daughter of Samuel Means Cooley & Margaret Rusk Cooley

1861 – 1865 – Civil War – Leroy was held as a prisoner by the confederates (1863)
1863 – 1865 – Refugees at Fort Scott, Kansas

1865 – Leroy begins construction of two story home on Center Creek

1880 – Lum marries Elmeda Hester Motley

1906 – 1912 – Lum's family homesteads in Dora, New Mexico Territory – return to Jasper Co., Missouri

1921 – Oscar marries Ethel Grace Sims

Chapter 1 – Acknowledgements

Bi-centenary Memorial to Jerimiah Carter who came to the Province of Pennsylvania in 1682
A Historical-Genealogy of his descendants down to the present time
By Thomas Maxwell Potts
Published by the Author
Canonsburg, PA 1883

Carter Cousins 1681 – 1989 Volume 1
By Marie Thompson Eberle & Margaret Shipp Henley
Timbercreek Ltd.
Miami, Oklahoma 1989

The Diary of Calvin Fletcher 1817 - 1866
By Calvin Fletcher
Indiana Historical Society
Indiana University Press

Encyclopedia of American Quaker Genealogy Volume II – Pennsylvania
by William Wade Hinshaw & Thomas Worth Marshall Editor
Genealogy Publishing Company
Baltimore, Maryland 1991

History of Hampshire County, Virginia - From its earliest settlement to present
By Maxwell Hu & H. L. Swisher
A Brown Boughner, Printer
Morgantown, West Virginia 1897

History of Jasper County, Missouri and its people Volume II
Mineral Township
By Joel Thomas Livingston
Lewis Publishing Company
Chicago, New York, San Francisco 1912

Journal & Letters of Phillip Vickers Fithian 1773 – 1774
A Plantation Tutor of the Old Dominion
University of Virginia Press
Charlottesville, VA

Hopewell Friends History 1734 – 1934 Frederick County, Virginia
Records of Hopewell Monthly Meetings and Meetings Reporting to Hopewell
Two Hundred Years of History and Genealogy
Compiled from Official Records by Joint Committee of Hopewell Friends
Assisted by John W. Wayland
Printed by Heritage Books in 2007

Virginia Genealogist April-June 1997   Volume 41   Number 2
Article by Thomas Katheder
Virginia Genealogist October-December 2003   Volume 47   Number 4
Article by Thomas Katheder

Bureau of Land Management website – Sales of Public Lands with Township & Range

Genealogy Libraries – Morman Genealogical Libraries; New England Genealogical Society

Genealogy Websites – Ancestry.com; Family Search; My Heritage; Find-a-Grave; Genealogy Bank; newspapers.com; Wikitree

Jasper County, Missouri Plat Maps

State Records & Archives - Birth & Death Certificates; Wills and Deeds

US Census Records – early Census records only list the Head of Household by name, with a date range given for other members of the family.

Chapter 2 – Dates

The subject of dates is a Pandora's Box of misinformation. The Julian Calendar began on January 1st in the year 45 BC during the reign of Julius Cesear. This calendar continued to be used for fifteen hundred years. Every fourth year was a leap year which resulted in three extra days accumulating every four hundred years. Over the centuries the dates designating the Winter Solstice and the Summer Equinox no longer matched the actual dates that these celestial events occurred.

In 1582 Pope Gregory XIII corrected the calendar by removing ten days and not adding an extra day if the centennial year was not divisible by 400. The years 1600 and 2000 were both divisible by 400 so these years included a February 29th and were leap years. The years 1700, 1800 and 1900 were not divisible by 400 so these years did not include a February 29 and were not leap years. By not adding three days every four hundred years, dates on the Gregorian calendar continue to match celestial events. Different countries made the change to the Gregorian Calendar at different times with the English making the change in the mid 1700's. The English needed to remove eleven days in order to bring their calendar back in sync with celestial events.

For centuries, the English had used a regnal year on legal documents. The year was expressed as the '*year in the reign*' of the monarch. To convert the regnal date to the calendar year one needs to know when the monarch's rule began.

Elizabeth I	ruled from November 17, 1558 until her death on March 24, 1603.
James I	ruled from March 24, 1603 until his death on March 27, 1625.
Charles I	ruled from March 27, 1625 until he was deposed and decapitated on January 30, 1649.

England was without a monarch from January 30, 1649 until the monarchy was restored in 1660. During this time Oliver Cromwell acted as Lord Protector of the Commonwealth until his death on September 3, 1658. Oliver Cromwell was followed by Richard Cromwell. Parliament invited Charles II to return after nine years in exile.

Charles II	ruled from May 29, 1660 until his death on February 6, 1685.
James II	ruled from February 6, 1685 until overthrown on December 23, 1688.

England was without a monarch until Parliament designated co-regents Mary II and her husband William III. Their rule lasted from February 13, 1689 until William III's death on March 8, 1702.

Anne	ruled from March 8, 1702 until her death on August 1, 1714.
George I	ruled from August 1, 1714 until his death on June 11, 1727.
George II	ruled from June 11, 1727 until his death on October 25, 1760.
George III	ruled from October 25, 1760 until his death on January 29, 1820.

Quakers opted to use numbers to designate the month instead of the Julian names which they considered to be pagan words. Early twentieth century genealogists thought that they needed to 'correct' Quaker handwritten dates. They assumed that the 1st month meant March not January. On at least one Certificate of Transfer from the Ashwith Monthly Meeting in Yorkshire County, England to the Middletown MM in Bucks County, Pennsylvania the date was written as:

> *"… meeting at Askwith in the County of York and Kingdom of England this 26th day of 5th month called July 1683."*

Several other Certificates of Transfer from the Settle MM located in the Yorkshire countryside include in parentheses the words (*English Account*) after the date.

Prior to the reign of Elizabeth Ist the majority of the English peasantry were illiterate. During the sixteenth century, English was just beginning to be used as a written language. A few pages of the Bible had been translated into English and writers such as William Shakespeare were producing works written in English. Under James Ist the entire Bible was translated into English. The newly developed printing press allowed for mass reproduction of the King James version of the Bible. This Bible fostered an increase in literacy. The proliferation of trade guilds whereby individuals were paid for their labor also contributed to an increased need for literacy.

Illiterate individuals had little need for a calendar. The Catholic Priests recorded statistics about births, marriages and deaths and told the peasantry when to celebrate Holy Days. For forty-six years, during the reigns of James Ist and his son Charles Ist the regnal year began in March. The concept that the regnal year changed with each new monarch may not have been fully understood. Many of the early quaker leaders were not highly educated. The individuals who wrote the Certificates of Transfer using March as 1st month may have been the first literate person in their family.

It is unknown how many colonial Quaker documents were written with 1st month indicating March or if this was a rarity, with the 1st month usually meaning January. In the *Encyclopedia of American Genealogy,* Thomas W. Marshall comments that he did not think the labeling of March as 1st month was very widespread. The use might have been limited to parts of New Jersey, Pennsylvania, and the rural English Countryside. Quaker documents viewable on Ancestry.com are recorded assuming that 1st month meant March.

The Gregorian calendar was adopted by the English in September 1752. It has been assumed that 1st month meant January for all dates after 1752. Early twentieth century typed copies of documents show that an attempt had been made to 'correct' older dates. Should January and February be recorded as the first two months of a year as on the calendar or as the last two months as in a regnal year? Most secondary documents list two possible years (example: 1702/1703). Quaker dates prior to 1752 should be consider approximations.

In this Scrapbook most of the names and birthdates for Carter family members living in Bucks County, Pennsylvania and in Frederick County, Virginia come from *Carter Cousins* by Marie Thompson Eberle and Margaret Shipp Henley. This source has been cited by many other researchers. Most of the information shows up in several genealogy databases with the original source being the work of Eberle and Henley. Some of the names have been corroborated by Wills, Deeds, and county tax records. A second often cited source is the *Bi-centenary Memorial to Jerimiah Carter* by Thomas Maxwell Potts. These two sources clash at times making different family connections. Every researcher has made their own interpretation of the limited original data so different conclusions are possible. Information found in secondary sources is often not documented, but has been repeated as if it were factual.

Chapter 3 – Quaker Documents

Most images of Quaker documents are images of copies recorded in a Public Registry. The handwriting was done either by a quaker scribe or by the county clerk. These are not images of original documents. One clue is if the document starts in the middle of a page following information about another individual. Another clue is if the signatures of witnesses all look like they were written by the same person. The entire document including all signatures had been written by a clerk. A third clue is the word *'seal'* surrounded by curlicues. The original piece of paper probably had a few drops of candlewax embossed by a stamp next to the signature. When monarchs passed away their clay seal was immediately broken. Individuals could have had their own wax seals.

Researchers are often disappointed to see a large X in the middle of a signature with the words *'his mark'* or *'her mark'*. This does not necessarily mean that the person was illiterate. Instead the signature was written by a clerk and the X indicates that this is not an original signature nor is it a forgery. This document is just a copy written into a Public Registry. The bound journal made it easier to relocate information by date and location. Original pieces of paper had probably been folded in half, then in thirds and small stacks of folded documents were then tied with string and stored in a drawer. Original deeds would have been kept by the buyer as proof of ownership of the land.

The subject of dates arises again concerning the date on an image of a Will. Most Quaker Wills end with wording similar to: *'Signed, Sealed and Published this day, month and year.'* This sounds like it should indicate the date that the will was written but instead in some cases the date may be when the will was recorded in the Public Registry. Many of the wills are then *'proved'* a few days later although some are not proved for several weeks or months. The term *'proved'* means that some of the witnesses have attested (or sworn) that this was the Last Will and Testament of the deceased. *'Proved'* does not mean when the will was finalized. A Probate Inventory and Sale of Personal Property usually took place after the will was proved.

Codicils were used to make changes to the original will. Instead of re-writing the entire will, the individual just added a codicil to amend or change the distribution of his property. Some wills include a line disclaiming any previous will(s) that the individual may have created. Since there only appears to be only one surviving version of a will, it seems that wills were not recorded in a Public Registry until after the individual died.

There are at least four slightly different images of the Will of James Carter Sr. Two typed copies are credited to Hinshaw's efforts in the early twentieth century. The other two copies were handwritten. One typed and one handwritten copy each bear the date September 16, 1812 which has been included in genealogy databases as James Carter Sr.'s date of death. The other two copies each bear the date July 24, 1812. On both dates, Mahlon Carter acting as the Executor of his father's estate, filed probate records with the Court. The son would not be filing probate records while his father was still alive. September 16, 1812 was not James Carter Sr. date of death. July 24, 1812 was probably when the traveling Circuit Judge came to town to provide annual legal services. James Carter Sr. most likely passed away before the July 24th date even though that is the date on one handwritten copy. Mahlon organized probate documents before the Circuit Judge arrived. During five months traveling around the county, the traveling journal had been subject to rain, wind, dust etc. After the Circuit Judge returned to the Courthouse in Leesburg, the documents were re-copied into a pristine new bound ledger with the September date.

Among the images of early Quaker documents some of the handwriting appears to have been done with quill pens while other images look more like the handwriting was done with metal tip pens. The 'quill pen' images have bolder lines and larger lettering. Some words run together while other words have a break in the middle. These documents include the words *'ye'*, *'thence'* and *'said'*. The dates are always written as day, month then year. The language usage has a 'Shakespearian vibe'. Documents which look like they were written with a metal nib have finer lines and smaller more scrunched lettering. They rarely have the words *'ye'* or *'said'*. Dates are usually written as month, day then year. The 'metal nib' documents lack the 'Shakespearian vibe'.

In the *Encyclopedia of American Quaker Genealogy*, William Wade Hinshaw explains that during the early twentieth century, quakers began compiling old documents in preparation for their two hundredth anniversary. Old documents were deteriorating and barely legible. Various individuals worked on different collections. Some worked on Pennsylvania documents while others worked on Virginia documents, or Ohio documents etc. From this work in compiling documents William Hinshaw is credited with creating the typed copies of old quaker documents. It seems that some of the documents were also rewritten by hand. Unfortunately those rewritten documents are not correctly labeled as twentieth century re-copying.

In the *Hopewell Friends History 1734 – 1934* there is a good list of the various Quaker Monthly Meeting places. The mother church is listed along with the Monthly Meetings which reported back to that church. The mother church for the Hopewell MM was in Cecil County, Maryland. Hopewell MM was the mother church for Fairfax MM located at Waterford in Loudoun County, Virginia. One might have expected the Fairfax MM to have been located in Fairfax, Virginia not in Waterford. Goose Creek MM was located in Lincoln about eight miles southwest of Waterford. Then another eight miles southwest of Lincoln, the South Fork MM was located near modern Unison. Amos Janney is credited with starting the Fairfax MM. The early Fairfax MM did not report back to a mother church so the area was considered in the 'verge' of the Hopewell MM.

Secondary sources usually locate the Goose Creek MM at Unison not at Lincoln. When in 1835 the Monthly Meeting was disbanded for lack of membership, it was the South Fork MM that was disbanded not the Goose Creek MM. Per the *Hopewell Friends History,* the Goose Creek MM was still in existence in the early twentieth century. Secondary sources claim that the behavior of members at the Goose Creek MM was troubling. There were non-approved events such as summertime horse races down main street complete with betting, public drinking and the shooting off of firearms. One cannot be sure whether the location was Lincoln or Unison.

The typed compiled records for Fairfax MM includes information from South Fork MM and Goose Creek MM. Likewise the typed compiled records for Hopewell MM includes information from Apple Pie Ridge MM and Monoquacy River MM. The handwritten compiled records for Middletown MM includes information from the Falls MM and Wrightstown MM. Early records for Chester, Pennsylvania appear to be lost or no longer available. Per a list of records at Swarthmore College, some early Chester quaker records should be available under the label Concord MM, Kennett MM or Chichester MM. The available New Garden MM records for Chester County do not begin until about 1730. Welsh quaker records in Pennsylvania are under the label Gwynedd MM or Uwchlan MM.

These compiled records lead to confusion as to which Monthly Meeting an individual was a member of and where the original information should be located. Example: The handwritten compiled Middleton Monthly Meeting contains information which should have been recorded in the Falls MM since the individuals were living closer to Neshaminy Falls than to Newtown.

Partial List of Quaker Meeting Places – extracted from *Hopewell Friends History 1734 – 1934* and *Encyclopedia of American Quaker Genealogy*

Pennsylvania
Abington – Montgomery Co., PA
Bradford – PA – w/ Sadsbury, Uwchlan & Robeson formed East Caln MM
Byberry – 1683 – Philadelphia Co., PA
Buckingham – 1720 – Lahaska, Buckingham Twp, Bucks Co., PA
Caln –1784 – Chester Co., PA
Center – Chester Co., PA
Chester = Chichester - Delaware Co., PA
Concord – Chester Co., PA
Darby Creek – 1682 – near Philadelphia, PA
Duck Creek – Smyrna, Lancaster Co., PA
Exeter – 1781 – Berks Co., PA

Falls – 1683 – Neshaminy Falls, Bucks Co., PA
Goshen – Chester Co., PA
Gwynedd – prev. North Wales – Montgomery Co., PA
Horsham – Montgomery Co., PA
Kennet – Kennet Square, Chester Co., PA – originally New Castle
Little Britain – Lancaster Co., PA
Maiden Creek – Berks Co., PA
Middletown – 1683 – Newtown, Bucks Co., PA
New Garden – Chester Co., PA
Philadelphia – 1682 – Philadelphia, PA
Providence – Montgomery Co., PA
Radnor – Haverford, PA
Richland – Bucks Co., PA
Solesbury – Bucks Co., PA
Upland – Chester, PA
Uwchlan – 1720 – in Welsh Tract – near Chester, PA
West Grove – Chester Co., PA

Delaware & New Jersey

Burlington – 1678 – Burlington Co., NJ
Chesterfield – Burlington Co., NJ
Evesham – 1760 – Moorestown, NJ
Haddonfield – Camden Co., NJ
Kingwood – Hunterdon Co., NJ
Moorestown – NJ – prev. known as Chester
Mount Holly – Burlington Co., NJ
Salem – 1636 – NJ
Upper Eveshaw – later Medford – near Haddonfield, NJ
Wilmington – Newcastle Co., DE

Maryland

Bush River – Harford Co., MD – west side of Susquehanna River
Cecil – 1698 – Cecil Co., Md
Deer Creek – Harford Co., MD
East Nottingham – Cecil Co., MD – mother church of Hopewell
Gunpowder – Baltimore Co., MD
Monoquacy River – 1762 – MD
Nottingham – 1730 – Cecil Co., MD – formed from E. Nottingham & W. Nottingham & Bush River
Pipe Creek – Carroll Co., MD

Virginia & West Virginia

Alexandria – 1802 – Woodlawn, Fairfax Co., VA – moved to Alexandria, VA
Back Creek – 1777 – Gainsboro, Frederick Co., VA
Bullskin – Charles Town, Jefferson Co., VA – renamed Berkeley
Center – 1819 – Winchester, VA
Crooked Run – 1759 – Nineveh, Warren Co., VA
Dillon's Run – 1800 – Hampshire Co., WV
Fairfax – 1735 – Waterford, Loudoun Co., VA – started by Amos Janney
Goose Creek – c.1750's – Lincoln, Loudoun Co., VA – started by Jacob Janney
Gravel Springs – SW Frederick Co., VA
Great Cacapon – Hampshire Co., WV
Hopewell – c.1744 – 7 mi NE Winchester, Frederick Co., VA – J. Chenowith, A. Hollingsworth & A. Ross
Little Cacapon – Hampshire Co., WV
Lupton – Lower Ridge, Apple pie Ridge – Frederick Co., VA
Middle Creek – 1778 – Arden, Berkeley Co., WV
Mills Creek – 1761 – Berkeley Co., WV
Mount Pleasant – 1771 – Frederick Co., VA SW of Winchester

North Fork – Hampshire Co., WV
Potts = Gap – c.1768 – Hillsboro, Loudoun Co., VA
Providence – Montgomery Co., PA
Ridge = Apple Pie Ridge – SW of Winchester, VA
Smith's Creek – c.1738 – Shenandoah Co., VA
South Fork – Beaverdam Creek, Unison, Loudoun Co., VA
Tuscarora – Martinsburg, WV

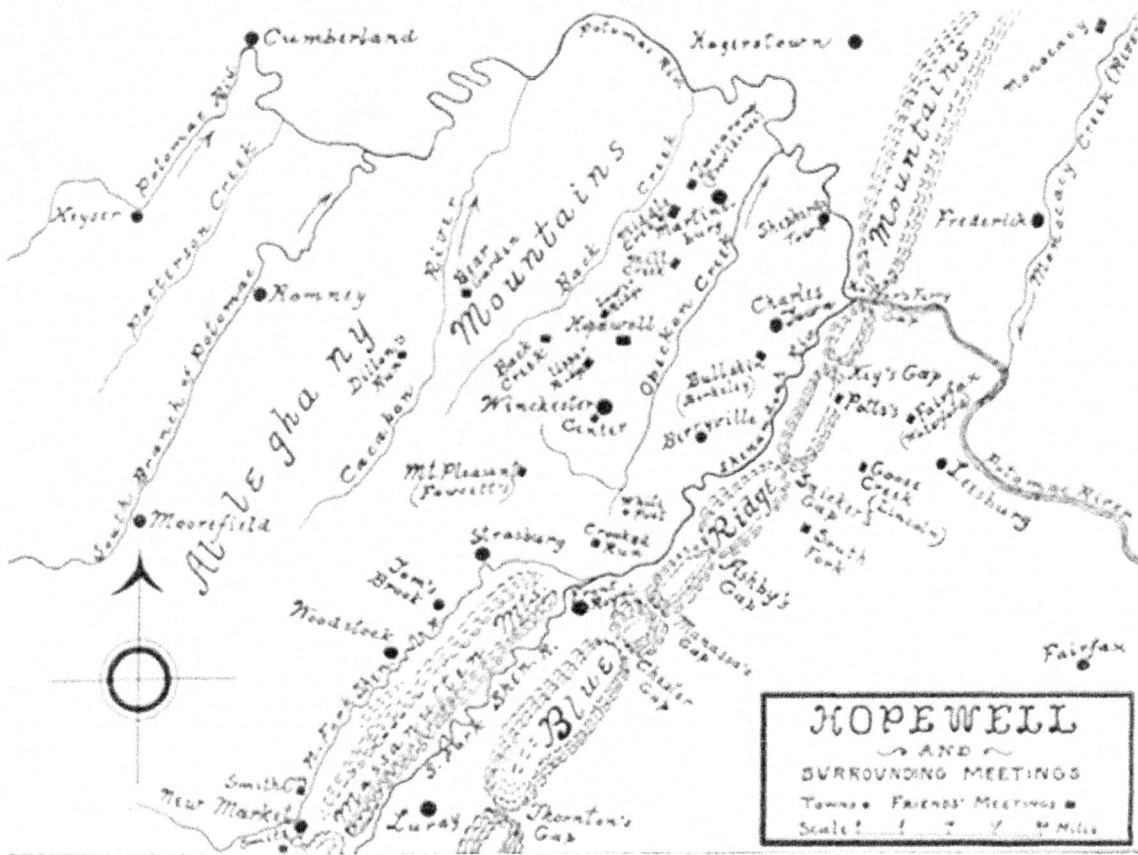

Map from *Hopewell Friends History*

Chapter 4 – Introduction

This is a scrapbook collection of facts and family lore about Leroy Carter. Included is information about his immediate descendants and his ancestors going back to the original Carter immigrants who arrived in North America in the 1680's. For years this Carter family could only be traced back to western Loudoun County, Virginia. Finally realizing that a date cited as a birthday was not correct allowed for the connection with two previous generations. An attempt has been made to weed out misinformation.

English families in the seventeenth and eighteenth centuries usually named their first son after the paternal grandfather, the second son after the maternal grandfather and the third son after the father. This practice resulted in multiple individuals with the same name – fathers, sons, cousins, and members of different families. When life expectancy was less than fifty years this naming practice did not create too much confusion. As life expectancy increased this naming convention created identity problems. Younger individuals would often add a modifier to their name to distinguish themselves from an older individual. Examples: William Carter of Wapping, Charles Carter of Cleves and Robert Carter of Nomini.

In the 1800's middle names came into use to distinguish a new baby from an older relative with a similar name. The repetition of names has resulted in facts being attributed to the wrong individual. Some researchers have added the mother's maiden name as a child's middle name. Some researchers have added a person's occupation as a middle name. Leroy Carter's ancestors followed the naming convention until James Carter 2nd and his wife Sarah Jane chose to use biblical names. The full truth may not be known, but interesting details link the family to significant events in American History.

Cartar or Carter as a surname originated as a description for individuals who pushed hand carts. The last name traces back to both Roman and Norman usage. Many Carter heraldic emblems include greyhounds as a sign of speedy transport. Other emblems display chariot wheels. The existence of over twenty heraldic emblems suggests multiple origins as honors to different Carter families. On Wills recorded in Pennsylvania the family name was usually spelled Cartar but once family members moved to Virginia and beyond the spelling is Carter.

The Carter family journeyed across the Atlantic Ocean in small seventeenth century wooden ships. Voyages usually took two months. Longer sailings often resulted in food shortages, outbreaks of disease, and the filling of the ships' hold with waste. There are accounts of smallpox outbreaks which resulted in multiple deaths at sea. The

Carter's were people of grit and perseverance, they overcame obstacles to carve out a life in the wilderness. They crossed a continent on horseback and by walking along side wagons pulled by oxen. Carters' established communities and commerce sought fortunes and lost much along the way but always remained a family.

At the beginning of the sixteenth century, Martin Luther posted his list of suggested reforms for the Catholic Church. One reform was to end the practice of Papal Indulgences whereby a sinner could pay a large sum to the Catholic Church to have his sins absolved. This practice of priests and popes praying to God on behalf of a person who paid for the Papal Indulgence upset the Christian beliefs of many. Another contentious issue was the mandatory payment of tithes to the Catholic Church. The protestant Anabaptist movement originated in the Black Forest region of the Holy Roman Empire. The Anabaptist believed a person should consent to baptism. They stopped the ritual of sprinkling holy water on babies. As the Dark Ages ended the Catholic Church emerged extremely wealthy while European peasants were struggling to survive.

When German Princes tried to create a unified nation out of the Holy Roman Empire, the residents of the Black Forest region did not want to be forced under the control of outside Princes. Unlike most of Medieval Europe, the residents of the Black Forest had enjoyed semi-autonomy. Not being under the control of a local prince had contributed to a sense of self responsibility. That sense of self carried over to the religious belief that each individual possessed an inner light and could communicate directly with God. There was no need for priests or popes to intervene and pray on an individual's behalf. The notion that a church hierarchy was unnecessary scared society elites. The upper classes expected to be treated with deference and respect. Equality was a frightening concept to those who had only known privilege. In the seventeenth century there were mass migrations of Anabaptist away from the Black Forest. Some migrated eastward, some migrated northward, crossing the Channel into England.

The term Anabaptist has loosely been used to denote several religious sects including the Huguenots, the Mennonites, the Amish, and the Society of Friends. In most colonial texts the term Anabaptist refers to the Society of Friends. Englishman George Fox is credited with starting the Friends of the Truth in mid-seventeenth century England. The name was later changed to Society of Friends. Members have long been referred to as the Quakers. After seeking answers from various priests, ministers and teachers, George Fox concluded that he could become a minister without first acquiring a college degree. Following Jesus Christ's example of preaching out in the open, George Fox traveled around England and Wales preaching a life of simplicity and peace. He preached that everyone possessed an inner light of Godliness, and that individuals should look for that inner light in others. Many of his early converts were females who often became preachers. The early services were a gathering of individuals listening to a preacher. By the eighteenth century colonial quaker services were often quiet contemplative times where anyone could speak if they desired.

Early Society of Friends burial grounds in England included grave markers carved with the name and dates of birth and death. George Fox's grave was marked with a headstone. Several of the old burial grounds have since been converted into landscaped gardens. In at least one cemetery the grave markers were moved over next to a wall, so they no longer designate the actual site of burial. In the American colonies the quakers did not erect grave markers, nor did they place field stones to mark the site of graves. Instead, they kept written records of who was buried within the burial ground.

The Society of Friends in England endured a period of 'sufferings' in the mid-seventeenth century. The Quaker Act of 1662 made it illegal to refuse to swear an oath of Allegiance to the Crown. Quakers would not use the word 'swear', instead they would 'attest' to the truth. The refusal to use the word swear was one of their most ardent beliefs. The Conventicle Act of 1664 made it a crime to hold secret meetings. The Quakers openly professed their faith with many of their services held outdoors. Many quakers were jailed, often for refusing to swear allegiance. Some quakers openly denounced the ministers of other faiths, or engaged in other deliberately provocative behavior.

In the seventeenth century it was a common practice in England for poor parents to send their children into indentured servitude. The child was expected to learn a trade with which they would be able to earn a living. The child's apprenticeship might begin as young as age eleven with the child remaining an indentured servant until they reached the age of twenty-one. Some early quakers owned slaves, and those who could afford the expense hired servants. Members of the Society of Friends became early and very vocal opponents to slavery. Prior to the Civil War many of the safe 'depots' on the Underground Railroad were quaker farms.

English men were not considered responsible adults until they reached the age of majority – twenty-one years of age. English Common Law did not allow men to own or inherit land until they reached the age of majority. Men usually did not marry until after they had established a means of earning a living, with most men marrying in their mid to late twenties. Girls were considered marriageable at the age of eighteen. Most girls married between the age of eighteen and twenty and often to a man a few years older than themselves. There are records of girls as young as sixteen getting married, with an adult guardian attesting that the girl was old enough to marry. These young girls were often orphans being raised by relatives.

Females did not own land with the exception of widows inheriting land in order to care for their underage children. However, the sale of land required the wife's signature, which was usually indicated by an X. Females simply were not present at the document signing and the male witnesses attested that the female had given her consent. Also, females were not considered capable of conducting business on their own. Men handled the business and legal matters on behalf of females.

Quakers kept detailed written records of births, marriages, and deaths in bound journals, but only for individuals who were members of the Society of Friends. For non-quaker immigrants to North America the records are usually only land transactions, wills, and tax rolls that were copied into a Public Registry.

Writing with a quill pen an 'e' is easier to form than an 'a'. To prevent ink blots the writer needs to have the quill pen in motion as the tip touches the paper and continue in motion as the quill is lifted away. Many of the swirls and extra 'e's at the beginning or end of words are attempts by the writer to prevent ink blots. Seventeenth century documents are often difficult to read due in part to breaks in the middle of words, words which are linked together, and the legalese of the time. The swirls at the bottom of documents may have been a way to drain excess ink from the quill to prevent ink from drying inside the quill. An attempt to keep the quill usable as long as possible.

In the seventeenth century the spelling of words including names often varied wildly. The copy of his 1714 Will starts with James Cartar's name spelled Carter but ends which his name spelled Cartar. Documents exist showing Cartar as the spelling of the last name for both James and his sons William, John and Benjamin, but land deeds usually have the family name spelled Carter. First names are often abbreviated – as an example 'Samuel' would be written as Saml with the 'l' being raised. 'The' was written as y^e. The small 'c' looked more like a small 'i' with an accent mark above it. The small 'd' looks more like a small 'c' followed by a closing parenthesis 'c)' with a long tail.

Quaker Wills usually start with praise to God, followed by referring to one's wife as *'dearly beloved'*. The wife is given the right to continue to live on the estate and is often provided a small annual stipend. The eldest son receives most of the property, is expected to maintain the estate and pay the stipend to his mother. If an individual had been successful then he might provide other pieces of land to younger sons. Otherwise younger sons and grandsons received cash. Daughters and granddaughters usually only received a small amount of cash and possibly a feather bed or a milk cow. Stepchildren were not included in the will.

King Charles II of England owed a substantial debt to William Penn's late father Sir William Penn. Instead of trying to recover the 16,000 pound debt, the younger William Penn asked for a grant of land in North America. William Penn was a friend of the Duke of York. He surprised his colleagues by joining the Society of Friends. In 1681 he received a charter from King Charles II to form a new colony in North America as a refuge for the persecuted Quakers. William Penn requested the release of numerous prisoners, both members of the Society of Friends and other religious dissidents. He also recruited individuals from a wide variety of labor guilds. William Penn wanted his colony to quickly become independent from England and not to remain reliant on resupply ships.

The Carter family story in North America begins with the arrival of James Cartar to the newly chartered Province of Pennsylvania in the early 1680's. The exact date of his arrival is not known, ship manifests only listed the names of a few passengers. Most of the original settlers arrived in 1682 aboard the twenty plus ships that made the crossing. The next few years brought hundreds of additional settlers. James Cartar's kinsman William Carter of Wapping arrived in July 1682 aboard the ship *Providence*. John Lash was also listed as a passenger. Lash was probably related to Catherine Lash who had married William Carter in London on April 1, 1675. William and Catherine were probably James Cartar's parents. The family most likely arrived in Pennsylvania at the same time as William Carter of Wapping. Wapping is a neighborhood of east London. William Carter of Wapping was a London Solicitor and as a friend of William Penn, he actively helped recruit migrants. The Cartar family were not members of the Society of Friends. The family had been recruited for their blacksmithing skills. James Cartar, Robert Carter and his son John Carter are noted as being blacksmiths.

William Penn arrived in Pennsylvania in October 1682 aboard the ship *Welcome*. First order of business was to negotiate a peaceful treaty with the Leni Lenape Indians. As a term of the treaty, the Indians could continue to use the land for hunting. After the settlers acquired hogs, the Indians 'hunted' and killed the domesticated hogs.

William Penn proposed the form of government with a constitution defining the rights of the settlers. The document was a Charter of Privileges allowing all men the right to vote. This Charter of Privileges reflected wording similar to the Magna Carta written in 1215 to protect the landed gentry from capricious behavior by a monarch. Concepts in the Magna Carta were later incorporated into English Common Law over the centuries. Unique to the Charter of Privileges there would be no standing army nor required military service. Prisoners were to be taught a trade with which they could earn a living. Education was intended to teach skills useful for employment. This included education for the children whose families were not members of the Society of Friends.

William Penn designed a wide street plan for the City of Philadelphia. He included public squares and parks with plenty of outdoor space. He believed green outdoor space would be healthier for citizens than the cramped squalor many had left behind in London. North of the City of Philadelphia, William Penn set aside 40,000 acres for the Welsh. The Welsh quakers who settled in this area came mostly from North Wales. In this Welsh Tract the settlers tried to speak and conduct business only using the Welsh language, at least for a while. Eventually English speakers moved into sections of the Welsh Tract. An additional 15,000 acres were set aside for German speakers. This German Tract is known as the Germantown section of Philadelphia.

William Penn also granted several tracts of land in Bucks County to the Society of Free Trade. These business tracts were located near Doylestown, New Britain, Hilltown and Durham. James Claypool, who served as the Treasurer of the Society of Free Trade wanted to establish a glass house to manufacture bottles, drinking glasses and windowpanes. He also wanted to establish a cordage mill and a metal works.

Chester County and the town of Chester lie to the southwest of the City of Philadelphia. The town of Chester became the poorer neighborhood. There were smaller lots and individuals who could not afford to buy land were allowed to rent lots in Chester. Chester may also have been the site of the first wharf where the majority of the early migrants came ashore. Bucks County, which lies to the northeast of the City of Philadelphia was first settled as a wealthier enclave. Some of the earliest settlers had purchased their land from William Penn before leaving England. William Penn located his own estate in Bucks County. Not all of the settlers to Bucks County were wealthy. The Certificate of Transfer for Martin Wildman called him a poor man, industrious and generous but very poor.

William Penn was not considered a very good, or detail oriented manager. After less than two years, Penn left the Colony and returned to England. Willian Penn was dismayed to discover many more religious dissidents in jail. He renewed his effort to get prisoners released from English and Welsh jails. When he finally returned to his colony eighteen years later, Philadelphia was a vastly different highly prosperous city.

The majority of the early immigrants to Pennsylvania were quakers, and they dominated the government for some time. Infractions which resulted in a person's name being recorded in the quaker minutes included fornication, public drunkenness, and bearing firearms. Sex outside of marriage seems to have been a major community issue. There were also numerous citations for men drinking too much. Otherwise quaker communities were relatively safe places to live. Quakers willingly paid taxes to build public facilities such as schools, churches, and court houses. They worked together to keep dirt roads passable. Quakers balked at paying taxes to support a military or pay restitution to soldiers for their service.

In only a few years the Pennsylvania Colony was thriving with the settlers producing most of the food and goods they needed. The colony was then able to export extra goods to the colony on Jamaica which remained dependent on resupply ships. Philadelphia became a thriving successful port city.

Not to romanticize conditions, seventeen century life was not easy. The first Welsh settlers to arrive in Pennsylvania dug caves along the riverbanks to live in until they could build a log cabin. Once a family moved into their new cabin, they would rent out the cave to the next wave of settlers. The cabin was usually one small room with a large stone fireplace. The fireplace was used for both heating and cooking. Sparks from the fire could easily burn structures down or catch long skirts on fire. Plus, there was the constant inhalation of wood smoke. The first settlers did not bring livestock with them. When a dairy cow was obtained from another colony, the milk and cream would be shared by several families. Within a few years any farmer who wanted livestock was able to obtain cows, hogs, sheep and horses.

The location where a family obtained water, whether from a natural spring or directly from a river or later from a dug well, influenced their chance of developing agues and fevers. Waste was dumped into the rivers creating sanitation problems. Philadelphia has a long history of annual yellow fever outbreaks. Over the years several attempts have been made to clean up the rivers and creeks and to stop the dumping of trash into the waterways. Work of all forms was labor intensive. Caring for animals and garden patches, hand sewing, cooking and butter churning, plowing fields, felling timber, and chopping firewood – all manual labor. In the early days walking was the only form of transportation until the settlers acquired horses.

James Cartar probably arrived as a young child along with his parents, whom I assume were William Cartar Sr. and his wife Katherine. James probably also had a brother - William Cartar Jr., and several uncles – Edward Carter, Robert Carter and William Carter of Wapping. James also had at least two sisters who were mentioned but not named in William Carter of Wapping's will. A 1687 map of Bucks County by Thomas Holmes shows both William Carter and Robert Carter owning land along the east side of Neshaminy Creek near the falls in the Warminster township. In March 1712 a portion of the Warminster township was disjoined to become the Southampton township. The early immigrants who arrived in 1682 had probably settled temporarily in Chester County. Then as more immigrants arrived a group of the earlier arrivals would move further inland. The Thomas Holmes map of Bucks County looks like a planned community. Each parcel of land was connected to a river or creek – giving each landowner water rights. Newtown was laid out as a town surrounded by farms. William Cartar's land lay between land belonging to quakers Henry Paxson and John White. The earliest Cartar blacksmith forge had probably been in Chester County. After the family moved to Bucks County, the blacksmith forge was probably located in the town of Durham.

Some historians assume that the William Carter land in Bucks County belonged to William Carter of Wapping, but he was known to have built his home near the wharf in downtown Philadelphia. His home was located between Second Avenue and Chestnut Street which were connected by Carter Alley. Most historians consider William Carter of Wapping to be the only William Carter among the original immigrants. He was a wealthy, well connected friend of William Penn. In Philadelphia he actively engaged in the affairs of the city, serving as a Sheriff in 1686, an Alderman starting in 1701, an Associate Judge, and even the Mayor of the City of Philadelphia in 1710. In 1721 he was Clerk of the Market, collecting rents from vendor stalls at the Capitol.

The City Council for Philadelphia was designated a Corporation and William Carter of Wapping served as an Alderman for about twenty years. Each year the Corporation would elect one of their members to serve as Mayor for the following year. Concerns of the Corporation included bridges, waterways, wells and street maintenance. In 1687 the Corporation decided that "... *ye caves on the banks were esteemed to be worth the building.*" They decided to assess property tax on caves being used as homes. The caves had been dug into the sides of the Delaware River and served as protection from the elements until a more suitable house could be built. The city of Philadelphia was divided into wards for tax purposes – Mulberry, Walnut, Roxborough, Southwark East and Southwark West, etc. Dwellings, servants, negros, horses, cows, rents and mills were taxable.

The Corporation dealt with complaints about carts that were overloaded with wares. The carts were traveling too fast causing the roads to develop ruts which then needed to be repaired. Some citizens laid cobbles on the roads in front of their homes in an attempt to reduce the problem. There are records of problems with an old well which would best be resolved by digging a new well, but the old well needed to remain usable until the new one could be dug. The Corporation dealt with the same type of issues city councils continue to deal with, how to raise funds and provided the community with needed services.

William Carter of Wapping married widow Mary Sutton on July 28, 1721 as recorded in the Philadelphia Arch Street MM. His name appears on many land deeds and transactions. In his six page will written in December 1738, William Carter of

Wapping lists his kinsmen Robert Carter, Edward Carter, and William Carter deceased. He provided for the two unmarried daughters of William Carter. This will suggests that there was an older second William Carter among the early settlers of Pennsylvania. Actually, there appear to have been at least three early William Carter settlers. One died in December 1718, one died in June 1729 and then William Carter of Wapping died in December 1738. The deaths of the first two William Carters plus one Katherine Carter are listed in the Philadelphia MM under the heading: *Burials of Such as not Friends*. Today that title seems a bit derogatory but actually it was just quaker shorthand. Until city and county governments were better organized, the Quaker Monthly Meeting Records included the deaths of non-quakers. William Carter of Wapping did not have any children so he made generous donations to the City of Philadelphia.

In April 1717 William Carter Jr. was *'admitted to freedom'*. In May 1717 his wife Elizabeth was also *'admitted to freedom'*. They were allowed to become members of the Society of Friends. The Katherine Carter who died in July 1720 was noted as the widow of William Carter. Some researchers claim that Katherine Carter was the first wife of William Carter of Wapping. Since she died first, she would not have been called his widow. The *Bi-Centenary Memorial to Jeremiah Carter* lists a second Katherine Carter who arrived as a servant to John Blunston. She was most likely an underage, indentured servant. In Philadelphia she first married Edward Turner and later married John Baldwin. From these small bits of information, I have concluded that James Cartar's parents were probably the William Carter who died in 1718 and the Katherine Carter who died in 1720. There were other early Carter immigrants to Pennsylvania, many were members of the Society of Friends and most came from the area around London. Some historians suggest that the Carters were descendants of Ancel Carter, who has been described as a North London Grocer.

Early in the seventeenth century, Ancel Carter owned Oake Farms in North London. Today Oake Farms is located near the town of Kettering in Northamptonshire County. Ancel Carter held a Royal Patent as a Vintner – an importer of wine who agreed to pay the crown five percent. Since there were a limited number of patents, this was a lucrative business. Bootleggers did not have royal patents and if caught bootlegging the punishment was torture and death. History suggests that Ancel Carter may be the relative who financed John and Thomas Carter's migration to the Virginia Colony in 1635. Anyone who paid for a migrant's passage was entitled to a headright of 50 acres of land in the Virginia Colony. Thomas and John Carter first settled in the Norfolk area. Then in 1650 when the Northern Neck was opened to English settlement, Thomas Carter patented over 10,000 acres and created Barford Plantation. Thomas Carter sold half of his Northern Neck land to John Carter who started Corotoman Plantation. John Carter's second son Robert was the well documented 'King' Carter of Colonial Williamsburg infamy. Many but not all of the Carters of colonial Virginia were the descendants of

Thomas and/or Robert Carter. Descendants of Thomas and Robert Carter dominated the tidewater and eastern counties of colonial Virginia. Descendants of the Cartars from Pennsylvania migrated to the western areas of Loudoun and Orange Counties. The heirs of Ancel Carter may have financed the migration of some of the early Carters who settled in Pennsylvania.

James Cartar's family may actually have had their origins in Yorkshire County, England. Vikings had invaded the area and remained, becoming known as the Norman invasion. Vikings were known for their blacksmithing skills, especially for making swords. A farm in Easingwold may have been home to the earliest members of this Cartar family. In Yorkshire the names William Carter and Robert Carter repeat over the centuries. DNA analysis of modern descendants suggests a large Scandinavian heritage, without any known Scandinavian names in the family tree. One Viking trait that seems to have been passed down is strong shoulder and bicep muscles. Many of the original immigrants to Bucks County, Pennsylvania came from Yorkshire, England. The Monthly Meeting records for Settle, a town near the Yorkshire Forest, contain the names Heaton, Hayhurst and Wildman. The names Easingwold and Easington refer to the same English town.

Chapter 5 – James and Susannah Cartar Family

James Cartar married Susannah Griffith in the fall of 1702 in Bucks County, Province of Pennsylvania. The exact date was not recorded in Quaker minutes. James Cartar was not a member of the Society of Friends, so for Susannah the marriage was considered *'out-of-unity'* and she was subsequently disowned. Since the Griffith family home was near Neshaminy Falls, the record of Susannah being disowned should have been in the Falls MM, but that record no longer seems to be available. Being disowned does not mean being shunned. The disowned individual was encouraged to attend meetings, admit their transgression, ask for forgiveness and ask to be readmitted.

Some sources list James Cartar's birth year as 1675, other sources list the year as early as 1670 without any documentation. I suspect that his brother William Carter Jr. was probably older than James. If the parents married in 1675 then William Jr.'s birth was circa 1676 and James birth circa 1678. James Cartar had probably been born in London, England. As an adult, James Cartar worked as a blacksmith, which means that his father William Sr. and brother William Jr. were probably also blacksmiths. The birth dates for the children of James and Susannah were not recorded in Quaker minutes. James Cartar listed his children in his will.

Susannah Griffith was the daughter of John Griffith and his wife Catherine. Various sources claim that she had been born in Pembrokeshire County, Wales on October 4, 1681. Her older sister Ann had also been born in Pembrokeshire five years earlier. These birth records come from the Parish of Egglows and list the child's names along with the father's name but not the mother's name. Egglows is an English mispronunciation and misspelling of the Welsh town Eglwyswrw - a small parish near Cardigan on the north coast of Pembrokeshire. I doubt that these parish records are actually for this family. The Griffith last name is quite common in Wales. If the family was from northern Pembrokeshire then one would expect that they only spoke Welsh. Parish records in Wales were probably Catholic records. Quakers in Pennsylvania did not use the term parish.

Wales has a long history of having been invaded, first by the Romans, then by Vikings, by the Flemish and by the English. The Romans mined iron ore, copper, and gold. The English extracted coal. Henry Tudor, who became Henry the VII of England, was born at Pembroke Castle on January 28, 1457. *"A future King of Wales who could speak no English."* By the seventeenth century the southern coasts of Pembrokeshire and neighboring Carmarthenshire County were home to many English speakers. English continues to be widely spoken along the southern coast.

The Griffith family settled in English speaking areas of Pennsylvania which suggests that the family was either English or they migrated from the southern coast of

Wales. Some researchers have tried to link the family to the famous Welsh Prince of Gwynedd – Llywelyn Gruffudd who was born circa 1223. Llywelyn Gruffudd was the only Welsh King to rule over all of Wales at a time when part of England was Welsh territory. His son David later lost the Cotswolds' in a battle with the English. John Griffith's parents are believed to have been Llewelyn and Mary Griffith. Some sources provide other names for his parents. Susannah and Ann also had a sister Mary about whom very little is known. Some websites have also added another sister Sarah, born in February 1679 in Pembrokeshire about whom less is known. Some websites spell Catherine with a 'K' and list her as Katherine Ann William from Merionethshire, Wales - an area which only spoke Welch well into the twentieth century. The John Griffith family had probably settled in Chester before moving to Bucks County. Early Chester, Concord, Chichester or Kennett MM records no longer seem to be available.

There was a second John Griffith who arrived in Pennsylvania after 1700 along with his brothers Griffith and William Griffith. These Griffiths were members of the nonconformist Welsh Baptist Sect from Trevelyan located near Cardiff in South Wales. They settled in Chester County. It has been suggested that these brothers were also descendants of Llywelyn Gruffudd.

There was a third John Griffith who died in Bucks County in 1738. His will was dated 4 month 1st day 1738 and proved on September 9, 1739. He was a miller married to Ann and his will lists three children – Hannah, Sarah and Samuel. His estate was to be sold with his wife receiving one third and his three children splitting the remaining two thirds. There were several John Griffiths both in Wales and in Pennsylvania during the seventeenth and eighteenth centuries. The existing records are difficult to read and confusing as to who is directly related to whom across the centuries.

John Griffith's older brother was Howell Griffith. Howell was incarcerated in the Carmarthenshire Jail for preaching the quaker religion. Some sources claim Howell was incarcerated in Haverfordwest jail in 1684. Haverfordwest is the largest town in southern Pembrokeshire. Howell Griffith's name was included on the ship's log, possibly because he was a quaker preacher. John Griffith's family most likely arrived in Pennsylvania at the same time as Howell Griffith's family – approximately June 1684. Howell is believed to have settled in Chester. There do not appear to be any records of either family moving to the Welsh Tract. Secondary sources claim Howell Griffith was married to Gwendolyn Ann and their known children include: Ann, Abraham, Evan, Diana, Patience, Ellen, Catherine, and John. It is unknown if this John Griffith was the individual who died in Bucks County in 1738.

John, Howell, and Howell's son Abraham were cordwainers. The cordwainer guild worked with leather mostly crafting new shoes. By contrast the cobblers guild repaired old shoes, often replacing the soles. As William Penn had envisioned, Philadelphia quickly became a thriving port city. The residents were able to raise and craft most of the products they needed and then the surplus was shipped to Jamaica to supply some of that colony's needs. In only a few years the farmers and craftsmen were earning considerably more than they might have expected to earn had they remained in England or Wales.

This new wealth allowed some men to purchase larger tracts of land and move away from crowded Chester. On March 3, 1689 approximately five years after arriving in Pennsylvania, Howell Griffith purchased a lot on High Street in Philadelphia. Howell probably semi-retired as a cordwainer, but he most likely continued preaching. High Street was later renamed Market Street. Market Street was a fashionable location in the heart of the English speaking city. Years later Benjamin Franklin and his wife Dorothy built their new house on Market Street.

In March 1696 John Griffith purchased 290 acres in Bucks County from Israel Taylor. Israel's father Christopher Taylor was one of the gentlemen to whom William Penn had allocated large tracts of land for redistribution to others. An earlier researcher had drawn a star on the Thomas Holmes map of Bucks County. The star was on one of several parcels labeled *'Taylor'*. The land was above Neshaminy Falls next to land labeled *'Widdow Hurst'*. This may indicate ownership by Mary Rudd Hayhurst, the widow of prominent quaker preacher Cuthbert Hayhurst Jr. In a letter William Penn referred to his friend as *'Cut Hurst'*. This parcel of land was near land owned by the Plumly family and across the creek from the land owned by William Cartar.

Quakers in Southampton Township were members of the Falls MM. After moving to Bucks County, John Griffith semi-retired as a cordwainer. He continued to make a few pairs of shoes for family but not extra pairs for export. He served on a Bucks County Grand Jury in 1696. Two years later he was asked to be a Constable for Southampton Township, but he *'pleaded his age'* and was excused from service.

On May 7, 1696 Susannah's older sister Ann Griffith married James Heaton. James Heaton had been born on December 25, 1674 in Yorkshire England. He was the second son of Robert Heaton Sr. and his wife Alice. The marriage was considered out-of-unity because James Heaton had been disowned by the quakers. Heaton family lore suggests that James Heaton had fathered a child but didn't marry the mother. A typed copy of *Bucks County Common Plea Court Records* has a judgement against James Heaton for fathering a child with his cousin Mary Scaife, who at the time was under eighteen years of age. The child John Heaton was born circa 1695. James Heaton was ordered to pay three pounds plus the court fees. It might have been James' older brother Robert Heaton Jr. who had been the actual rogue. As the second son, James might have agreed to assume the disgrace to protect the family's good name and reputation. If the Egglows Parish birth record was for this Ann Griffith, she would have been about twenty years old when she married.

James Heaton and his brother Robert Heaton Jr. are credited with building the first grist mill in Bucks County. The mill was located on Chubb Run in the valley south of the Middle Lots. The area was later renamed Langhorne Manor. In 1709 the Heaton brothers built a second grist mill on Core Creek. This mill was located at Bridgetown between Durham Road and Neshaminy Creek. There are accounts of farmers from New Jersey crossing the Delaware River by raft in order to bring their grain to one of the Heaton Mills to be ground into flour.

On June 6, 1702 as recorded in the compiled Middletown MM Men's Minutes, John Griffith asks the Quaker elders for advice. His daughter Susannah had 'entangled' herself with a man who was not a member of the Society of Friends. In September 1702 a group of quaker ladies spoke with Susannah trying to convince her not to marry outside of the faith. They reported back that Susannah's mind seemed to be made up. If the birthdate of October 4, 1681 is correct then Susannah would have been about twenty-one or twenty-two when she and James Cartar married. I suspect she was probably closer to eighteen. She certainly sounds more like a giddy teenager than an adult. This opens the possibility that Susannah was not born until after the family arrived in Pennsylvania. If only early Chester MM records were available. I also suspect that there were other children besides Mary, Ann and Susannah. Many children died young from smallpox, whooping cough, agues, fevers and other diseases.

In 1702 John Griffith sold 50 acres of his Southampton land to his daughter Mary and son-in-law Samuel Griffith. Samuel Griffith later sold the 50 acres to James Cartar who bequeathed it to his second son John. Samuel Griffith's parentage remains undetermined, however he might have been the son of the third John Griffith noted above. From this land transaction it appears that Mary was probably older than Susannah. At least she had married earlier. Mary's birth does not appear to have been recorded in the Parish records at Egglows which adds to my doubt that those records were for this family. Since Mary and Samuel were both quakers, one would expect to find record of their announcement of intention to marry in the Monthly Meeting either in one of the Chester congregations or the Falls MM.

Samuel and Mary Griffith are difficult to trace. There were several Samuel Griffiths and also several Mary Griffiths in Bucks County. Most of the available records appear to be for the next generation(s). There was a Samuel Griffith noted as a shoemaker who acquired 300 acres in the New Brittain township of Bucks County on July

28, 1738. This date coincides with the possibility that he received a portion of the third John Griffith's estate.

In 1704 James Cartar purchased 250 acres in Solebury Township of Bucks County from Francis White. Solebury township along the Neshaminy Creek is located north of Northampton township. Then in 1706 John Griffith sold most of his remaining 240 acres in Southampton Township to his son-in-law James Cartar. John Griffith reserved about three acres for the use of himself and his wife. This included land for firewood, a meadow, a garden plot, and the east end of the dwelling house. The Griffiths missed their daughter and wanted to have some influence on the education of their grandchildren. In 1709 James Cartar sold the 250 acres in Solebury township to George Brown.

Secondary sources claim that Catherine Griffith died about 1708. One would expect her burial to have been recorded in the Falls MM. Quakers usually waited a full year before remarrying. On October 6, 1709 John Griffith received permission to marry twice widowed Elizabeth Vail Gach. The marriage was recorded in New Jersey, on October 20, 1709. Most researchers consider the marriage to have been a Civil Ceremony, but the couple appear to have been members of the Woodbridge MM. Quaker marriages might be included in county records in New Jersey. The couple settled in Woodbridge township in East Jersey. John Griffith's name appears in the Woodbridge MM records in support of the building of a new meeting house.

John Griffith died on August 20, 1713 in Woodbridge. His will was recorded and proved in Bucks County, Pennsylvania. This will is clearly for Susannah's father. Son-in-law James Heaton was one of the executors along with his second wife Elizabeth. The will names his daughters: Susannah Carter, Ann Heaton, Mary Griffith and Martha Griffith. Martha Griffith was probably Elizabeth's young daughter. The will also mentions cousin Abraham Griffith. Ephraim Heaton, the younger brother of Robert Heaton Jr. and James Heaton was one of the witnesses to the signing of the will. There is no mention of Sarah Griffith, she was probably the miller's daughter, a sister of Samuel Griffith.

To complicate matters further, on the Find-A-Grave website a headstone in the First Presbyterian Church Cemetery of Elizabeth, New Jersey has been cited as being for this John 'Cordwainer' Griffith. The faded inscription says *"John Griffith Born in New Castle, England and died in this town"*. The same Find-A-Grave image lists his birth place as Eglafing, Bavaria, Germany. Confusing. Welch, English or German? I think information about several John Griffiths has been merged together and may be difficult to untangle. It makes no sense for a body to have been transported about ten miles from Woodbridge for burial in Elizabeth, New Jersey. The grave marker states that the body buried in Elizabeth, died in Elizabeth. Susannah's father was probably buried in a quaker burial ground with no grave marker. The death of John Griffith may have prompted James Cartar to write his own will in order to protect his family should he pass away unexpectedly.

The known children of James and Susannah:

1.	William Cartar	born circa 1703	d. March 1749
2.	**John Cartar**	born circa 1705	d. before 1742
3.	James Cartar II	born circa 1706	d. 1758
4.	Richard Cartar	born circa 1707	d. circa 1787
5.	Joseph Cartar	born circa 1709	d. 1781
6.	Ann Cartar Hibbs	born circa 1710	d. after 1766
7.	Benjamin Cartar	born circa 1712	d. before November 1748

Seven children born in about thirteen years of marriage. The order and dates of their births are just estimated. James Cartar's Will was recorded with the date of December 1, 1714. William was named as his eldest son. The rest of the children are listed as: John, Ann, James, Richard, Joseph and Benjamin. This may not be their birth order. Most researchers have placed Richard as the youngest.

James Cartar named Jeremiah Langhorne as one of the Executors of his will. Langhorne was a prominent landowner, a member of the Council of Bucks County, the Colonial Assembly and a Justice of the Peace. His name appears on several Bucks County Wills as either Executor or witness. Jeremiah Langhorne was also an original investor and part owner of the Durham Iron Company. Jeremiah Langhorne never married. He owned several negro slaves whom he named in his own will providing them with small parcels of land. Most of his landholdings went to his nieces and nephews. Langhorne Manor was named after Jeremiah Langhorne.

In 1727 the Durham Iron Company installed the first blast furnace for producing 'pig iron'. There had been an earlier iron works which had produced smaller batches of 'sponge iron' in the centuries old process known as 'iron bloomery'. Sponge iron was produced at lower temperatures than pig iron. Sponge iron still had impurities and needed to be hammered and reheated several times. This process of hammering and reheating was known as 'working the iron' which produced 'wrought iron'. As a blacksmith James Cartar would have worked sponge iron to create wrought iron objects.

James Cartar died before March 1715 when his will was proved (see Chapter 11). The surviving copy of his will is in a bound ledger book, so the handwriting is that of a clerk. At the top of the will his name is written as James Carter, but at the bottom the spelling is James Cartar. Eldest son William was slated to inherit 200 acres and a white mare when he turned twenty. William was then expected to be able to pay each of his five youngest siblings 15 pounds of silver money when they matured. Second son John was to inherit 50 acres when he turned twenty-one. Daughter Ann was to inherit a feather bed, and the executors were instructed to build her a new house on his plantation. The residual of his personal Estate was to be divided equally among his youngest sons – James, Richard, Joseph, and Benjamin.

To his dearly beloved wife Susannah, James bequeathed a feather bed of her choice plus a docile horse with saddle and bridle. Also, she would receive one third of James' estate for the maintenance of herself and the education of their children. The math is a bit fuzzy but eventually those forty acres were to be shared by the surviving younger sons. Somehow Susannah managed to care for, feed, clothe and keep her children out of trouble for the next five years. Susannah must have had some assistance with difficult tasks such as felling trees for firewood. These seven children all survived to become adults and raise children of their own.

On August 6, 1720 Susannah Cartar married widower Robert Heaton Jr. as recorded in the Middletown Monthly Meeting - *"marriage of Robert Heaton and Susannah Carter orderly accomplished."* The *Bi-centenary Memorial to Jeremiah Carter* lists Susannah Carter as the widow of Henry Carter. Henry was a brickmaker who was buried on 27th day 3rd month 1709. Thomas Potts does not include the maiden name of this second Susannah Carter nor does he provide the names of her children.

Susannah had been accepted back into the Quaker fold. First she had needed to admit that her first marriage was wrong and then listen to that marriage being condemned. Susannah became stepmother to Robert's four surviving children. It would have been a noisy household with so many teenagers. Two of Robert's daughters soon married. Grace Heaton married Jeremiah Croasdale on September 22, 1720 and then Sarah Heaton married Joseph Walker on January 3, 1722. Susannah seems to have remained close to her stepdaughters per her own will written more than forty five years later.

Robert Heaton Jr. inherited land in Northampton township. Besides being a farmer and miller, Robert Heaton Jr. served two terms in the Pennsylvania legislature. About six months after marrying, Susannah gave birth to a son. As noted in the Middletown MM on April 3, 1721 *"Robert Heaton hath had a child born about six months after marriage, which being a public scandal upon truth."* Both Susannah and Robert Heaton Jr. were disowned by the Society of Friends. Robert Heaton Jr. vehemently protested that he had done nothing wrong. He named the child Robert Heaton III. Quakers living in Newtown and in the Northampton township were members of the Middletown MM.

Robert Heaton Jr. had been born on June 3, 1671 in Clapham Parish, of West Riding in Yorkshire County, England. He was the eldest son of Robert and Alice Heaton. The Heaton family had been members of the Settle Monthly Meeting. Gentleman Robert Heaton Sr. purchased over a thousand acres directly from William Penn before leaving England. The Heaton family arrived in Pennsylvania aboard the ship *Lamb* on October 22, 1682. Robert Heaton Sr. purchased over 200 acres in Bucks County from original purchaser Robert Holdgate. The Heaton family appears to have been relatively wealthy, owning several parcels of land. Robert Heaton Sr. died in Bucks County in July 1717. Alice Heaton died in July 1727 as recorded in the Middletown MM. Alice Heaton had probably been a member of the Robert Heaton Jr. and Susannah household from the time of her husband's death until her own death.

Robert Heaton Jr. had married Grace Pearson on May 8, 1700. On April 6, 1706 the Middletown MM records a discussion with Robert Heaton Jr. concerning a claim by former servant Elizabeth Seelock. She had come forth with a charge that Robert Jr. had committed adultery with her. Robert was not dismissed for this infraction.

Grace Heaton and five of their children died in 1719. Secondary sources claim that the winter had been bitterly cold and then a smallpox epidemic swept through the colony. Grace Heaton died in February 1719. The five children died in the fall. The quaker MM records the deaths as the date of burial. The dates of birth are recorded in the compiled Middletown MM but one cannot be sure of the month, because of the 1st month dating controversy. Note that the birthday given for the eldest son Joseph was before the first marriage date – no explanation, nor any explanation for his being named Joseph.

Known children of Robert Heaton Jr. and Grace:

1.	Joseph Heaton	b. February 3, 1697	
2.	Sarah Heaton Walker	b. September 28, 1701	d. 1768
3.	Grace Heaton Croasdale	b. August 6, 1703	
4.	Elizabeth Heaton Noble	b. August 15, 1705	
5.	Alice Heaton	b. October 30, 1708,	d. September 1719
6.	Robert Heaton III	b. 1710	d. September 1719
7.	Mary Heaton	b. 1712	d. September 1719
8.	Thomas Heaton	b. 1714	d. September 1719
9.	Isaac Heaton	b. 1716	d. October 1719

Susannah and Robert Jr.'s known children:

1.	Robert Heaton III	b. circa February 1721	d. May 26, 1764
2.	Alice Heaton Plumly	b. August 30, 1723	
3.	Anna Heaton Dunn	b. July 5, 1726	d. August 16, 1813

Most sources have Alice as older than Robert III, but a photocopy of a few pages from a history of the Robert Heaton family supplies the dates of birth for both Alice and Anna. This history does not provide Robert Heaton III's birthday but does state that he was only nineteen when he married Jemima Nelson in 1740, which would imply the birth year of 1721. Today it seems odd to reuse the names of children but to the quakers they were honoring an ancestor. In this case Robert Heaton Jr.'s father Robert Sr. and his mother Alice. Alice Heaton, the daughter of Susannah, married John Plumly Jr. in 1739 and they had eleven children. Anna Heaton married Ralph Dunn Jr. out of unity. The Middletown MM record dated December 7, 1744 - *"Informed Robert Heaton hath been at the marriage of his sister who went out from amongst Friends with her marriage."*

In his will written on March 17, 1743 (see Chapter 11), Robert Heaton Jr. bequeaths to his wife Susannah the east end of his dwelling house with all the household goods, the garden and firewood plus a cow and heifer. Susannah was also to receive twenty pounds annually during her natural life. To his daughters Sarah Walker and Grace Croasdale he gave 50 pounds each. To his daughters Elizabeth Noble and Alice Plumly he gave 5 shillings each. To his unmarried teenage daughter Anna Heaton he bequeathed 170 pounds. To his son and heir Robert Heaton III he bequeathed the remainder of his estate. Robert Heaton Jr. made no mention of his Cartar stepchildren although William Cartar was one of the witnesses to the signing of the will. He also does not mention Joseph Heaton.

On the Wikitree website Alice Heaton, the daughter of Grace Pearson, was listed as the wife of John Plumly Jr. who was the son of John Plumly and Mary Bainbridge. The first Alice Heaton died in 1719 when she was only eleven years of age. It was the second Alice Heaton, the daughter of Susannah, who married John Plumly Jr. in 1739. It was the second Robert Heaton III who purchased 378 acres in Orange County, Virginia from John Frost. If his birth was in 1721, then Robert Heaton III would not have been eligible to purchase land until after he turned twenty-one in 1742. The land may have only been an investment, it is questionable as to whether he actually ever lived in Virginia. He had two infants sons to care for in Pennsylvania. On March 25, 1742 Robert Heaton III's name appears on a Fredericks County Road Work Order to lay out a road from Parkins Mill to Kersey Ferry. This may simply indicate that his name is on the county record as the owner of the land on Back Creek, even if he was not actually living in Virginia. After his father died in 1743, Robert Heaton III spent the rest of his life in the Pennsylvania Province.

On January 6, 1740 the second Robert Heaton III married Jemima Nelson, who is listed as the daughter of Henry Nelson and his second wife Alice Wildman Nelson. On some websites Jemima has been given the middle name of Wildman. When they married Robert Heaton III was nineteen and Jemima was only sixteen. It seems Robert Heaton III was following in the behavior of his father pressuring young ladies. Jemima wisely insisted on marriage first. Henry Nelson attested that Jemima was old enough to marry. Jemima Nelson is believed to have been born on January 23, 1724. The Quaker birth record lists the name as Jeremiah Nelson. Was Henry Nelson so desperate for a son that he named his fifth daughter Jeremiah? Robert Heaton III and Jemima had two sons: Robert Heaton IV was born in 1740, and Thomas Heaton was born in 1742. The naming of their second son Thomas suggests that Jemima's biological father's first name might have been Thomas. The name Thomas Wildman does not show up in the existing quaker records. In colonial times if an infant's mother died the family would ask another mother who was nursing her own child to take in and nurse the infant. If Jemima's last name wasn't Nelson it need not have been Wildman either.

In Henry Nelson's Will his daughter's name is spelled Gemimah. The birth record with the name Jeremiah appears to have been an early twentieth century recopy – the date is listed month, day, year. The whole controversy over Gemimah's parentage may have been caused by an early twentieth century copyist misreading the original script and assuming that the name was Jeremiah not Gemimah. When someone added the middle name Wildman that added to the speculation about her parentage. Since Henry Nelson had named his own son Thomas, his father's first name might have been Thomas. When Gemimah died in 1742, she and Robert Heaton III were living in the Byberry township located north of the City of Philadelphia. Robert Heaton III married Ann Carver on April 2, 1747, as recorded in the Middletown MM.

Children of Robert Heaton III and Gemimah

1.	Robert Heaton IV	b. November 24, 1740
2.	Thomas Heaton	b. October 26, 1742

Children of Robert Heaton III and Ann

1.	Isabel Heaton	b. May 24, 1748
2.	Susannah Heaton	b. May 11, 1750
3.	John Heaton	b. June 30, 1752

Some genealogy websites erroneously list James Carter 'blacksmith' and Susannah Carter as being members of the Quaker Hopewell Monthly Meeting in Virginia or as members of the Opequon Friends. It is unlikely that either of these two individuals were ever in Virginia. Their namesake grandchildren and great grandchildren were more likely the individuals who joined the Hopewell Society of Friends near Winchester.

James Cartar 'blacksmith' died a decade before white settlers began moving into the northern and western sections of the Virginia Charter.

Benjamin Franklin moved to Philadelphia in 1723, a seventeen year old runaway from indentured servitude at his older brother's print shop in Boston. At first, he worked for other printers, then in 1729 Benjamin began printing the *Pennsylvania Gazette* newspaper. From 1732 to 1749 he printed annual editions of *Poor Richards Almanac*. Franklin's target audience were the residents of the City of Philadelphia, Bucks County, Chester County and Philadelphia County, in the Province of Pennsylvania.

As Philadelphia became crowded, many quakers chose to move to the New Jersey Colony, and then down the coast to the Maryland Colony, rather than moving further inland. In 1722 Robert Carter of Williamsburg, Virginia aka 'King' Carter (unrelated) acting as land agent for Lord Fairfax, began surveying the Indian lands in the northern portion of the Virginia Charter. The British Governor of the New York Colony had recently signed a second 'Great Wampum' treaty with the Iroquois. This treaty assured that the Iroquois would remain north of the Potomac River. In exchange the Iroquois thought they were securing the Ohio Country as their hunting grounds forever. By 1722 the Tuscarora of the North Carolina piedmont had already moved north to become known as the sixth tribe of the Iroquois. The Algonquins of Virginia were not a party to the treaty, and as white settlers moved into the northern Virginia Territory, the Algonquins moved into Ohio.

Sixteen year old George Washington participated in the land surveys of what became Loudoun, Berkeley, and Hampshire Counties. As the land was surveyed starting from the southeast and heading to the northwest, Robert Carter along with a half dozen other wealthy Virginia plantation owners patented large tracts of land. They subdivided the land into approximately 200-acre plots which were then offered for lease. The lease terms were for 99 years or three generations. Robert Carter hoped to attract Huguenots who were starting to settle in central Pennsylvania. Robert Carter wanted future generations to own land, not just the eldest son. Robert Carter ended up owning about 300,000 acres before his death on August 4, 1732 at the age of 69. Quakers were attracted to the northwestern portion of Prince William County which was first renamed Fairfax County and then later renamed Loudoun County.

After quaker leaders Alexander Ross and Morgan Bryan became aware that Robert Carter was having the Indian lands surveyed, they decided to ask for a land grant. They went to the governor and council of Virginia in 1730 and received a grant of 100,000 acres along the Opequon River near modern Winchester. This newly available land attracted more quakers settlers. The area was originally part of Orange County, then a portion of Orange County was renamed Frederick County in 1738. Frederick County wasn't officially organized until 1743. As settlers purchased land, the acreage was first surveyed to prevent later property line disputes. Brothers Joseph, Benjamin, James II and Richard Cartar plus half-brother Robert Heaton III all purchased some land and lived in northern Virgina near the Opequon River.

When Lord Fairfax arrived from England following the death of Robert Carter, he assumed that he owned all of the land listed in his English Charter. This caused some confusion as to the ownership of the 100,000 acre land grant to the quakers. In October 1754 Lord Fairfax re-granted the lands to the Quakers already living on the acreage in what was then Frederick County, Virginia Colony.

White settlement in Berkeley and Hampshire Counties remained limited due to the constant threat of Indian attack. The French and Indian Wars started in 1754 with the Iroquois wanting to force the Algonquins out of the Ohio Country. During the seven years of fighting, British Redcoats occupied New England residences. They took over homes, farms, and food supplies without compensation. No individual landowner was prepared to feed hundreds of extra mouths for years. After the fighting ended, England decided to keep a standing army on the North American Continent and expected the colonies to pay for their deployment. Colonists felt that they had contributed sufficiently to the war effort and that idle soldiers were more of a threat than a form of security. The behavior of the Redcoats created resentment and a growing desire for independence from Britain. When the Constitution of the United States was drafted in 1789 to replace the weak Articles of Confederation, a Bill of Rights for individuals was included. Article III of the Bill of Rights *"Assures that troops may not be quartered in private homes without the owner's consent."*

Details of the lives of the children of James and Susannah:

William Cartar was the eldest son of James and Susannah. Therefore he was probably born in the fall of 1703 about one year after his parents married. William would have been about seventeen when his mother married Robert Heaton Jr. As a teenager he might have worked at one of the Heaton mills. In *Carter Cousins,* Eberle and Henley claim he married Sarah Plumly in 1732. Sarah Plumly born in 1713, was the daughter of John Plumly Sr. and Mary Bainbridge Plumly. In the Middletown MM there is a notation dated May 6, 1721 of John Plumly being seen frequently overtaken by strong drink and of quarreling and fighting. Per the Thomas Holmes map of Bucks County, the Plumly family owned land along Neshaminy Creek near the land purchased by John Griffith. William inherited 200 acres of that land from his father. William was also bequeathed a white mare. William was expected to help provide for his younger siblings.

In the *Bi-Centenary Memorial to Jeremiah Carter,* Sarah Plumly's husband is listed as the son of John Carter and Grace White Carter. Secondary sources state that this John Carter was the son of Robert Carter. There were several John Carters in Pennsylvania. Argument in favor of this family connection is the birthyear of 1707 for William which is closer to Sarah Plumly's birth year of 1713. Also, John and Grace were quakers, as there is a record of their intention to marry in the Middletown MM. Argument against this family connection is the cited birth years for their children. Nathaniel and Robert were born in 1705. John and William were born in 1707. Ann and Martha were born in 1709. Three sets of twins were possible but I think information about several families has been intermixed.

The will for John Carter, yeoman of Bucks County was dated 20th March 1709/10 and proved 17th of May 1710. A typed abstract lists his wife as Grace and his children as Robert, William, Mary and Martha. The witnesses were Grace Carter, Jeremiah Langhorne and Francis White. Hence the Nathaniel, John and Ann cited above either were not this John Carter's children or they died before 1710. The will of Mary Paxson was dated 10th month 25th Day 1718 and proved on February 23, 1719. Mary Paxson lists her daughters as Mary Appleton and Grace Carter. She lists her granddaughters as Rebecca and Susanna Appleton, Mary and Martha Carter, Mary Chase and Elizabeth Aldridge. She lists her grandsons as Robert and William Carter. These two wills provide proof of a second William Carter. It is uncertain which William Carter/Cartar actually married Sarah Plumly.

Circumstantial evidence points to Eberle and Henley being correct. First there was the proximity of the family properties. John and Mary Plumly would have known James and Susannah. They could observe William's management of his inherited lands. They had years to form an opinion about his character and whether he would be a good provider for their daughter even though his was not a quaker.

The known children of William and Sarah:

1. James Cartar   b. circa 1733
2. Sarah Cartar   b. circa 1735
3. Mary Cartar   b. circa 1737
4. William Cartar Jr.   b. circa 1739

Naming their first son James and not John, with a second son named William and no Robert is an argument supporting lineage to James and Susannah instead of John and Grace. William Cartar died in March 1749 in Southampton township. John Plumly Jr., acted as the executor of his estate which went to Sarah for the care of their underage children. If the location and number of acres could be positively identified then it might be possible to settle the dispute as to which William actually married Sarah. William Cartar had probably spent his entire life in Bucks County working as a farmer and a miller. Sarah Plumly Cartar married Jonas Deyn Preston in 1751.

William and Sarah's son William Cartar Jr. could possibly be the William Carter who married Mary Hayhurst on September 26, 1771. Mary Hayhurst was the daughter of William Hayhurst. A second possibility for Mary's husband was the eldest son of Joseph Cartar and his second wife Rachael. Born circa 1746 in Virginia, this William grew up near his grandmother Susannah Heaton in Northampton township. These two William Cartars were first cousins. Per the naming convention, Mary probably married the son of Joseph and Rachael. Mary and William named their first son Joseph and their second son William. There might have been other unrelated William Carters.

William and Sarah's daughter Sarah Cartar might have married a Hayhurst and therefore might be the Sarah Hayhurst who was a witness to Susannah Heaton's will. A second possibility for Sarah Hayhurst was the only daughter of Joseph and his first wife Catherine. Their daughter was born about 1741 in Virginia and per Eberle and Henley in *Carter Cousins,* she married William Hayhurst Jr. and gave birth to daughter Katherine Hayhurst before 1766. Eberle and Henley were referencing Susannah Heaton's will, a conclusion this author questions. Joseph and Catherine's daughter Sarah would have been over twenty one when Joseph and his second wife Rachael and their three children moved to Bucks County in 1764. Sarah was old enough to have already been married and there does not seem to be a record of her moving to Bucks County.

John Cartar was the second son of James and Susannah Cartar – more about his life in the next chapter.

Ann Cartar, the only daughter of James and Susannah, was bequeathed a feather bed in her father's will. Whether the executors of her father's will built her a house is unknown. Ann is usually listed as one of the younger children, but she is the third child mentioned in her father's will, which might put her birthyear as early as 1706. Ann Cartar married William Hibbs on September 2, 1728 as recorded in the Middletown MM. Since she was living with a stepfather, I suspect she was only eighteen when she married which would place her birthdate in the year 1710. In which case Ann would have only been about four years old when her father died. After Ann turned eighteen she and William Hibbs would have announced their intention to marry before a quaker meeting. They then waited for approval of the marriage before actually tying the knot.

Known children of Ann and William Hibbs:

1.	Susannah Hibbs	b. November 22, 1729	
2.	Hannah Hibbs Cooper	b. April 6, 1730	d. 1777
3.	Phebe Hibbs Smith	b. February 14, 1732	d. 1804
4.	Sarah Hibbs Blaker	b. January 4, 1734	d. 1805
5.	William Hibbs Jr.	b. October 27, 1735	d. 1789
6.	James Hibbs	b. October 7, 1737	
7.	Anne Hibbs Smith	b. September 12, 1739	d. 1825

Ann may have been the only one of James and Susannah's Cartar children to become a member of the Society of Friends. Some of Susannah's Heaton children joined the Quakers. Grandchildren living in northern Virginia also joined the Quakers. Ann Cartar Hibbs spent her entire life in Bucks County. Ann and her daughter Susannah Hibbs were named in the will of her mother Susannah Heaton in 1766. William Hibbs died in Northampton township in 1789.

James Cartar II should have been James and Susannah's third son per the naming convention. Most genealogy websites consider him to be one of the younger sons. He was probably born about 1706. Without documentation one source lists May 23, 1706 as his birthdate. James Cartar II upon reaching the age of majority could have taken over management of the land his father had bequeathed to Susannah.

An advertisement in the *American Mercury* newspaper dated Friday February 6, 1733 suggests that James Cartar was working as a brewer and smoking meat on the side.

James Carter
Who for several years past hath, and still continues to officiate as Master to George Emlen of the City of Philadelphia, Brewer, having a Commodious Conveniency of his own, professes to Smoke and Dry, for all person willing, either Bacon, Beef or Fish, after the best manner, very reasonable, and to be carried by him from Home and to Home. Any Person or Persons disposed to employ him in this Affair, may be informed at George Emblen's or at his own Dwelling back of Mr. A. Hamilton's Garden in Walnut-Street, and be fully satisfied.

If this advertisement was for James Carter II, he had probably started working for George Emblen as a teenage apprentice and then advanced to Master Brewer. The ad also suggests that James was living in the City of Philadelphia. In which case a younger brother possibly Richard might have managed the inherited land.

George Emlen was the son of George Emlen Sr. who had been one of the first immigrants. George Emlen Sr. laid out the City of Philadelphia according to instructions from William Penn. George Emlen Sr. was a brewer who ran the *Three Tuns Inn* on Chestnut Street between 2nd and 3rd. He was one of the early Alderman running the affairs of the City of Philadelphia. George Emlen Sr. died in Philadelphia in December 1710. George Emlen Jr., born in Philadelphia in 1695, was also a brewer operating a facility on 5th between Market and Chestnut streets. George Emlen Jr. died in 1754 in Philadelphia.

In the mid 1730's James Cartar II followed his younger brothers Joseph and Benjamin to Orange County, Virginia and purchased 300 acres. After moving to Virginia, James II married Hannah Chenowith in 1738. Hannah born circa 1713, was the daughter of John and Mary Chenowith from Baltimore County, Maryland. James Carter II was named in the will of his father-in-law and along with Thomas Chenowith acted as executors of his estate. John Chenowith was a member of the Hopewell MM. Members carried rifles to fight off attacks by wolf packs.

Known children of James II and Hannah:

1. Jane Carter   b. circa 1739
2. Ann Carter
3. Ruth Carter
4. Hannah Carter
5. James Carter III   b. October 14, 1750 in Frederick County, Virginia Colony
6. William Carter   b. circa 1752
7. John Carter   b. circa 1754

James Carter II wrote his own will on November 18, 1758, at which time his daughter Jane was over eighteen. The will was probated in Frederick County, Virginia on December 6, 1758. James describes his three hundred acres as lying *"on the southeast side of the road leading from Winchester to Belhaven."* Belhaven was the port area of Alexandria, Virginia. When Hannah died in 1764 her son James Carter III was about fourteen. In *Carter Cousins,* Eberle and Henley claim James Carter III married Ann Bowen and after the American Revolution began, they and several of their neighbors moved to Washington County, Pennsylvania. In Pennsylvania the family joined the Presbyterian Church.

Richard Cartar is usually listed as the youngest son but was probably the fourth son of James and Susannah. I suspect that Richard was born about 1707. Richard may have been the son who managed the land his father had bequeathed to Susannah. Richard and his brother James II probably moved to Virginia in the year 1736. He married Margaret Bruce in Orange County, Virginia. Richard was named in the 1747 will of his father-in-law John Bruce. He received a suit of wool clothing. In Virginia Richard first acquired 188 acres which was surveyed by James Wood on March 12, 1736. Richard acquired a total of 394 acres on Adams Creek a tributary to the Opequon River, which he and Margaret sold on September 30, 1765, to James Lindsey.

Richard and Margaret are believed to have moved to Berkley County, South Carolina Colony. A previous researcher identified Richard Carter by a distinctive X mark on deeds in both Frederick County, Virginia and Laurens County, South Carolina. Since the documents were most likely written by two different clerks, the distinctive X marks are just a coincidence. Berkley County was renamed Laurens County in 1785. On October 14, 1766, Richard and Margaret purchased a colonial plat of 200 acres on Cain Creek. On November 29, 1772, they purchased a second colonial plat of 300 acres also on Cain Creek. Then on August 5, 1777, Richard and Margaret used quit claims to divide their land among their five sons. The list of their sons may be backwards to their birth order. James should have been the eldest with John the second son per the naming convention. The eldest was probably born circa 1739.

Know sons of Richard and Margaret:

1. George Carter
2. Robert Carter
3. Joseph Carter
4. John Carter
5. James Carter

Secondary sources claim that George Carter was a British Loyalist during the American Revolution. He and his family escaped to Spanish Florida following the Revolution. Wills for Robert and John were probated in Laurens County, South Carolina.

When Robert Heaton Jr. died in 1743, his land in Pennsylvania was inherited by his son Robert Heaton III. On March 17, 1748, Robert Heaton III gave a Power of Attorney to James Carter II and George Hollingsworth of Frederick County, Virginia for them to sell his land on Back Creek. The land where John Frost was living. The same John Frost, from whom Robert Heaton III had originally purchased the land. Before selling the land, they needed to acquire a grant from Lord Fairfax as proof of ownership. Robert Heaton III died in Pennsylvania in 1764. After which Joseph Cartar returned to Northampton township to care for his elderly mother Susannah Heaton.

Joseph Cartar was probably the fifth son of James and Susannah Cartar. He would have been about eleven years old when his mother married Robert Heaton Jr. Joseph was approximately the same age as the first Robert Heaton III who had died the previous fall. Joseph seems to have been the curious kid who asked *'how do mills work'* and '*how does fermentation produce ale*', etc. Learning how things worked served him well as an adult. Joseph Cartar married Catherine Duncan on November 16, 1731, in Bensalem, Pennsylvania Province. Other researchers have speculated that her father was Edmund Dunkin. Bensalem township was located in south Bucks County, near Byberry township northeast of Philadelphia. If Joseph's birthday was in 1709 then he would have been about twenty-two when he married. Joseph was the first Cartar brother to move to Orange County, Virginia. Starting in the fall of 1734, Joseph managed to purchase over 600 acres along Opequon Creek with 456 acres surveyed on October 10, 1734 by Robert Brooke.

In Virginia, Joseph Cartar built several mills, a tavern known as an 'ordinary', and a distillery. Settler Lewis Neill who started his own mill, complained to Lord Fairfax that *"Joseph Carter was hogging all the water."* Joseph had learned from his stepfather where to located a mill in order to take advantage of the power of a waterfall. Joseph and his sons built five mills along the Opequon River and Red Bud Creek. These included a sawmill, a flour mill, a flax oil mill, a flax breaking mill and a paper mill. The flax breaking mill exposed the pliable inner fibers which were woven into linen. Poor sanitation practices resulted in water being unsafe to drink. Unclean water may be the cause of many of the agues and early deaths. Quakers crafted their own ale, beer, and spirits. They were expected to drink sparingly, with no public display of drunkenness.

Known children of Joseph and Catherine:

1. James Carter	b. August 19, 1732, in Bucks County, Pennsylvania, died October 27, 1798, in Frederick County, Virginia.	
2. Edmund Carter	b. circa 1734	d. before 1781
3. Joseph Carter Jr.	b. circa 1736	
4. Richard Carter	b. circa 1738	
5. Benjamin Carter	b. circa 1740	d. 1796
6. Sarah Carter	b. circa 1742	

Catherine Duncan Cartar died in 1742. Then Robert Heaton Jr. died in July 1743. Concerned about the welfare of his mother, Joseph Cartar went back to Bucks County, Pennsylvania. Joseph appears to have been the more successful of the brothers. Benjamin, James II and Richard all lived nearby along the Opequon. They may have nominated Joseph to go back and check on their mother's welfare. Joseph's eldest son James was only eleven and his daughter was a toddler. He most likely had an agreement with one or more of his brothers to look after his businesses and his children while he traveled to Pennsylvania. Joseph Cartar was issued a Pennsylvania license to marry in November 1744 and shortly thereafter married Rachael Mead. After marrying Joseph and Rachel returned to Frederick County, Virginia. Susannah's youngest son Robert Heaton III remained in Pennsylvania.

Known children of Joseph and Rachel:

1. William Carter   b. circa 1745   d. June 1784 Bucks Co., PA
2. Ann Carter   b. circa 1748
3. John Carter   b. circa 1753   d. Sept 28, 1793 Bucks Co., PA

The birth order and parentage may not be correct. The list comes from Eberle and Henley in *Carter Cousins*. In Susannah Heaton's Will she bequeaths legacies to William, Richard and Ann the offspring of Joseph. She does not mention John. Joseph's younger half-brother Robert Heaton III died in 1764. Joseph Cartar left his land and mills in Frederick County to the care of his five older sons. He returned to Bucks County with Rachel and their three young children to look after his elderly mother. Joseph is listed in the tax rolls of Northampton township in 1764. When Joseph Cartar died in 1781 in Northampton township his sons living in Virginia inherited the Frederick County land. Per secondary sources Joseph, Benjamin, James and Richard were living in Virginia. Edmund had passed away prior to 1781.

Joseph Cartar's eldest son James inherited 456 acres plus the Red Bud Paper Mill. James was expected to pay one hundred fifty pounds of gold or silver lawful currency to his brother John. This suggests that John was Joseph Cartar's youngest son and that Joseph did not have any additional land to bequeath to him. Joseph's will also directed James to pay twenty five pounds to his own son Joseph and another twenty five pounds to his niece Katherine the daughter of Edmund.

James continued to operate the paper mill in partnership with his son John. Per articles in the *Republican Constellation* newspaper published in Winchester, James & his son John dissolved their partnership in 1816, with John refurbishing the mill before moving to Warren, Ohio. In 1818 the Red Bud Paper Mill was leased by Smith & Barbour. Smith & Barbour promised to continue producing the fine quality paper and stationery that the mill was known for. Per the *Winchester Gazette* newspaper, James and Arthur W. Carter conveyed 126 acres of the Opequon Manufacturing Company to Daniel Annin in 1823. Arthur William Carter was the son of James and the grandson of Joseph. He had been born on May 14, 1772 in Frederick County, Virginia.

Joseph's son Benjamin fathered a dozen children with two wives. Benjamin's eldest son named Joseph was born circa 1759. Benjamin married his second wife Rachel Burnet on May 6, 1784. Benjamin appears to have spent his entire life in Frederick County. He left behind very little in the way of a paper trail. Details of the lives of Joseph's other children is sketchy.

Benjamin Cartar was probably James and Susannah's youngest son. Benjamin was born circa 1712. Benjamin married Margaret Hollingsworth in Orange County, Virginia. Margaret was the daughter of Abraham Hollingsworth and Ann Robinson Hollingsworth. The Hollingsworth family were early members of the Hopewell Monthly Meeting. Two months after surveying land for Joseph Cartar, Robert Brooke recorded surveying 376 acres for Benjamin Cartar on December 16, 1734. At the time he purchased land Benjamin should have been over twenty-one which fits with a birthday before the fall of 1713. Benjamin had probably accompanied Joseph and his family when they moved to Virginia, in order to help his brother build a cabin.

Known children of Benjamin and Margaret:

1. Samuel Carter   b. after 1734
2. Thomas Carter   b. before 1748

Benjamin died before November 1748 when Frederick County, appointed Isaac Hollingsworth as guardian for underage Thomas Carter. Thomas Carter later married Mary Chambers and moved to Berkley County, South Carolina where his uncle Richard Carter had previously moved. Mary Chambers was the daughter of William Chambers whose Frederick County land had been regranted by Lord Fairfax in 1754.

Williamsburg, *The Virginia Gazette*   Monday April 10, 1752

Just IMPORTED in the Rachel, Capt. Armstrong, from London, and to be sold at a reasonable Rate, at the Unicorn's Horn, by the Subscriber, in Williamsburg.
A fresh assortment of Drugs and Medicines, Etc. consisting of best Jesuit Bark, Ipecacuanha, Rhubarb, Oil of Turpentine, Tartar Emetic, Spermaceti, Sarsaparilla and China Roots, Allom, Antimony, Brimstone, Etc. Etc. Likewise Bateman's and Stugbton's Drops, Daffey's and Squire's Elixirs, Freeman's Cordial, Golden and plain Spirits of Scurvy-Grass, Turlington's Drops, Universal Balsam, Anderson's and Lockyer's Pills, Eaton's and Helvetius's Styptics, Borax, Coperas, Prussian Blue, Red, and White Lead, fine eating Oil, Florence ditto, French and Pearl Barleys, fine French Hungary and Lavender Waters, Cinamon, Cloves, Mace, Nutmegs, Black Pepper, best Durham Mustard, Scotch Snuff, white and brown Sugar-Candy, Barley Sugar, Carraway-Comfits, Sugar Plums, Spanish Liquorice, Candied Eringo and Angelica Roots, preserved Citron, Salt Petre, Epson and Glauber's Salts, Gold-leaf and Dutch Metal, Vermillion, best Londen-made Lancets, Smelling-Bottles with and without Cases, Anchovies, Capers and Olives, Pumice Stone, Sponge, Jug Corks, Ratsbane, Etc. Etc. Etc.   James Carter

An interesting list of the drugs and medicines available in the colonies in 1752. The proprietor James Carter of Williamsburg, Virginia was probably a descendent of either Thomas Carter of Barford or Robert Carter of Corotoman. Shop keepers in Philadelphia could have imported a similar array of products. It was the spices – cinnamon, cloves, mace, nutmeg and black pepper from the East Indies that had prompted European exploration. For centuries very expensive small quantities of spices were transported overland to Cairo Egypt and then distributed throughout Europe. Christopher Columbus thought that he could reach China and the Spice Islands by traveling west. After all Copernicus had insisted that the earth was round and Viking sagas told of lands discovered by sailing to the west. The Portuguese had discovered the Azores by sailing west. Columbus miscalculated the circumference of the earth and was disappointed at being unable to locate the Spice Islands on his three voyages. The Caribbean was the location where he was sure the islands should be. Then in 1498 Portuguese explorer Vasco da Gama ventured around Africa's Cape of Good Horn and found the route to the Spice Island. Soon the Portuguese were bringing shiploads of spices back to Europe. During the reign of Elizabeth I her sanctioned 'privateers' brought captured Spanish ships filled with cane sugar to English ports.

Following the French and Indian Wars which lasted from 1754 to 1761, England needed cash. In 1764 England imposed a Sugar Tax on the colonies. The colonists protested and the tax rate was reduced. To raise more funds England passed the Stamp Act in March 1765. The Stamp Act was intended to go into effect in November of 1765. The colonist detested the Stamp Act more than the Sugar Tax. The Stamp Act required that every piece of paper be taxed depending on how that piece of paper was intended to be used. The first pages of legal documents were taxed at a higher rate than personal correspondence. Identical sheets of paper were to be taxed at different rates. The tax had to be paid with British coin, not with colonial paper money. One major problem was the lack of actual British coin in the colonies. Six of the colonies had independently appealed to the crown to try and get more coin delivered. Most of the colonies were printing paper currency, and bartering for goods and services was commonplace. In the Virginia Colony, wooden tobacco dollars were printed and exchanged as cash. Wooden tobacco dollars had been introduced as a form of credit. When plantation owners shipped their crop of tobacco leaves to England, they were provided with the wooden dollars as a temporary payment. Instead of paying for the crop with actual currency, buyers in England paid with a return shipment of merchandise. When these goods arrived back in Virginia, the plantation owners could use the wooden dollars to 'purchase' these goods. Soon the wooden dollars were exchanged as cash. Anyone holding tobacco dollars could use them to purchase items of the returned merchandise. Spanish and French coins were also in widespread use in tidewater Virginia. With an outcry of 'No taxation without representation' the Stamp Act was repealed in March 1766 a year after it had been passed.

Benjamin Franklin owned one of the print shops printing currencies for Philadelphia. Beginning in 1767 Benjamin Franklin printed the *Pennsylvania Chronicle* newspaper which expressed revolutionary sentiment. Franklin's view of Britain had shifted, and his opinions were published in the newspapers of other colonies.

Susannah Griffith Cartar Heaton died on December 30, 1770. She was in her late eighties. An exceptionally long life. Her death was recorded in both the Byberry MM of Philadelphia and the New Garden MM in Chester. Both records refer to Susannah as a *'very ancient widow'*. When English settlers first arrived in Virginia in the early 1600's, life expectancy was about fifty years. Poor sanitation, diseases and the complications of childbirth caused many early deaths. Susannah outlived two husbands and five of her sons. Joseph Cartar, Richard Cartar and their sister Ann Hibbs plus their half-sisters Alice Plumly and Anna Dunn outlived their mother. All ten of Susannah's children had survived to become adults, marry and raise children of their own. Remarkable!

Susannah wrote her Last Will and Testament on January 15, 1766 mentioning several of her grandchildren who were living nearby in Pennsylvania (see Chapter 11). Her son Joseph Cartar was named the sole Executor. Susannah had very little in the way of a Personal Estate to bequeath to her heirs. It was more the thought than the amount – grandmother gave her young grandchildren an inheritance. To her daughter Ann Hibbs, she gave her clothes. To granddaughter Susannah Hibbs she bequeathed her feather bed. Susannah Hibbs was Susannah Heaton's oldest biological grandchild. She gave a bond that was in arrears to son-in-law John Plumly Jr. so that he might try to collect the past due amounts. She provided five pounds to granddaughter Mary Plumly and another five pounds to Katherine Hayhurst. She bequeathed five pounds each to grandchildren: William, Richard & Ann Cartar – the offspring of Joseph Cartar. To her grandchildren by Robert Heaton III – Isabel, Susannah and John Heaton she gave an equal part of her remaining estate.

When writing her new will Susannah seems to have left off her granddaughter Mary Plumly. The legacy to Mary was then added at the top of the page – in a 'Prized Place'. This anomaly suggests that Susannah was beginning to show age related mental decline and possibly vision loss. This Last Will voided all previous wills. Susannah had probably written several wills. The first might have been after James Cartar passed away. After the death of her son Robert Heaton III, Susannah would have needed an updated will with a new Executor. Ann and Susannah Hibbs were probably the primary caregivers and companions to Susannah Heaton, while Joseph Cartar provided the financial management. Susannah's Will wasn't proved until almost a month after her death, it might simply have been forgotten or misplaced. Other than possibly a brief childhood in Wales, Susannah spent her entire life in the Province of Pennsylvania.

Not all of the names on Susannah's Will have been positively identified. Ann Hibbs was her daughter by her first husband James Cartar. Susannah Hibbs was her unmarried granddaughter. Mary Plumly was the daughter of Alice Heaton and John Plumly Jr. Ezra Croasdale a witness to the will was the son of stepdaughter Grace Heaton Croasdale. James Cooper another witness was the spouse of granddaughter Hannah Hibbs. The third witness Sarah Hayhurst has not been positively identified. She was probably Susannah's granddaughter. She might have been either the daughter of eldest son William Cartar and his wife Sarah Plumly, or the daughter of Joseph Cartar and his first wife Catherine Duncan. In either case Katherine Hayhurst was Susannah's great granddaughter.

Four of Susannah's Cartar sons moved to Orange/Frederick County, Virginia with grandchildren by sons Joseph and James II continuing to live in Virginia. Her three grandsons, by her second son John moved to western Loudoun County, Virginia where grandson James Carter raised a large family along the banks of the south fork of Beaverdam Creek. Some of Susannah's descendants moved from Virginia to South Carolina, while others moved to Ohio, Indiana, Missouri and beyond. Her 2G grandsons participated in the 1849 California Gold Rush. Susannah Griffith was an original immigrant to the newly founded Province of Pennsylvania and in less than one hundred years after her death her descendants had crossed a continent and settled in California, Oregon and many territories in between.

Three years after Susannah Heaton's death the Boston Tea Party occurred on the night of December 16, 1773. Subsequently, Britain blockaded Boston Harbor. The First Continental Congress convened in Philadelphia from September 5, 1774 to October 26, 1774 to address colonial grievances and demand that England adhere to the Charter Rights of the Colonists. Colonists expected to be treated as loyal British citizens.

Chapter 6 – John and Alice Cartar Family

John Cartar was the second son of James and Susannah Cartar. He was born circa 1705 and would have been about fifteen when his mother remarried. He inherited 50 acres in Southampton township from his father. John married Alice Nelson on October 14, 1731 in the Christ Church in downtown Philadelphia. Alice Nelson was disowned by the Middletown MM on October 4, 1733 *'for marrying unknown to her parents.'* Alice Nelson born on June 30, 1713 was the second daughter of Henry Nelson and his first wife Alice Hayhurst. The Hayhurst name is also spelled Hairst, Hearst and Hurst. Her maternal grandfather was Cuthbert Hayhurst Jr. who had been a quaker preacher in Settle, England. Cuthbert Hayhurst Jr. was an ardent follower of George Fox and had been repeatedly fined and jailed. Before migrating Cuthbert Jr. purchased 500 acres along Neshaminy Creek directly from William Penn. His Certificate of Transfer from the Settle MM in Yorkshire, England was dated June 7, 1682. Cuthbert Jr. and his brother William died shortly after their arrival. They settled on low marshy ground and soon developed agues and fevers. A secondary source list the burial date as March 2, 1683. Alice Hayhurst's mother was Mary Rudd Hayhurst from Slaidburn Parish, Yorkshire. Mary Hayhurst died in 1686 in Bucks County, Pennsylvania.

Alice Nelson's mother Alice Hayhurst Nelson had been born in Slaidburn Parish in 1679. Alice Hayhurst married Henry Nelson on December 16, 1708 as recorded in the Middletown MM (see Chapter 11). After giving birth to two daughters, Alice Hayhurst Nelson died in 1713. Her first daughter Mary had been born on November 6, 1709 and died on November 11, 1711. As his second wife, Henry Nelson married Alice Wildman on October 23, 1719. Alice Wildman Nelson had been born in England in 1687. She was the daughter of Martin and Ann Wildman.

Henry Nelson appears to have done quite well after moving to Newtown, Pennsylvania in the early 1700's. He had been able to purchase several parcels of land. He performed various civic duties, which included serving on a Grand Jury, serving as a tax assessor and as a constable. Henry Nelson served a single term in the Pennsylvania legislature in 1720. Even though he was prosperous, religious and civic minded, Henry Nelson had a drinking problem. On January 6, 1718 Henry acknowledged his disorderly conduct after drinking too much strong liquor. Henry Nelson was disowned by the Middletown MM in 1726 because of his drinking problem.

Henry Nelson's will was probated on April 11, 1744 in Bucks County, (see Chapter 11). He provided his second wife Alice Wildman with the use of his 450 acre plantation in Middletown Township for the rest of her natural life. The estate would then go to his son Thomas Nelson. Thomas was also to receive land and a mill in Newtown. His daughter Alice Cartar received the seventy-six acre plantation near Wrightstown where she and her sons were living. Henry Nelson had acquired the land from John Ross and his wife Elizabeth Griscom Ross who were the parents of Betsy Ross. History credits Betsy Ross with designing and sewing the first flag of the United States of America. Per Henry Nelson's will after Alice's death the land would go to her son Henry Cartar. It seems that Henry Nelson had not been in contact with his daughter for some time. Alice Cartar had married widower Joseph Yates on September 20, 1742 and had given birth to son Robert Yates in 1743. Infant Robert Yates was not mentioned in his grandfather's will. In the spring of 1746 the Yates family moved to western Loudoun County, Virginia Colony.

Also in Henry Nelson's will his daughter Ann Wilson was to receive 50 acres in Briston township. Daughter Letitia Joly was to receive a 61 acre plantation in Newtown which after her death would go to her son Nelson Joly.   After they reached the age of majority the grandsons – Henry, John and James Cartar plus Robert and Thomas Heaton were to receive 10 pounds each. Robert and Thomas Heaton are referred to as the sons of Gemimah. Grandsons Henry Wilson and Nelson Joly were to receive 20 pounds each. Granddaughters Elizabeth Wilson and Alice Joly were to receive 10 pounds each. It is unlikely that the Cartar brothers ever received their inheritance from their grandfather Henry Nelson. No one in Bucks County knew where Alice Cartar had moved or if the Cartar brothers survived to the age of twenty-one.

In his will, Henry Nelson specified that his negro be well clothed and set free from servitude. Quakers treated slaves much the same as they treated indentured servants. Servitude was a time in a young person life during which they were expected to learn a trade with which to earn a living. Henry Nelson was literate but some of the spelling in his will suggest that he might not have been very well educated. Example: the word acres is spelled with a 'k' – akors; he used the word 'foloweth' instead of follows and his spelling of his daughter's name Gemimah seems unique.

Known children of Henry and Alice Hayhurst Nelson:

1.	Mary Nelson	b. September 6, 1709	d. September 11, 1711
2.	Alice Nelson	b. June 30, 1713	d. circa 1777

Known children of Henry and Alice Wildman Nelson:

1.	Ann Nelson	b. August 6, 1720
2.	Letitia Nelson	b. December 19, 1721
3.	Jeremiah Nelson	b. January 23, 1724 – (daughter – Gemimah)
4.	Thomas Nelson	b. April 27, 1726

Alice Nelson Cartar had been disowned by the Society of Friends after she married John Cartar. Not marrying another quaker probably displeased Alice's very religious father. John and Alice had three sons whose names are recorded in Henry Nelson's will: Henry, John and James in that order. Per the naming convention one would expect the first born son to be named after the paternal grandfather, the second son after the maternal grandfather and the third son after the father. However, John's two brothers Joseph and William had each named their first son James in 1732 and 1733 respectively. Naming their first son after Henry Nelson might have been a gesture to repair the family relationship. Susannah Heaton already had two grandsons named James Cartar. She would have understood the desire to repair the family relationship since she had needed to repair the relationship with her own parents after marrying out-of-unity. At least five of Susannah's grandsons were named James Carter.

Very little is known about John Cartar other than he inherited 50 acres. This land was part of the original purchase by John Griffith. John Griffith sold the 50 acres to Samuel Griffith who in turn sold it to James Cartar. James bequeathed the land to his second son. Researcher Thomas Katheder wrote an article for *The Virginia Genealogist* Volume 47 Number 4 dated October – December 2003 claiming that John Carter was a blacksmith like his father. However there was another John Carter, the son of Robert Carter who was cited as a blacksmith. The two John Carters were probably cousins. Without his father to teach him the trade of blacksmithing it is doubtful this John Cartar became a blacksmith. John Cartar may have served as a constable for Newtown township in March 1728. He would have been about twenty-three at the time. With several individuals bearing the same name it is difficult to say with certainty to which individual a record applies.

The known children of John and Alice:

1. Henry Cartar   b. circa 1733
2. John Cartar   b. circa 1735
3. **James Cartar**   b. circa 1737

It is unknown when John Cartar died nor when or why Alice and her sons moved to the property in Wrightstown. Wrightstown was a wilderness community on the western flank of Bucks County. The family should have been able to continue living on the fifty acres John had inherited. The only stipulation would have been to pay the annual taxes. Henry Nelson with his numerous land acquisitions should have been able to advise his daughter. It is possible that John's death was a traumatic memory for Alice and she wished to move away from the daily reminder of his death. John Cartar's estate was not probated until 1750 by Robert Heaton III and John Plumly Jr. The death of William Cartar in 1749 and the subsequent settlement of his estate may have prompted John Plumly Jr. to look into the status of the adjoining fifty acres. Land that was near John Plumly Jr.'s own inherited land. On March 22, 1750 the Bucks County Court appointed administrators to settle John Cartar's estate. Robert Heaton III and John

Plumly Jr. posted bond with the court. Heaton signed the following statement: *"I Robert Heaton of Northampton in the county of Bucks, Yeoman, do solemnly, sincerely and truly declare and affirm that Alice Carter, widow of John Carter, late of Newtown in this county, is not resident within the Province of Pennsylvania, but in some part of Virginia or Maryland."* In Bucks County Probate Court on June 12, 1750, Robert Heaton III signed a statement that he had reviewed John Cartar's accounts, debts and inventory as required by the bond. He and John Plumly Jr. could not locate any of John Cartar's personal estate to inventory.

When James Cartar II and Richard Cartar moved to Virginia in 1736, they left the forty acres in Southampton to the care of one of their older brothers. Then when John passed away, William would have managed the entire 290 acres. His 200 acres, John's 50 acres plus Susannah's 40 acres being sure that annual taxes were paid. As Henry's uncle William would have considered it his responsibility to look out for the interests of his underaged nephew, just as the Executors of his father's estate had looked out for his inheritance.

Alice Cartar married widower Joseph Yates on September 20, 1742 in a New Jersey civil ceremony. The Yates name is sometimes spelled Yeats or Yeates. Thomas Katheder in the above cited article suggests that quakers went to New Jersey in order to marry outside of the quaker religion. He also hypothesizes that Alice may not have waited a full year after John's death before remarrying. Hindsight suggests that Alice and Joseph were both emotionally distraught. Their relationship helped each other heal. In the Wrightstown MM record dated February 1, 1746, *'Joseph Yeats continues his request to come under the care of Friends.'* He was asking to be re-admitted as a quaker. Then in March 1746 *'Joseph Yeats requests certificate to Monthly Meeting at Opeckon in Virginia.'* The blended Cartar/Yates family moved to western Loudoun County in 1746. Several other quaker families from Bucks County had already moved to the area possibly lured by the 99-year leases being offered. Some researches note that Joseph Yates was not included in his father's will. Joseph's younger brothers Peter and Robert inherited their fathers extensive land holdings near Newtown.

Alice Yates presented a certificate from the Middletown MM with her last name as Cartar and was received at the Fairfax MM on April 28, 1746. Alice had been accepted back as a member of the Society of Friends. Alice Yates name appears often in the Fairfax MM records. She seemed to have thrived in her new home. On April 30, 1757 Alice made a request for her children to be admitted as a birthright since their mother was a quaker. She received the answer that 'yes' her children did have a birthright.

There doesn't seem to be a record of Joseph Yates presenting a certificate of transfer. However, the Fairfax MM records have a request by Joseph to be released as an overseer on December 25, 1756. The overseer was the person who conducted the Monthly Meeting attempting to keep the meeting on agenda. Overseers also spoke to any individual who was accused of committing an infraction. They would invite the individual to come to meeting, confess their transgression and ask for forgiveness. Acting in the capacity of overseer meant that Joseph was a member of the Fairfax Society of Friends.

The Yates family settled on 165 acres along Catoctin Creek near Waterford, Virginia. The Cartar brothers grew up a part of the Fairfax Quaker community. They attended quakers schools and church services, while working the land of their stepfather. Joseph Yates died in 1761 and Alice was listed as head of household the following year with two tithable males living with her – her sons James Cartar and Robert Yates.

Henry Cartar seems to have lost out on two inheritances – 50 acres in Southampton Township from his father James Cartar and 76 acres in Wrightstown plus 10 pounds currency from his grandfather Henry Nelson. There are quaker records of a Henry Carter requesting a transfer from the Fairfax MM to the Hopewell MM near Winchester, Virginia on March 31, 1759. Henry Carter was received in the Hopewell MM and then disowned on August 3, 1761 for 'attending marriage contrary to discipline.' This Henry Carter was probably Alice Yates eldest son. The fate of his brother John Carter has not been determined.

Henry Carter was a witness when James Carter acquired land in 1764. In *The Virginia Genealogist* Vol 41, Thomas Katheder cites the Marty Hiatt and Craig Roberts Scott article *Loudoun County, Virginia Tithables*. They claim that Henry Carter along with James Carter Sr. were listed as tithable in the years 1765, 1767, 1768 and 1769. Henry's name disappeared from the list after 1769. White men over sixteen and negroes over twelve were tithable. There were a number of John and Henry Carters so connecting documents with the sons of John and Alice is problematic. There was a Henry Carter who served in the Virginia Militia, but whether or not this was Alice's son has not been determined.

Joseph Yates had been born circa 1694 in Newtown, Bucks County. The inclusion of Webster as a middle name was probably added by earlier researchers – not by his parents. His father was James Yates and his mother was Agnes Webster. Agnes' brothers John Webster and Peter Webster lived in Falls Township. Per his father's will written on December 31, 1730 Joseph had three brothers: James, Peter, and Robert. He also had four sisters: Agnes, Isabel, Sarah and Margaret. He married Margaret Rigg

Pearson on November 30, 1721. Widower Joseph Yates married widow Alice Nelson Cartar on September 20, 1742 in a civil ceremony in New Jersey.

Known children of Joseph and Margaret:

1.	Joseph Yates Jr.	b. circa 1725	
2.	Jane Yates	b. circa 1727	
3.	Hannah Yates		
4.	William Yates	b circa 1737	d. before March 1827
5.	Providence Yates		d. before August 1761

Known children of Alice and Joseph:

1.	Robert Yates	b. circa 1743	
2.	Benjamin Yates	b. circa 1745	married Phebe Wildman
3.	Issac Yates	b. circa 1749	
4.	Alice Yates	b. circa 1750	married Isaiah Myers on Oct 15, 1777.

Joseph Yates' Will was recorded on August 29, 1761 and the will was proved in November 1761 (see Chapter 11). He named his children in his will but does not mention or provide anything to his Cartar stepsons. To his wife Alice he provided a feather bed plus a grey mare and a new riding saddle. Alice also gets the profits from his plantation for the next twelve years. After that time she will receive one third of the profits as long as she remains a widow. After the twelve year period his son Robert is to receive ownership of the 165 acres minus his mother's 1/3 profit. Son Benjamin is to receive ½ of the profits from the cleared land, meadows and orchards for seven years plus ten pounds once he is twenty-one. Son Isaac is expected to attend school to learn a trade plus he will receive ten pounds once he is twenty-one. Daughter Alice is to receive a feather bed and four milk cows. Daughter Jane is to receive five pounds when she reaches eighteen. His children from his first marriage are to receive five shillings each. Since Providence had previously passed away her children were to receive five shilling each. Joseph Yates Jr. remained in or returned to Warwick, Bucks County, where he was taxed in 1759.

Chapter 7 – James Sr. and Hannah Carter Family

James Carter Sr. was probably the youngest son of John Cartar and Alice Nelson Cartar. His was born circa 1737. He married Hannah Eblen on June 26, 1765, out-of-unity in Fairfax. Fairfax might refer to the town of Fairfax, Virginia or to the quaker Fairfax Monthly Meeting located in the town of Waterford. As noted in the Women's Fairfax MM on July 27, 1765, *"Hannah Eblen having married out of the unity of friends to a young man a member of this meeting we therefore in conjunction with our men friends conclude to draw up testimony against them..."* Both James and Hannah were disowned on August 31, 1765.

Hannah was the eldest child of John William Eblen and Mary Warner Eblen. The Eblen name is also spelled Eblin. Hannah had been born in Chester, Pennsylvania on January 2, 1746. The Eblen family with nine children transferred to the Fairfax MM community on November 29, 1762. The family presented a certificate from the Chester MM dated January 29, 1762. James Carter Sr. was soon smitten with Hannah. She was several years younger than James.

Known children of John and Mary Eblen:

Hannah Eblen Carter	b.	2-1-1746	m. James Carter
Eliza Eblen Parker	b.	14-10-1748	m. Joseph Parker
Mary Eblen Pyatt	b.	14-4-1750	m. John Pyatt II
Rachael Eblen Sloan	b.	30-7-1753	m. John Sloan – dis 1773
Samuel Eblen	b.	18-7-1755	dis 1774 bearing arms
Elizabeth Eblen	b.	12-7-1757	
John Eblen	b.	16-4-1759	m. Ann Whitaker – mou 1782
Isaac Eblen	b.	6-5-1761	dis 1784 quarreling
Sarah Eblen Chapman	b.	circa 1764	m. Thomas Chapman – mou 1792

The Quaker abbreviations 'dis' and 'mou' come from the early twentieth century typed combined records. 'Dis' – either meant disciplined or disowned. 'Mou' – stood for married out of unity which also meant disowned.

James Sr. acquired 295 acres in western Loudon County, from quaker Thomas Dodd. In the Virginia Archive this deed transfer is listed as an L&R – a *Lease & Release*. This was not one of the 99 year leases. There are two Indenture documents signed on November 16, 1764 and November 17, 1764 respectively. Copies of these documents available for a fee from the Virginia Archive are barely legible. The fading documents with cramped writing are confusing to decipher (see Chapter 11).

The first Indenture was for a one year lease. James Carter Sr. paid Thomas Dodd five shillings cash which Mr. Dodd acknowledged receiving. James Carter Sr. agreed to make a rent payment of one pepper corn due on the Feast of Saint Michael. This rent payment due on September 29th is often seen in lease agreements and refers to a nominal payment as proof of completion of the lease term. A description of the land places the 295 acres on Beaverdam Creek which was a branch of Goose Creek and mentions property lines of neighbors Richard Blackburn and Benjamin Grayson Jr. The acreage was described as a number of 'poles' between oak and hickory trees. A pole or rod used as a land measurement equals 16.5 feet. 160 square poles equals one acre.

The second Indenture signed on the next day has Thomas Dodd and his wife Sarah Dodd relinquish their claim to the land after a payment of forty pounds which Mr. Dodd acknowledged receiving. Henry Carter, John Eblen, Peter Eblen and three other men witnessed these two transactions. The signatures all look to be in the same handwriting as the body of the documents, so these are copies of entries made in a bound journal by a clerk – not images of the original documents. James Carter Sr.'s signature is not displayed on either Indenture. Thomas Dodd signed the original documents over to James Carter Sr. When the traveling Circuit Court Judge came to town James Carter Sr. showed the documents to the Judge, who copied them into his traveling journal. After the Judge returned to Leesburg, the documents were recopied into a new bound journal. Showing the documents to the traveling Circuit Judge was the way the deed transactions were recorded with the county.

Over the centuries there have been several ways for transferring land ownership. The earliest method required the two parties to meet on the actual land and give an oral transfer before witnesses. By colonial times the transfer of a deed required written documentation and the recording of the transfer in a public registry. In colonial Virginia there was a requirement that the transfer be recorded within six months of the transaction. This could be a problem when living in the wilderness and the traveling Circuit Judge only come to town once a year. A *Lease and Release* method of transferring land did not require registration in a public registry. By signing a lease first, the buyer then had an interest in the land, after which the seller could release his interest in the land effectively transferring title to the buyer.

Nowhere on either the lease or sale is there mention of a third party or quit rents. Thomas Dodd owned the land having purchased it on September 18, 1757 during the French and Indian Wars when prices paid for farm produce were high. He sold it to James Carter Sr. who then had full ownership of the acreage. Thomas Dodd was able to negotiate and sign the lease without his wife, but her consent and signature were required for the actual sale. Sarah Dodd's signature includes the words *'her mark'*. Sarah Dodd was probably literate, but simply not present at the sale. The six male witnesses attested that Sarah Dodd had given her consent. The rent price of five shillings and the sale price of forty pounds for 295 acres sounds quite low but following the end of the French and Indian Wars the colonies were probably in a recession. Wars tend to cause inflation which results in higher prices for farm produce because an army needs to be feed and supplied. The Virginia Militia had been heavily involved in the French and Indian Wars. Once fighting ended a recession followed with lower prices for farm produce and land.

Having owned the 295 acres for only seven years, Thomas Dodd may not have made very many improvements. The sale mentions *'farms, orchards, and edifices'* but that was standard legalese. There is no mention of an actual cabin, cultivated fields or planted orchard. The term orchard probably referred to apple trees. Colonist planted apple trees not so much for fruit to eat but rather for cider apples with which to make both cider and vinegar. With a wide variety of uses, vinegar was the best medicine available. In a 1758 letter to his nephew Colonel George William Fairfax, Lord Fairfax mentions wanting grafts from apple varieties: Golden Pipen, Non-parel, Aromatick, and Medlar. Some of these varieties may have been better eating apples.

Alice Yates was probably quite happy for her thirty year old son to marry Hannah – future grandchildren. When James Carter Sr. and Hannah Eblen married, Hannah was already pregnant. Both were disowned by the Society of Friends on August 31, 1765. The quaker record refers to James Sr. as *"being one of their own."* From his teens James Sr. had grown up a part of the Fairfax quaker community. Alice Yates died circa 1777. James Sr. and Hannah raised a large family along the banks of Beaverdam Creek. Over the years the local town had several names – first Butterfield, then Union and finally Unison.   In 1829 a name change was requested by the Post Office since there were other towns also known as Union, Virginia.

Known children of James Sr. and Hannah:

1. John Carter   b. December 31, 1765.
2. Henry Carter   b. March 31, 1768.
3. Ashur Carter   b. July 3, 1770, died infancy.
4. Asa Carter   b. July 4, 1771.
5. Ruth Carter Newlon   b. March 9, 1774.
6. Dempsey Carter   b. July 18, 1776. Declaration of Independence had just been signed. American Revolution had started.
7. Eden Carter   b. August 30, 1778.
8. Tamer Carter   b. December 15, 1780, died infancy.
9. Faey Carter   b. July 17, 1782,   died infancy.
10. Taly Carter   b. July 17, 1782,   died infancy.
11. Sarah Carter Yates   b. March 26, 1784.
12. Mahlon Carter   b. September 11, 1787.
13. **James Carter 2nd**   b. June 28, 1791.

This list of names and birthdates was first seen on the Morman Genealogy Library Data Base years before Ancestry.com was founded. Tamer, Faey and Taly were listed as possible children names.

On February 16, 1810 James Carter Sr. purchased an additional 50 acres from neighbor William Vickers and his wife Anne. This land was to the west of his original homestead and he apparently provided the land to one of his married sons. That same year he purchased 154 acres in Hampshire County, Virginia which today is part of West Virginia. His eldest son John moved his family to Hampshire County.

Details of the lives of the children of James Sr. and Hannah:

The first son, John Carter, was named after both of his grandfathers – John Cartar and John Eblen. Hannah was pregnant when she and James Sr. married, so a date of birth in December 1765 or in January 1766 would seem appropriate. Other family trees have him married to Martha W. King and residing in Albemarle County, Virginia or in Campbell County, Virginia. I don't think this John Carter ever used the middle initial 'B' nor was he married to Martha W. King. I believe her spouse was a different individual. When his father acquired 154 acres in Hampshire County, John moved his family to that property. James Carter Sr. bequeathed the land along the Southfork of the Potomac River to his eldest son John.

The 1810 US Census has a John Carter living in Hampshire County with two sons under 10; two sons between 10-15; one daughter 10-15. John and his wife were both over 45.

The 1820 US Census has a John Carter with one son 10-15; one son 16-18 and three sons 16-25; one daughter 16-18. Both John and his wife are over 45.

The 1830 US Census has a John Carter with one son under 10; one son 20-29; two females 20-29. John was over 60 and his wife are over 70. (The young son might have been a grandson and one of the females a daughter-in-law.)

There is a Letter of Administration and a Probate Inventory for the estate of John Carter who died without a will in Hampshire County, Virginia (see Chapter 11). The Letter of Administration starts with a document date of October 25, 1841 and lists the names Albert, Robert and John Carter. The Probate inventory lists five heirs to John Carter's estate: Albert, Robert, James and John Carter plus Hannah Bilbes who also received a widow's share of the estate. Hannah was probably a second wife who had remarried after John Carter's death. In the 1830 Census John's wife was listed as over seventy. After John Carter passed away Hannah married Henry Bilbes. It appears that Henry Bilbes insisted on a widow's share of John Carter's estate. This request prompted the sons to file a Letter of Administration and detail the distribution of their father's estate.

A history of Hampshire County mentions several Carter families. The history starts with seven year old James Carter who arrived in Hampshire County in 1810 along with his family. The family settled near Hanging Rocks. The father wasn't named but could have been John Carter. He arrived sometime after the 1810 Personal Tax was assessed in the Spring and before the 1810 US Census data was collected in August. Among the descendants of James Carter and his wife Mary, the history lists John W. Carter a merchant in Pleasant Dale. Pleasant Dale is near Hanging Rocks to the east of Romney, West Virginia. The final settlement of John Carter's estate in January 1847 was held at a Court of Hampshire County in Romney. From the Census records there appear to have been several additional children not listed in the Probate records. Some may have died young, and some may have moved away. These pieces of data seem to be for John the eldest son of James Sr. and Hannah. There were several John Carters in Hampshire County, and more in other Virginia Counties. Making definitive connections is difficult without documentation corroborating names and birthdays of children.

Second son Henry Carter was named after his great grandfather Henry Nelson and his uncle Henry Cartar. Some family Trees have Henry Carter married to Sarah White on December 13, 1785 in Albemarle County. Again, I question this connection to Albemarle County. Henry inherited the land where he was living located west of the original 295-acre homestead. Henry may have died on August 31, 1840. In the 1830 US Census for Union in Loudoun County, Henry is listed as being over sixty. Living with him was a female over sixty and one over forty, plus a male over forty and six grandchildren between infant and twenty years of age. The 1830 Census only lists the name of the head of household. Henry Carter seems to have remained in western Loudoun County as his son and grandchildren were buried in the Southfork Burial ground with carved headstones. It is easy to confuse Henry with his uncle Henry Carter. Henry and his wife probably had other children. Non-quaker individuals did not leave very much of a paper trail.

Known son and grandchildren of Henry and his wife:

1. Richard Carter   b. August 26, 1790, married Deborah Newlan.
   1. William M. Carter   b. December 5, 1816, died August 12, 1891.
   2. Alfred N. Carter   b. circa 1821, died 1890.

Asa Carter married his first cousin Cinthia Parker in June 1797. Cinthia Parker was the daughter of Eliza Eblen Parker and Joseph Parker. She may have been a few years older than Asa. Asa inherited about 44 acres of the original homestead from his father. The description of the dividing line between the lands bequeathed to Asa and Mahlon indicates that this parcel of land was the northeast corner of the original homestead.

Known children of Asa and Cinthee:

1.	Havilah Carter	b. October 16, 1798.	D. December 18, 1860
2.	Asahel Carter	b. November 20, 1799.	D. September 21, 1851
3.	Lucinda Carter	b. July 26, 1801.	D. February 21, 1853
4.	Dedan Carter	b. June 1, 1803.	D. May 15, 1865

5.	Ardalas Carter	b. March 22, 1805.	D. June 30, 1889
6.	Hannah Carter		
7.	Addison Carter	b. circa 1810	d. about 1900
8.	Craie Carter	b. circa 1812	
9.	Julina Carter	b. February 9, 1812.	D. October 28, 1887

The children were born in western Loudoun County. In 1812 Asa Carter moved his family to Hampshire County. On June 8, 1814, Asa used the land in Loudoun County as collateral for a loan in order to purchase additional land in Hampshire County. The loan for $600 was acquired from Isaac & Samuel Nichols, with a bond held by Benjamin Grayson. Asa had until October 1, 1816 to repay the loan or Benjamin Grayson could sell the land. Cinthia's signature was required to use the Loudoun County land as collateral. Her name has an X in the middle with the words *'her mark'*. Cinthia had not returned to Loudoun County, instead the men who witnessed the document attested that Cinthia had given her consent. Asa repaid the loan. After his youngest brother James 2nd decided to move to Ohio in 1817, Asa sold the forty-four acres to his brother Dempsey for $2,200. Asa's family also made the move to Ohio. Cinthia Parker Carter died in Ohio on October 5, 1825. Asa Carter died on March 26, 1844. The one location in Ohio positively connected to Asa Carter was in Plain Township of Franklin County to the east of Columbus.

Ruth Carter married John W. Newlon in 1799. John Newlon died about 1829 and Ruth Newlon died about 1847.

Known children of Ruth and John:

1.	William Carter Newlon	b. circa 1802	
2.	Samuel C. Newlon	b. January 29, 1804	d. February 18, 1874
3.	Nimrod Newlon	b. December 4, 1805	d. September 6, 1876
4.	James Newlon	b. circa 1809	
5.	John Newlon	b. circa 1812	
6.	Sarah Newlon	b. September 10, 1814	d. October 12, 1889

Dempsey Carter was born about two weeks after the Declaration of Independence was signed. Dempsey was still unmarried when his father wrote his will. Dempsey later married Mary Anne. Dempsey inherited the southern third of the homestead including the house his parents had lived in. The Hinshaw typed copy of James Sr.'s Will gives Dempsey his choice of *'houses'* to live in, I interpreted the word to be *'horses'* not *'houses'*. His compensation for looking after his mother was the horse of his choice. The homestead property probably had several cabins, with a new cabin built as each son married. Dempsey was later swindled out of his land and his brothers attempted to restore the ownership. Those documents list the land as over one hundred acres. In some documents Dempsey is spelled Demsey without the letter 'p'.

In the 1820 US Census for Loudoun County, Dempsey and his wife were both listed as being between 26 and 45. They also have three children – one daughter and two sons between the ages of 16 and 26. These children might have been Dempsey's stepchildren. In the 1830 US Census there was only Dempsey and his wife. Dempsey Carter is the only name in either census. I haven't located Dempsey's Will, but his estate took some time to probate between 1845 and 1850. His brother Eden was the executor of his estate. There was a committee to inventory his assets, collect rent that was due, pay off his debts and finalize his accounts. The probate documents suggest that his wife preceded him in death and any children were no longer living in Loudoun County.

Eden Carter married Susannah Hann on December 15, 1803. Their minister was William Williamson per Loudoun County Marriage Records. Susannah Hann had been born on February 14, 1786. Eden inherited the land Mahlon was living on, which appears to be a separate parcel of land James Carter Sr. had acquired. He spent his working life as a farmer in Loudoun County. He served as the executor of his brother Dempsey's estate. His son Francis Marion Carter moved to Williams County, Ohio. After retiring Eden and his wife also moved to Williams County, Ohio. Susannah died on April 29, 1855 and Eden died on August 15, 1857 in Ohio. They probably had other children than the three names linked to them.

Known children of Eden and Susannah:

1.	Margaret Carter	b. circa 1827	
2.	Francis Marion Carter	b. April 11, 1828	d. November 11, 1885
3.	Susannah Amanda Carter	b. April 10, 1834	

Sarah Carter married James Yates in 1811. James Yates was born about 1780. Sarah Yates died in Ohio in 1850. James Yates died in January 1860.

Known children of Sarah and James:

1.	Lucinda Yates	b. September 1807	d. June 9, 1875
2.	Joel Yates	b. January 5, 1809	d. December 25, 1875
3.	Carter Yates	b. August 26, 1811	d. July 13, 1888
4.	Hannah Yates	b. September 14, 1814	d. April 1, 1859
5.	Eden Yates	b. February 17, 1820	d. February 7, 1900
6.	Jemima Carson Yates	b. March 10, 1823	d. March 11, 1884
7.	Sarah T. Yates	b. May 11, 1827	d. August 27, 1992

Mahlon Carter married Catherine in 1808. Mahlon appears to have inherited the northwest corner of the original homestead where Eden was living on at the time James Sr. wrote his will. Mahlon acted as the executor of his fathers' estate. He filed probate papers with the traveling Circuit Court Judge on July 24, 1812. Mahlon died about 1839 having remained in Loudoun County.

Known children of Mahlon and Catherine:

1.	Troyless Carter	b. August 10, 1808	d. May 12, 1888
2.	Salathiel Carter	b. circa 1810	
3.	Emya Carter	b. circa 1812	d. circa 1890
4.	James Carter	b. circa 1815	d. June 2, 1866
5.	Hannah Carter	b. circa 1817	d. March 22, 1866

Details about the life of the youngest son James 2nd will be discussed in the next chapter.

Quakers in general did not participate in the American Revolution. Hannah's brother Samuel Eblen was an exception. Samuel Eblen was disciplined twice by the Fairfax Monthly Meeting for taking up arms. Samuel was disowned on March 26, 1774 for joining the Virginia Militia, reinstated on May 28, 1774, and disowned again on June 28, 1777. Secondary sources claim that Samuel Eblen served under Captain Henry for three months in 1777 and was present at Burgoyne's Defeat. He served another three month in 1781 under Major Riley as they pursued Cornwallis towards Williamsburg, Virginia.

Following the American Revolution the cash strapped newly formed United States government had no way to repay its debts. There was the loan from the French, and loans from wealthy plantation owners, plus the need to pay restitution to the soldiers who had done the fighting. To solve the latter need, the military forged further west into Indians lands that were part of the North Carolina and Virginia Charters. The military surveyed the land and plotted out 40-acre parcels which were distributed to the soldiers as payment for their service. Some of the soldiers accepted the land and moved into the area that today is eastern Tennessee and eastern Kentucky, displacing the Algonquin once again.

To repay the wealthy landowners who had helped finance the American Revolution, the Second Congress of the United States created 'The Sinking Fund' as Bill # 30 on November 7, 1791. The Sinking Fund created a system of incremental payments designed to slowly pay down the debt. John Adams the Second President of the United States signed the bill into law. The name James Carter was on the list of Virginia contributors being repaid. This James Carter was the grandson of either Robert 'King'

Carter or Thomas Carter. James Carter Sr. was successful enough as a farmer to have been able to purchase three additional parcels of land. He did not have the tens of thousands of dollars that James Carter was slated to be repaid by the Sinking Fund.

James and Hannah's son Asa was only five when the American Revolution began. Children Eden, Sarah and Mahlon were born into the new Union governed by the Articles of Confederation. The Constitution of the United States of America was written and ratified in 1789. James Carter 2nd was born into the new United States of America.

The Carter Family Bible

A Quaker Bible printed in Berwick, Northumberland, England in 1793 was given to James Carter 2nd on September 16, 1798 when James 2nd was only seven years old. The bible was an English translation of a Swiss bible from the Church of Neufchatel which included arguments by the Reverand M. Ostervald. James Carter Sr. had signed the top of the first blank page and followed his signature with the September date. Below his name he wrote *'and Hannah his wife'* followed by the same date. About halfway down the page, Asa Carter signed his name followed by the same date. Below his signature Asa wrote *'Cinthia Carter'* followed by the same date. The bible had probably been ordered by Cinthia Parker before her marriage. The couple married in June 1797, and later they decided that they did not have need for two bibles. If Asa's father would pay for one bible, that would give the young couple a little bit of cash. James Carter Sr. was in his sixties and expected his youngest son to read the bible aloud.

When he was sixteen, James Carter 2nd added this comment to the back of his bible:

> *James Carter his book don't steal this*
> *book for fear of shame for in it is the*
> *oners name and if this book you do steal*
> *hit is a book you can't conceal   February 15th Day 1807*

Most people get a chuckle from the spelling of 'owners' and the use of the word 'hit', plus the lack of punctuation. James 2nd may have been upset with an older sibling for taking his bible without permission, but he did not write the note in a moment of anger. There are no ink blots, he took his time composing and writing the message. James Carter 2nd received a good basic quaker education. As good an education as a wilderness community could provide with limited resources.

Researcher Thomas Katheder, after having the opportunity to view the Carter Family Bible, wrote an article in the *Virginia Genealogist* Volume 41, Number 2 in 1997. The article contains several erroneous statements. James Carter Sr.'s birthday is not written anywhere in the Bible. Inexplicably, Mr. Katheder assumed that September 16,

1743 was James Carter Sr.'s birthdate. It is unknown how he came up with the year. In a footnote to the *Virginia Genealogist* article, Mr. Katheder admits that this date might not be correct. He provided the date to the Morman Genealogical Library where it was regarded as a fact. The date is incorrect by several years and has thrown researchers a curve ball. Alice Nelson Cartar Yates could not have been James Carter Sr.'s mother since she had been married to Joseph Yates for a year.

Mr. Katheder wrote another article for the *Virgina Genealogist* Volume 47, Number 4 in 2003. He changed James Sr. year of birth to 1741 and makes the family connection that Alice Yates was James Carter Sr.'s mother. That information has not been added to genealogy databases. Researchers have also assumed that James married shortly after turning twenty-one. With Henry Carter as a witness to the deed transfer, he also had to have been over twenty-one, which leads to the speculation that Henry was older than his brother. In a small wilderness farming community, there may have been a lack of marriageable females, which might explain Henry Carter's transfer to the Hopewell Monthly Meeting.

The bible was covered with buckskin and buried during the Civil War to keep it away from the unfunded Confederate volunteers who were raiding family farms for supplies. Mr. Katheder claims the bible was buried to keep it away from Union soldiers. Union soldiers were not raiding family farms in southwest Missouri. The bible remained buried for about three years. Time underground yellowed the pages. More than one hundred years later the bible retained a strong musty earthy odor. Part of the smell might have been due to the deteriorating buckskin cover. Some of the entries for birthdates of children appear to be James 2nd handwriting, other entries were probably in Sarah Jane's handwriting. Leroy's handwriting may be the least legible. James Walter Sr. inherited the bible so later entries were in his handwriting.

Names, Dates of Birth and Dates of Death Listed in the Carter Family Bible

James Carter was born the 28th Day of June In the year 1791
Sarah Carter his wife was Born the 7th Day of December In the year 1789
Eden Carter Son of James Carter And Sarah his wife was Born the 5th Day of August In the year 1812
Lemuel Carter was Born the 14th Day of February 1814
Salathiel Carter was born May 5th Day 1816
Washington G Carter was Born November the 17th Day 1818
Julina Carter was born October 24th 1821
Sarah Jane Carter was born February 5th 1825
James Gilbert Leroy Carter was born April 22nd 1826
Alfred Gipson Carter was born September 18th 1829
Harriett Meria Zerna Carter was born April 29th 1835

Harriett Meria Zerna Carter Deceased March 7, 1842 at 2 o'clock AM. 6 years 10 months and
Sarah Jane Carter Deceased June 20th 1825 Aged 4 months and 15 Days when Departed this Life
Eden Carter Deceased October the 4th Day Aged 2 months when Departed this Life
James Carter Deceased October the 9th Day 1845
Sarah Carter Deceased January the 27th day 1854

James Carter And Sarah Myers was Married the 24th Day of October In the year 1811
Sarah Jane Jones Daughter of Julina was born November the 4 1840 being the granddaughter of James
& Sarah Carter
Hariet Meria Dickison was born July 16th 1847

James Gilbreth Leroy Carter and Mary Means Cooley were Married July 22, 1849
Mary Means Cooley Died April 8, 1902
James Gilbreth Leroy Carter Died Nov. 8, 1914

There is another page listing the births of some grandchildren which is barely legible.

James Carter Sr.'s 1812 Will

The exact date of James Carter Sr.'s death is unknown. Most genealogy websites list September 16, 1812 as his date of death. Of the four known images of his will, two were handwritten, plus there are two typed copies credited to Hinshaw. None of these images are of the original will. One handwritten copy dated September 16, 1812 clearly states at the top that James Carter was already deceased. This was probably the courthouse copy. A second handwritten copy dated July 24, 1812 was probably the traveling Circuit Judge's copy. On that same date, Mahlon filed probate documents. I suspect James Carter Sr. died before his youngest son turned 21 on June 28, 1812. He might have passed away late in the year 1811 or in 1812, before July 24th.

The two handwritten copies of the will have the word 'seal' surrounded by curlicues next to James Carter Sr.'s signature. In the middle of the signature is an X with the words *'His Mark'*. The signature was not original, the word seal indicates that this is a copy made by a clerk. Not an original, not a forgery, just a copy of the signature written by a clerk. Most likely the original will was written on loose sheets of paper. While in town the Circuit Court Judge made a copy in a bound journal. After the Judge returned to the courthouse in Leesburg, the 'worst for wear' traveling journal was copied into a new journal. The original documents on loose sheets of paper had been folded in half then in thirds. A small stack of these folded legal documents would have been tied with string and stowed in the Judge's saddlebag, until they could be filed in a drawer back at the courthouse.

The first time I read a typed copy of James Carter Sr.'s will, I suspected that he had not written the entire document. Stuck in the middle was wording directing the youngest son James Carter 2nd to work for his older brothers for wages. That wording does not appear in other copies of the will.

In his Will (see Chapter 11) James Carter Sr. gives his wife Hannah continued use of the house plus all the furnishings. Hannah also gets the profits from the farm minus an annual payment of $100 to Dempsey. Dempsey gets his choice of a horse and will inherit the farm after his mother's death. Eldest son John received the 154 acres he was living on in Hampshire County. Henry received the land he was living on but is expected to pay his sister Ruth $200 within two years. Asa received the 44 acres he was living on. Eden and Mahlon were expected to trade the land they were living on. A description of property lines mentions trees, rocks, neighbors and distances measured in poles. Both Eden and Mahlon were expected to pay $100 each for two years to their youngest brother. James 2nd is to receive $840 of which $400 was to be paid by his brothers. The remaining $440 was to come from the sale of his father's personal property. Sarah Yates was to receive $40. Ruth Newlon was to receive $320 of which $200 was to be paid by her older brother Henry. Both John and Mahlon were named as executors, but the job fell to Mahlon since John was living in Hampshire County.

The sale of James Carter Sr.'s personal property needed to raise about $600.00 to pay the legacies bequeathed to his children. The probate documents show that James Carter Sr.'s farm operation included horses, cows, hogs, sheep, wheat, rye and corn. By Mahlon's accounting he raised $765.08 but paid out $255.15 ½ which included 7½ % commission of $57.37 ½ cents for his efforts. It took two years to settle his father's estate. A net of $509.92 ½ was about ninety dollars short of fulfilling the Legacies. The final probate document with the court was filed on October 10, 1814. A Loudoun County Court ruled on May 17, 1815 to record the probate documents and then the Court finalized James Carter's estate of August 14, 1815.

James Carter Sr. asked to be buried in the Southfork Burial Grounds. With the last line of his will James Carter Sr. asks his children to *"suppress emotions of discontent with respect to the division of my estate and to endeavor to live in love and harmony with each other"*.

The 1812 Will mentions a property line to the north of the old homestead which abutted land belonging to William Carter (no relation). William R. Carter moved to Loudoun County in 1785 after having served in the American Revolution. He was married to Margaret Jury Carter. Their children included sons Jesse Carter and William Jury Carter plus daughter Rhoda. Jesse Carter and his father moved to Preble County Ohio in 1815. William Jury Carter was married to Mahalia. He sold the land in western Loudoun County to George Keen in July 1821. George Keen built a two-story stone house on the property, replacing the small log cabin. That piece of land had several names over the decades: *Meadow Brook, Gray Stone,* and *Faraway Farm.* Interestingly

Faraway Farms was the name Robert Carter III aka Colonel Carter of Nomini had called one of his inherited properties. After his eldest son died in London, Colonel Carter sold off some of his land holdings to pay off his son's debts. History is unclear if this was the same land leased by Thomas Blackburn or Benjamin Grayson – two prominent early quaker leaders in the South Fork MM.

After George Keen arrived in western Loudoun County, he began acquiring as much land as possible. Many of the properties he purchased had been leased land. It appears that the great grandchildren of Robert 'King' Carter preferred the upper-class society of Manassas, Virginia to owning land in the wilds of western Loudoun County. Raised with wealth and the comradery of their social status, many had married cousins. There were so many intermarriages that historians have difficulty untangling who is related to whom and how.

Notice in the Philadelphia *Pennsylvania Gazette* Sunday July 4, 1745

To be sold, by the Trustees appointed by an Act of the Assembly of Virginia, at Fredericksburg, at October Fair, the following valuable Tracts of Land, viz. Eight Thousand Acres and upwards on Opequon, in the County of Frederick. 8,000 Acres on the Branches of Goose Creek, in the Counties of Fairfax and Prince William. 6,000 Acres on the Branches of Bull-Run, in Prince William County. Also 100,000 Acres on the Branches of Roanoke, to be disposed of by Charles Carter. Any Persons inclining to purchase any of the above mentioned Lands, are desired to send in their Names, with the Quantity of Acres they would have, to the Subscriber, living near the Falls of Rappahannock.   Charles Carter

Charles Carter was attempting to unload some of the excess land his father had acquired. More than 120,000 acres was just too much for one man to manage. The grandchildren seems quite happy with less land around Manassas. A few thousand acres was more than enough for any one person to manage.

James Carter Sr.'s will gives no indication of where James 2nd and Sarah Jane were living. New cabins had been built on the homestead as each son married. James Sr. bequeathed his youngest son one thousand dollars minus one hundred sixty dollars he had already provided. The $160 was probably for a marriage bond, paid to the minister who performed the ceremony. The minister was expected to record the marriage at the Courthouse. James Carter 2nd and Sarah Jane Myers marriage wasn't recorded in Leesburg.

Some websites erroneously claim that James Carter 2nd married Mary Howell when he was only sixteen. James Carter, the son of Peter Carter of eastern Loudoun County married Mary Howell. Peter's son was about seven years older than James Carter 2nd. Part of the confusion comes from the name of their minister – John

Littlejohn. This was the same traveling minister who had performed the marriage of Asa Carter and Cinthia Parker. John Littlejohn is best known to history as the owner of the farm in Alexandria, Virginia to which important government documents were spirited in 1812 after the British Redcoats laid siege to Washington, DC. As the British began burning government buildings, documents were hurriedly removed. Included in the stash of government papers were copies of the Declaration of Independence, copies of the Constitution and the large portrait of George Washington that Dolly Madison had instructed to be cut from its frame at the White House.

When Loudoun County split off from Fairfax County the dividing line was the Difficult Run. Later the dividing line was moved west to the Sugar Run. Peter Carter owned land between the Sugar Run and the Difficult Run, so without moving his land changed counties. Per the Loudoun County Marriage Records there was a third James Carter in Loudoun County who married Rachel Jenkins on October 12, 1820 with the ceremony performed by John L. Dogg. Only the marriages of Asa & Cinthia and Eden & Susannah were recorded with the Loudoun County Clerk's Office.

The contract wording in James Carter Sr's will led me to suspected that James Carter 2nd worked the land that Asa had inherited while Asa moved his family to Hampshire County. Recent perusal of '*Sims Index of Hampshire County, Virginia Personal Tax List 1800 – 1814*' sheds new light on where James 2nd and Sarah Jane were living. The Sims Index is a typed copy of a deteriorating handwritten journal.

The Index divides Hampshire County into an upper or western section and a lower or eastern section. Numbers beside each individuals' name represent the number of taxable white men, the number of common horses, and the number of taxable **negro** slaves who are over the age of twelve. Mills and business licenses were also taxed. The Carter last name shows up in both the upper and lower sections. The Virginia Legislature did not pass tax legislation in 1808 so no personal tax was collected that year.

Upper	*1809*	*Henry Carter*	*1 – 1*
Upper	*1810*	*John Carter*	*1 – 1*
Upper	*1812*	*Henry H Carter*	*1 – 1*
Lower	*1806*	*Joseph Carter*	*0 – 1 – 1*
Lower	*1807*	*Joseph Carter*	*0 – 2 – 2*
Lower	*1809*	*Joseph Carter*	*0 – 2 – 2*
Lower	*1810*	*Joseph Carter*	*0 – 3 – 2*
Lower	*1811*	*Joseph Carter*	*0 – 3 – 2*
Lower	*1811*	*James Carter*	*1*
Lower	*1811*	*John Carter*	*1 – 4*
Lower	*1812*	*James Carter*	*1 – 2*
Lower	*1812*	*John Carter*	*1 – 5*

Lower	*1813*	*Asa Carter*	*1 – 2*
Lower	*1813*	*James Carter*	*1 – 3*
Lower	*1813*	*John Carter*	*1 – 5*
Lower	*1814*	*Asa Carter*	*1 – 2*
Lower	*1814*	*James Carter*	*1 – 3*
Lower	*1814*	*John Carter*	*1 – 5*

Joseph Carter appears to be a free negro who managed to buy some of his family members. The Henry(s) and John Carter taxed in the upper section of Hampshire County were NOT the sons of James and Hannah. They might have been James' brothers. There are no details as to where they were living prior to 1809 or after 1812.

I interpret this document to show that James Carter 2nd accompanied his older brother to Hampshire County. In the summer of 1810, James 2nd helped John's family build their cabin. He remained for about a year and wasn't taxed for owning a horse in 1811. James 2nd returned to Loudoun County and married Sarah Jane Myers. With cash from his father's will, James 2nd was able to buy land in Hampshire County. That is where he and Sarah Jane began raising their family. I no longer think that James and Sarah Jane lived on or worked the land Asa inherited in Loudoun County.

Among the Probate Inventory of personal property from James Carter Sr's estate, sons John, Asa, and James 2nd did not purchase any of their father's stuff. These sons had moved to Hampshire County before the sale took place. Mahlon purchased more items than any other individual. Henry, Eden and Hannah each purchased a few items.

Southfork Quaker Burial Grounds

Quaker members of the South Fork MM set aside land as a cemetery known as the Southfork Burial Grounds. Quakers did not erect grave markers nor did they mark gravesites with field stones. They kept written ledgers of the names of individuals who were buried in Southfork. The Unison Preservation Society website lists only sixty-seven grave markers in the Southfork Burial Grounds. All but two of these markers show a date of death after 1835, the year that the South Fork MM was disbanded for lack of membership. Most of these markers are for non-quakers who continued using the cemetery. The Find-A-Grave website lists one hundred thirty three grave markers. Twice as many markers as the Unison Preservation Society website acknowledges. A closer examination of these additional markers show some disturbing features. Many are made of irregular shaped pieces of stone. Some have drafting lines, but the letter spacing is inconsistent. The letter 'N' is purposely carved backwards and the letters 'DECEED' are included. 'DECEED' is not an actual word. In speaking the quakers referred to the deceased as *'the departed'*. In wills the word is often abbreviated as *"dec'd"*. These additional markers are not very respectful and were probably added to the cemetery in the twentieth century.

On the Find-A-Grave website there once was an image of field stones nestled together in the leaf litter which were purported to designate where James Carter and Hannah Carter were buried within the Southfork Burial Grounds. Early images show two stones with a faint carving of the initials JC and HC respectively. Those field stones were later pulled out of the ground and stood upright. More recently someone replaced those field stones with larger stone slabs standing erect about a foot apart.

Some family trees list a date of death for Hannah in 1798, but she was listed in her husband's will of 1812 very much alive. She was later recorded in the probate documents as purchasing a few items during the sale of her husband's personal estate. Hannah Eblen Carter probably died in the spring of 1821 before her son Dempsey and his wife sold the 103 acres. Per the Loudoun County, VA Court of Chancery Case No. M-1554 in 1839, Carter's Comm. vs. Drake's Exor. *Et al.* and M-1718 in 1850, Carter vs. Bilby *et al*, Dempsey had been defrauded in the sale and received the land back in a rescission action.

The Hannah Carter who died in 1798 might have been the second wife of Peter Carter. She was included in Peter Carter's will written in June 1794. Hannah would have been the stepmother to the James Carter who married Mary Howell. Her father John Whaley had been a foreman working for Robert Carter, managing several of his farms in northern Virginia. Robert Carter I[st] did not want to use valuable tidewater tobacco growing land for food crops. As he surveyed northern Virginia, he patented thousands of acres and started several farms near Manassas. Frying Pan Farm managed by John Whaley raised corn and cattle near modern Dulles Airport.

Chapter 8 – James Carter 2nd and Sarah Jane Myers Family

James Carter 2nd was the youngest child of James Sr. and Hannah Carter. Hannah was forty-five when James 2nd was born on June 24, 1791. His father was in his mid-fifties. James 2nd was probably treated as a spoiled baby. He was twenty-six years younger than his oldest brother John. He was four years younger than his closest sibling Mahlon. Anytime there were chores to perform, an older stronger brother was available to do most of the manual labor. Under the quaker naming convention one would have expected the third son to have been named James. It is possible that Hannah had given birth to another son the couple had named James, but that child died young. Some websites list James Carter 2nd as James Carter Jr. but to the family he has always been known as James 2nd without any middle initial.

James Carter 2nd married Sarah Jane Myers on October 24, 1811 in Loudoun County, Virginia. James 2nd was only twenty years old which was a tad young since men usually didn't marry until they had established a profession with which to earn a living. Sarah Jane's parents are unverified. In the Carter Family Bible her birthdate is listed as December 7, 1789. The Bible does not list where she was born. In Carter family lore she was always called Sarah Jane not simply Sarah. It is possible that she was the daughter of the Sarah Myers whose name appears in the Fairfax MM records as an attendee at several weddings.

Several German Myers families were members of the Fairfax MM including brothers Jonathan, Benjamin and William Myers. These brothers may have been the sons of Joseph and Phebe Schooley Myers of Hunterdon County, New Jersey. The Myers name is of German origin and at times it is spelled Mires, Miers, Myres, or Meyers in English records. There had been a large contingent of Germans who settle in the Germantown section of Philadelphia. Another large group settled near New Bern, North Carolina. The first generation settlers often continued to speak mostly German while the second and third generations became more anglicized. The Myers brothers in Loudoun County had anglicized first names. Some Anabaptist had migrated from the Black Forest area of the Holy Roman Empire to England almost a century prior to migration to North America. In his will William Myers refers to his wife Sarah and his daughter Sally. The names Patsy, Polly, Sally and Molly were often used as a childhood nickname. At the time of William Myers death, Sarah Jane would have been twelve years old, so this is one possibility for her parentage.

James Carter 2nd did not inherit any land from his father. Instead, he was bequeathed $1,000 minus the $160 his father had already provided. The couple's first three children were born in Virginia – probably Hampshire County not Loudoun County. Hampshire County is now part of West Virginia. Their next five children were born in Franklin County, Ohio. Their youngest daughter was born in Marion County, Indiana.

Known children of James 2nd and Sarah Jane:

1. Eden Carter   b. August 5, 1812,   d. October 4, 1812.
2. Lemuel Carter   b. February 14, 1814.
3. Salathiel A. Carter   b. May 5, 1816.
4. Washington G. Carter   b. November 17, 1818, in Franklin County, Ohio Country.
5. Julina Carter   b. October 29, 1821.
6. Sarah Jane Carter   b. February 5, 1825,   d. 1825 New Albany.
7. **James Gilbert Leroy Carter**   b. April 22, 1826.
8. Alfred Gipson Carter   b. September 18, 1829   d. August 1871.
9. Harriett Meria Zerna Carter   b. April 29, 1835, in Indianapolis, Marion Co., Indiana

James Carter 2nd moved his family to Franklin County, Ohio County circa 1817. Hamilton Twp., New Albany & Plain Twp. are possible locations. Land prices in Virginia were approximately $2.25 per acre with most parcels averaging 200 acres. Much of the land near Unison had been acquired as 99-year leases which were nearing expiration.

Following the War of 1812, Massachusetts, Connecticut, and Virginia all asked for a piece of the Ohio Country. They wanted to award land as restitution for military service. The military surveyed the Indian territory opening it up to white settlement. Only a few soldiers chose to move to Ohio, so the territory was soon opened to everyone. Land prices were offered at $1.25 per acre with a minimum of forty acres. Smaller garden plots were available for military widows. Low land prices and the uncertain future of the leased land in northern Virginia attracted settlers. By 1835 the quaker South Fork Monthly Meeting was disbanded for lack of membership.

James Carter 2nd took advantage of the offer of inexpensive land. There is only one record in the Bureau of Land Management of a James Carter purchasing land in Ohio between 1812 and 1830. There are two records of a James Carter receiving a military allotment and assigning the land to another individual. The military allotments were for different James Carters. The land purchase was on 11/14/1816 for Township and Range 010N – 019N SW1/4 Section 29. This was for 160 acres in Vinton County, south of Columbus. James Carter is listed as being from nearby Ross County, Ohio. This record is probably also for a different James Carter. Land records after 1830 were for different James Carter families. Land records with a middle initial are also for different James Carter(s). Some websites give James 2nd the middle initial 'C'. Per the Bureau of Land Management records, the James C. Carter who purchased land in Ohio was from Boone County, Kentucky.

Exactly when the family left Virginia is not certain, but after crops had been harvested in the early fall would seem like a good time. A second possibility would be early spring before planting began. The family may have moved several times, purchasing land from individuals and not through the Bureau of Land Management.

Exactly where the family lived is difficult to pinpoint, five of the children are listed as having been born in Franklin County, Ohio. The James Carter 2nd family moved out of Ohio in 1830 heading west to Indianapolis, Indiana. Their last residence appears to have been in Plain township of Franklin County located east of the city of Columbus. Family lore claims that there had been several years of severe flooding resulting in complete crop failures. Ohio has a history of tornados with the year 1828 recording extensive damage to the western half of Ohio. Strong winds can severely damage grain crop yields. Then there was a major cholera outbreak in the city of Columbus which killed over one hundred individuals.

On July 29, 1828 the Columbus newspaper lists a notice of a Sheriffs Sale at the home of James Carter in Plain township to occur on August 16, 1828. For sale would be one Mare and one Colt taken as the property of James Carter to settle the lawsuit by P. Mapes. It is uncertain if this was James Carter 2nd but it might have been.

Beginning in the 1830's a schism developed in quaker communities known as the Hittite Revolt. The more urbanized congregations desired a structured weekly service which included the reading aloud of scriptures. Other congregations did not want any changes. Heated debates caused congregations to split, some ousting half of their membership. Although the Carter family were not members of the Society of Friends, a rowdy discord among neighbors could have been a factor in the decision to move.

In 1840 Franklin County published a list of tax delinquent properties in The *Ohio State Journal* newspaper of Columbus, Ohio. Hundreds of names are on the list including James Carter and Asa Carter both owning lands in Plain township. James Carter owed taxes on 100 acres for the year 1830. Asa owed taxes on 275 acres for the year 1834. Hundreds of families moved away from flooded land that was unsaleable. If no one came forward to pay the delinquent tax, the county would reclaim the land and offer it for resale.

The National Road was under construction as the Carter family moved west. Begun in the spring of 1811, the six hundred mile long National Road stretched from Cumberland, Maryland to Columbus, Ohio, then on to Indianapolis, Indiana and finally to Vandalia, Illinois. Construction ended before the road was extended to St. Louis, Missouri. From the east the National Road followed the original Cumberland Trail through the Appalachian Mountains. The Trail had been used extensively during the French and Indian Wars. The Cumberland Trail was widened by Daniel Boone who lead covered wagons through the mountain pass as settlers moved into eastern Kentucky. In 1797 Ebenezer Zane established a rough wagon road from Wheeling, WV to Maysville, Kentucky. Sections of this old route were incorporated into the National Road. Construction was financed by the sale of Federal Lands. In the 1830's individual states took over construction. Eastern sections of the road used crushed rock to create a hard durable surface. Clay was used to surface other areas. Before the Civil War broke out, thousands of pioneers traveled the National Road heading westward looking for a better life. The National Road was completed to Indianapolis in 1837.

The James Carter 2nd family moved to Marion County, Indiana in 1830. James 2nd may also have purchased land in Hamilton County. Salathiel purchased land in Hamilton County from individuals. James, Lemuel and Washington purchased additional acreage in Washington Township of Marion County through the Bureau of Land Management.

James Carter 2nd name appears in several court documents (see Chapter 12). The first legal record is in the Marion County Circuit Court 1833 March Term. His name is on the list of store and tavern keepers who had been issued a business license since the September 1832 term. These businesses were taxable in 1833. James Carter 2nd had applied for a tavern license in December 1832 which was to expire on December 12, 1833. James 2nd and Sarah Jane operated the Rosebud Inn. Business licenses needed to be renewed each year. Only about half of the businesses were on the list for the March 1834 term. There may have been a large turnover of business owners in the 1830's with the influx of new residents.

Microfilmed pages of court cases are not a complete record of the case but are merely attorney filings pertaining to the case. Much of the handwriting is barely legible. First case: on September 14, 1833 James 2nd and three other men went to the court house and swore under oath that John Blackburn was an idle, vagrant. They felt that his wife and three children would suffer without assistance. The State tried John Blackburn for vagrancy but he was acquitted by the judge. The other three men had appeared in court but James Carter 2nd did not. The judge ruled that Blackburn could recover the court fees from Carter for failure to prosecute. A grand sum of $6.59 ½ cents. James 2nd may have been hiding from the court because he was being sued by merchants in another case. When James Carter 2nd did not pay the court costs, the judge issued a writ of execution to seize and sale some of Carter's property. After public notice, the Constable sold one pair of oxen for twenty cents. The judge issued a second writ of execution and once again the Constable auction off a wagon for $1.31. In March 1834 James Carter 2nd countersued the judge, the constable and the man who had been the highest bidder at both auctions seeking $500.00 in damages.

As for the second case, merchants Henry & James Nevill sought damages of $1,000 dollars, unable to locate James Carter 2nd the judge issued a writ and the constable was able to retrieve some of the merchandise. In March 1835 James Carter 2nd countersued. Among the merchandise listed were three bags of coffee weighing a combined total of 488 lbs., a chest of tea and a half barrel of sugar, a dozen axes and shovels plus a 25 lb. bag of shot and one keg of brimstone weighing 57 lbs. The large quantities of coffee, tea and sugar sound like they were intended for use in the tavern. Brimstone is another name for sulfur, historically called the burning rock. Sulfur flames burn at a high temperature. Why James Carter 2nd would need so much brimstone is unknown, but he may have been using it in brewing beer and or distilling whisky. His hiding from the court might have had something to do with alcohol production.

In regard to the first case concerning the unpaid court fees, when James Carter 2nd countersued he was overheard calling James Kimberlin a liar and challenging him to a duel. Kimberlin had been the highest bidder at both of the auctions, acquiring a wagon and a pair of oxen for a combined expense of $1.51. In April 1837 James Carter 2nd was charged by the State of Indiana with dueling.

The image of an irascible gun toting James Carter 2nd challenging another man to a duel is difficult to reconcile with the image of the teenager back in Loudoun County, Virginia who wrote in the back of his bible *don't steal this book for fear of shame*.

In 1837 Salathiel Carter sued Carson Nickers in a case of Replevin. Salathiel sold a mare and its colt to Nickers who then took a second mare and colt. The mare was valued at $75 dollars and the colt at $25 dollars. The suit asks for $300 dollars in damages.

Tucked inside the family bible was a small scrap of paper titled *Account of Sale of Lots in Fayetteville*. The Carter name is listed next to lots numbered 31 and 37. Fayetteville is a small unincorporated town in Lawrence County, Indiana southwest of Indianapolis. The town was platted in February 1838 by Ezra Kern. James Carter 2nd may have been considering moving away from Marion County before Gilbert Kemp's mill house burnt to the ground.

James Carter 2nd had a long running dispute with Gilbert Kemp the owner of a grist mill in southern Hamilton County. The reason for the dispute is unknown. Gilbert Kemp might have been shortchanging farmers in the quantity of flour per load of grain. There may have been mixing of wheat flour with corn meal or vice versa. Since James Carter 2nd and his sons owned land south of the mill, the complaint might have been about waste contaminating the water. Also there was a court case in the April 1838 term of Hamilton County Court which is alluded to as a reason for their dispute.

Gilbert Kemp's grist mill house burnt to the ground overnight on September 16, 1838. Kemp went to the Hamilton Circuit Court and accused James Carter 2nd of arson. James Carter 2nd was arrested and kept in jail for twenty four hours before appearing in custody before a Judge on September 25, 1838. After hearing the evidence the Judge acquitted James Carter 2nd.   In the court documents there are two pages which appear to be duplicates. Gilbert Kemp's mill was originally valued at one thousand dollars, then on the additional copies the amount was changed to four thousand dollars.

Gilbert Kemp wasn't satisfied with the acquittal so he appeared before a Hamilton Grand Jury claiming there was sufficient evidence to charge Lemuel and Salathiel Carter. The Carter brothers were tried for arson in the April 1839 term of the Hamilton Court. The venue was changed to the Marion Circuit Court in Indianapolis. The circumstantial evidence against them consisted of: they were seen talking with their father on the day the mill burnt. Then at 3 o'clock in the afternoon they were seen riding past the mill, heading to Noblesville. Afterwards the prosecution could not account for their whereabouts. The prosecution claimed the brothers made misleading statements as to where they went and at what time. Also, Lemuel must harbor bad feelings toward Gilbert Kemp since he was still living with his father. In summation because the brothers did not prove their innocence they must be guilty.

The defense lawyer for the Carter brothers was Calvin Fletcher, who claimed the prosecution case was insufficient. He proposed other hypothesis suggesting someone else had committed the crime. He mentioned a broken pen knife and a cigar stub. Oddly, he did not present any witnesses for the defense. Lemuel and Salathiel were convicted and the sentence included a $5.00 fine and two years of hard labor in the State Penitentiary. Fletcher appealed the verdict to the State Supreme Court. To stay out of jail pending the verdict, the brothers posted bond putting their land up as collateral.

The Indiana State Supreme Court rubberstamped the lower court decision without hearing any evidence. The brothers had already left Indiana. None of the documents indicate that Gilbert Kemp was ever awarded any amount for damages. On August 1, 1839, James Carter 2nd countersued Gilbert Kemp for false arrest and defamation of character. James Carter 2nd was awarded $2,000 in damages. It is unlikely that he ever received a penny from Gilbert Kemp.

In 1841 there were petitions to review the court case and discharge the liens against Elijah Brock and William Rice concerning the bonds the Carter brothers had posted. The Carter land had been sold by the state for $500. A petition with more than seventy signatures was sent to the newly elected Governor James Whitcomb.

Governor Whitcomb issued a pardon in favor of Lemuel and Salathiel Carter on September 19, 1846. The Carter brothers were no longer fugitives from the law. In his autobiography Calvin Fletcher claims that the Carter brothers did not receive a fair trial. Evidence was withheld, but he does not elaborate.   A modern Indiana Archivist could not locate any record of the brothers having served any time in the State Penitentiary. Family lore does not mention any time spent in Indiana, although that is where Salathiel and Charity met, married and their first two sons were born.

In 1839 Lemuel purchased 40 acres through the Bureau of Land Management. Lying along Blackberry Creek, the land was on the western edge of Jasper County, Missouri. The following year James Carter 2nd purchased land close to Georgia City. Today the Georgia City cemetery is the only indication that a town once existed. In 1842 James Carter 2nd traded for land along Center Creek which became the family homestead. Black flies were such annoying pests that the family plowed their corn fields at night. Since there were no mills nearby the corn had to be soaked and then grated for meal. To obtain staples the family traveled two hundred miles north to the trading post at Boonville on the Missouri River. The round trip using oxen to pull a wagon took about two months.

Details of the lives of the children of James 2nd and Sarah Jane:

Lemuel Carter was born on February 14, 1814, probably in Hampshire County, Virginia. Lemuel's education was not as formal as his father's quaker influenced upbringing. Lemuel first purchased land in Marion County, Indiana. He and his brother Salathiel left Indiana in 1839 after being convicted of arson. They forfeited their land in Indiana in order to stay out of the state penitentiary. In 1839 Lemuel purchased 40 acres on Blackberry Creek in Jasper County, Missouri. Lemuel married Isabelle Pyles.

Lemuel and his brothers Salathiel, Washington, and Alfred along with brother-in-law Thomas Jefferson Cooley participated in the 1849 California Gold Rush. Word reached Missouri in the fall of 1848 that gold had been discovered at Sutter's Mill near Sacramento, California. The Carter brothers along with dozens of other residents of Jasper County decided to go to California and try to strike it rich. In the 1850 US Census these men were listed with the occupation of 'G Hunter'.

Gold! Gold! Gold!

The last accounts from California of gold discoveries in that country are really astounding. We find in the Journal of Commerce two Letters dated at Monterey on the 29th June and 21 July last, from which we gather that the sands of the streams, which empty into the Sacramento, about 35 miles above Sutter's settlement – the one called the American Fork, and the other the Feather river – are literally full of gold dust, from the minutest particles up to pieces weighing over an ounce. The most of it resembles squirrel shot flattened out. The discovery had produced the greatest excitement in the country.

Columbia Herald-Statesman Friday October 6, 1848 page 3

It appears that in the first part of February last, Messrs. Marshall & Bennett were engaged with a party in erecting a sawmill for Capt. J.A. Sutter, on the American Fork of the Sacramento river, about forty miles above its mouth. In excavating tailrace, they removed the rock during the day, and let in the water after night, in order to wash out the loose sand and dirt, On the morning of the 10th, after shutting off the water, Mr. Marshall discovered the first gold lying upon decomposed granite in the bottom of the tailrace. It would seem that little doubt was entertained of its being the real "Simon pure'" for operation ceased on the mill, and all hand's commenced searching for gold, it was soon found that gold abounded along the American Fork for a distance of thirty miles. For a time the discoverers were the only ones aware of the fact, but the news finally spread through the settlements. But little credit, however, was gained by the report, though occasionally a solitary "gold hunter" might be seen stealing down to a Lunch, with a pick and shovel, half ashamed of his credulity. Sometime during the month of May, a number of credible persons arrived in town from the scene of operations, bringing specimens of the ore, and stating that those who were occupied in collecting the precious metal, were making from $3 to $10 per day. Then commenced the gold rush!

Columbia Herald-Statesman Friday December 29, 1848 page 1

Knowing how far the family had traveled and the difficulty of a journey over what were described as high Rocky Mountains, the brothers decided that traveling by horseback was their best option. They would get to California faster without their families. The married brothers promised their wives that they would return in one year, even if they had not discovered any gold. Leroy was not physically able to ride horseback for long distances, so he was unable to join his brothers. The brothers promised Leroy a share should they discover any gold. The location of their mining claim has not been determined, but it was probably near Sacramento.

Known children of Lemuel and Isabelle:

1.	Lemuel Carter (Lemma)	b.	1849	d.	1933
2.	Frank Carter	b.	1852	d.	1873
3.	Albert Carter (Alla)	b.	1855	d.	1881

During the year that Lemuel was away seeking gold, Isabelle spent time with her sister and brother-in-law in Daviess County, Missouri as recorded in the 1850 US Census. Upon returning from California, Lemuel joined his wife in Daviess County. He tried to settle down, but the urge to prospect for gold was too strong. Lemuel sold his properties in Daviess County to his brother Salathiel. Salathiel moved his family to Daviess County and Lemuel moved his family to Tehama County, California where he joined his younger brother Alfred. After Isabelle passed away on June 9, 1858, Lemuel left his children in the care of Alfred while he tried silver mining near Humboldt, Nevada.

In a letter to Leroy, Lemuel used his sons nicknames – Lemme, Frank, and Alla. Lemuel complained to Leroy that they should write more often. The sparsity of correspondence made it seem they did not like each other. Letters had not been delivered during the Civil War, especially since Leroy had temporarily relocated to Ft. Scott, Kansas. Lemuel bragged about the variety of fruit available in California. Lemuel ended one letter with *"now I have written a long letter about nothing a taul and I fine it as warisome a subject as I could of pict a pon...."* Isabelle, Lemuel, their three sons plus Alfred Gipson Carter were all buried in the Carter Vina cemetery, in Vina, Tehama County, California. Grave markers only list initials and years. Lemuel Carter had an adventurous life if not an easy life.

Salathiel Carter was born on May 5, 1816 probably in Hampshire County, Virginia. In the family bible, Salathiel's birth record includes the middle initial A. The author has not uncovered his full middle name. He married Charity Cook Brock in Indiana. The Brock family resided near Noblesville in Hamilton County about nine miles northeast of Indianapolis. Charity Brock born on March 8, 1816 was the daughter of Elijah Brock and his first wife Mary Way Brock. Charity Brock had been named after her paternal grandmother Charity Cook Brock.

Salathiel Carter first purchased land in Indiana. When the US Post Office was unable to deliver mail they would compile a list of unclaimed letters and publish a notice in the local newspaper. Salathiel's name appeared on the January 1838 list of unclaimed mail for the Noblesville Post Office. He left Indiana in 1839 after being convicted of arson. With a pregnant wife and one young son, it seem highly unlikely that Salathiel had participated in the arson. He purchased land in Jasper County, Missouri. An early Jasper County Plat Map shows Salathiel owning land abutting the western edge of the land owned by his father along Center Creek. After pursuing gold mining in California for one year, Salathiel began buying additional parcels of land through the Bureau of Land Management. This seems to indicate that the brothers had found some gold. He sold his land along Center Creek in the mid 1850's and took over the land his older brother Lemuel had acquired in Daviess County, Missouri.

Known children of Salathiel and Charity:

1.	Elijah Calvin Carter	b. circa 1837	d. circa 1896
2.	John Wesley Carter	b. March 22, 1839	d. May 24, 1917
3.	Amanda Jane Carter	b. circa 1841	d. May 30, 1873
4.	James Henry Carter	b. June 11, 1843	d. August 29, 1913
5.	Seth Meyers Carter	b. circa 1847	d. April 29, 1914
6.	Mary A. Carter	b. circa 1849	d. February 24, 1878
7.	Alfred Columbus Carter	b. December 23, 1854	d. April 26, 1923
8.	Nathan Stanford Carter	b. September 9, 1858	d. May 16, 1928

Daviess County, Missouri was a pro-Union area during the Civil War. Some of the land sales in Daviess County through the Bureau of Land Management were restitution for military service. Salathiel Carter died on October 24, 1876 in Gallatin, Daviess County, Missouri. Charity Carter died on April 13, 1889 in Gallatin, Daviess County, Missouri.

Washington G. Carter was born on November 17, 1818, after the family had moved to Franklin County, Ohio Country. Washington's middle name has not been positively verified but was probably George since he named his eldest son George. Washington married Julia Ann Cooley on June 4, 1848 in Jasper County, Missouri. Julia Ann had been born on February 20, 1826 in Crawfordsville, Indiana. She was the daughter of Samuel Means Cooley and Margaret Rusk Cooley. Samuel Cooley was from Pennsylvania while his wife Margaret had been born in Brown County, Ohio. Samuel Cooley was a schoolteacher and the first Judge in Jasper County, Missouri. Samuel Cooley was widely respected for his fairness in legal rulings.

Other genealogy researchers claim that Margaret Cooley's grandmother, Elizabeth McCray Vance was a Shawnee, with her parents being Blue Jacket and Rising Sun Kispoko. Blue Jacket aka Weyapiersenwah and Rising Sun Kispoko Techacha Morning Star were members of the Shawnee Turtle Clan, while some of their ancestors might have been Mohawk from Canajoharie, New York Colony.

Rather than being an actual Shawnee, it seems more plausible that Elizabeth had been kidnapped/rescued by Shawnee after warriors had attacked and killed most of her white family. As white settlers moved into Tennessee, Kentucky and Ohio there were numerous attacks on settlements, with very young children being taken by the warriors to replace their own child who had been killed. Raised by loving foster parents these children rarely wanted to return to white society. Often the return of white children was a condition of peace treaties. Many of the children had a difficult time transitioning back into white society. After being returned to white society some of the children returned to their native foster families. When they became adults some of these individuals tried to be peace liaisons between the two very different cultures. Elizabeth McCray married Patrick Vance in 1762 in Frederick County, Virginia. Their daughter Margaret Vance married David Rusk. Margaret and David's daughter Margaret Rusk married Samuel Means Cooley in Brown County, Ohio in 1825.

Washington Carter purchased land in Marion County, Indiana and Jasper County, Missouri. The Jasper County land totaled 456 acres between the towns of Webb City and Oronoco. The farm was on a small rise of land with a natural spring and a grove of oak trees. *The History of Jasper County, Missouri* published in 1883 by Mills & Company lists the farm as having 100 acres under cultivation, 200 acres in pasture and the remainder as timberland. The family raised hogs, cattle, and sheep.

Known children of Washington and Julia Ann:

1.	George Marion Carter	b. April 1, 1849,	d. December 4, 1887.
2.	Thomas L. Carter	b. July 24, 1852,	d. November 15, 1882.
3.	Selathiel Elmore Carter	b. June 16, 1855,	d. November 26, 1941.
4.	James Hamilton Carter	b. December 17, 1857,	d. March 2, 1916.
5.	Norris H. Carter	b. March 26, 1862,	d. September 10, 1862.
6.	Laura Malinda Carter	b. September 14, 1864,	d. February 4, 1936
7.	Alfred G. Carter	b. September 14, 1864,	d. December 11, 1903.
8.	William Leroy Carter	b. December 2, 1867,	d. October 14, 1914
9.	Mary Ellen Carter	b. June 16, 1870,	d. June 5, 1964, in CA.

During the Civil War, Washington and his family were forced by the Confederates to abandon their land in Jasper County, Missouri and seek refuge in Fort Scott, Kansas. Twins Laura and Alfred were born in Fort Scott. When the family returned to Missouri they found that all of their buildings had been burnt to the ground. They began rebuilding.

Sheriff's Sale

By virtue and authority of an execution issued from the office of the Clerk of the Circuit Court of Jasper County, Missouri, returnable to the Fall Term, 1867, of said court, and to one directed, in favor of Washington Carter, and against John Chamberlain, I have levied upon and seized the following described real estate as the property of said defendant: all the right, title, interest, and claim of said defendant in and to the following described real estate, lying and being in the county of Jasper and State of Missouri, to-wit: the N1/2 of the SE1/4, and lot No. 1 of the NE FR1/4 of sec 3, and the W1/4 of lot No. 1 of the NW FR1/4, and the NW1/4 of the SW1/2 of sec 4, town 29, range 30, containing in all 239 40-100 acres. And I will, on Tuesday, the 28th day of May, 1867, between the hours of 9 o'clock in the forenoon and 5 o'clock in the afternoon, at the courthouse door, in the town of Carthage, in the State of Missouri, sell at public vendue, for cash in hand, to the highest bidder, all the right, title, interest, claim, estate and property of the above named defendant of, in and to the above described property to satisfy said execution and costs. n20   S. H. CALDWELL Sheriff.

The Carthage Weekly Banner Saturday May 11, 1867

Grand and Petit Juries

The following is announced as the Grand and Petit Juries for the March term of the Jasper Circuit Court:

Grand Jury – A.B. Lewis, Jesse Shortess, J.R. Cabaniss, Augustus Roberson, D.M. Mason, John C. Webby, G.S. McCormick, Charles W. Engle, Thomas Conmer, Jerrey Carr, John K. Glassford, George Holt, Chas. Petit, Allen Scott, R.G. Sloan, John F. Baker, Columbus Carr, Jno. W. Confer.

Petit Jury – W.G. Carter, Thoms Blackwell, Samuel Sanderson, Wm. Williams, Ambrose McKee, Daniel Cogle, John S. McBride., B.B. Carmin, Woser Ancher, Geo. C. Kost, Joel S. Wells, F.A. Hendricks, F.W. Bristow, Henry Shepherd, T.J. Hollingsworth, Charles Mitchell, Joel Long, P.R. Johnson, Geo. P. Childs, J.D.P. Hendrick, J.H. Summers, D. Hulbart, John Green and John N. Hood.

The Carthage Press Thursday February 5, 1874 page 3

Washington served on the Petit Jury for Jasper County during the March 1874 term. Washington died on August 23, 1874 and Julia Ann died on December 4, 1887. They are buried next to each other in the Carter-Laxton Memorial Cemetery in Carterville, Missouri.

> *Mr. Washington Carter, one of the oldest citizens in southwest MO., died last Sunday morning. Mr. Carter was a gentleman who all respected and revered. He was a man of sound sense and whose opinions were respected by all. In his death the people of Jasper have lost a good citizen, and in the cause of reform and earnest advocate.*
> The *Carthage Press* Thursday August 27, 1874

Julina Carter was born on October 29, 1821. She was James 2nd and Sarah Janes's first daughter and the only daughter to survive to become an adult. Julina married three times; her first husband's was Daniel F. Jones. Daughter Sarah Jane Jones was born on November 17, 1840. Julina's second husband was Levi Dickerson. Daughter Harriet Dickerson was born July 16, 1847. Julina's third marriage was to Jonathon Rusk. They raised six children: Jeanette, Thomas, Jonathon, Walter B., Emma Paradine, and Frank. Julina Rusk died on January 16, 1892.

Alfred Gipson Carter was born on September 18, 1829 in Franklin County, Ohio. His family nickname was Gip. He participated in the 1849 California Gold Rush but did not return to Missouri, instead he moved to Tehama County, California. He staked a mining claim on Deer Creek near the town of Vina. In the mid 1850's his brother Lemuel moved his family to Vina. Alfred looked after Lemuel's children while Lemuel searched for silver in Nevada. Alfred married late in life. He and Ellen had three children Cora May, Emma and Wallace who all died young. Alfred died on March 12, 1871 in Vina, Tehama County, California.

Harriett Maria Zerna Carter was born on April 29, 1835, in Marion County, Indiana. She was the youngest child of James 2nd and Sarah Jane. In February 1842 she received an award from her schoolteacher for her 'studiousness'. She died on March 19, 1842 in Jasper County, Missouri. Harriett was one of three Carter family members who was buried in a small cemetery plot on land that the City of Carthage later decided would be a good location for a city park. The Carters were asked to move their cemetery. Three bodies were exhumed and reburied on private family property.

James Carter 2nd died on October 9, 1845 and was originally buried in the same Carthage cemetery as his daughter Harriett. Sarah Jane Carter died on January 27, 1854 and was buried alongside her husband in the private cemetery. As a teenager the author saw the small cemetery but has not been able to relocate the site. The dates of birth and death for both James Carter 2nd and his wife Sarah Jane Myers Carter were handwritten in the Family Bible. The dates are corroborated by information in the *History of Jasper County*. James 2nd passed away nine years before Sarah Jane. Find-a-Grave incorrectly lists both James Carter 2nd and his wife Sarah Jane Myers Carter as being buried in the Carter-Laxton Memorial Cemetery. The grave marker identified as Sarah Jane has the incorrect date of death – January 27, 1871. At least two modern markers for James Carter 2nd have been added to the cemetery at different times. As of 2024 the marker for James 2nd was turned sideways and lies at the feet of the marker for Sarah Carter. Original markers were made from white Carthage limestone often referred to as Carthage Marble. This soft limestone does not weather very well and many of the original markers are barely legible. The Carter-Laxton Memorial Cemetery has several mature oak trees, whose large surface roots are pushing and toppling grave markers.

In Ohio the Bureau of Land Management took over the sale of Federal Lands. The Bureau tried to stay ahead of white settlers by surveying land before settlers were allowed to purchase or move into a new area. The Bureau surveys used a grid system designated as Townships and Ranges. A north/south meridian line crossed an east/west base line. Townships designate an area of six square miles and how that area lies north or south of the base line. Ranges identify a tier of townships and how they lie east or west of the meridian. Each township of approximately 23,040 acres was divided into thirty-six Sections of 1 square mile or 640 acres. Each section could then be divided into half sections of 320 acres, quarter sections of 160 acres, half a quarter section of 80 acres or quarter of a quarter section of 40 acres. These portions of sections were designated by N, S, E, W, NE, SE, NW, or SW. Partial sections were known as Aliquot Parts and were used to describe irregular areas such as where creeks cut off a corner of land.

Since most of the land west of Ohio was first surveyed and purchased from the Bureau of Land Management, their website is a good source for original land purchases. One caveat is the possibility of several individuals with similar names. In land records, James Carter 2nd does not have a modifier attached to his name. Previous researchers have tried to add middle initials to his name (C, D, E etc.) because of land purchases for a James Carter with various middle initials. These were probably different individuals. The places where I am sure he purchased land were Franklin County Ohio, Marion County Indiana, Fayetteville, Lawrence County Indiana and Jasper County Missouri.

Known land purchase through the Bureau of Land Management:

Ohio

10/28/1835	Lemuel	017N – 004E	NW1/4NW1/4	Section 15	40	Marion Co.
03/20/1837	James 2nd	017N – 004E	NE1/4NW1/4	Section 14	40	Marion Co.
08/10/1837	Washington	017N – 004E	SE1/4NW1/4	Section 14	40	Marion Co.

Missouri

04/03/1848	Salathiel	028N – 032W	SW1/4	Section 4	80	Jasper Co.
11/01/1848	Alfred & JGL	028N – 032W	NE1/4NE1/4	Section 9	40	Jasper Co.
11/01/1848	Alfred & JGL	028N – 032W	NW1/4NW1/4	Section 10	40	Jasper Co.
11/01/1848	Alfred & JGL	028N – 032W	SW1/4SW1/4	Section 3	40	Jasper Co.
12/16/1850	Salathiel	028N – 032W	E1/2W1/4Trct 1	Section 4	80	Jasper Co.
12/16/1850	JGL & Salathiel	028N – 032W	NW1/4SE1/4	Section 28	40	Jasper Co.
12/16/1850	JGL & Salathiel	028N – 032W	NE1/4SW1/4	Section 21	40	Jasper Co.
12/16/1850	JGL	028N – 032W	NW1/4NE1/4	Section 9	40	Jasper Co.
09/01/1851	Salathiel	028N – 032W	W1/2SE1/4	Section 21	80	Jasper Co.
09/01/1851	Salathiel	028N – 032W	W1/2NE1/4	Section 28	80	Jasper Co.
07/01/1852	Salathiel	028N – 032W	NW1/4SW1/4	Section 9	40	Jasper Co.
03/10/1856	Washington	028N – 032W	NE1/4SW1/4	Section 1	40	Jasper Co.

06/16/1856	Salathiel	059N – 027W	NE1/4NW1/4	Section 36	40	Daviess Co.
06/16/1856	Salathiel	059N – 027W	W1/2SE1/4	Section 24	80	Daviess Co.
04/01/1857	Salathiel	059N – 027W	E1/2SE1/4	Section 24	80	Daviess Co.
05/15/1857	JGL	028N – 032W	SE1/4NE1/4	Section 9	40	Jasper Co.
05/05/1859	Salathiel	059N – 027W	W1/2NW1/4	Section 36	80	Daviess Co.
06/01/1859	Washington	028N – 033W	SE1/4SE1/4	Section 1	40	Jasper Co.
06/01/1859	Washington	028N – 033W	N1/2NE1/4	Section 12	80	Jasper Co.
06/01/1859	Washington	028N – 033W	SE1/4NW1/4	Section 12	40	Jasper Co.

The brothers went on a land buying spree after December 1850. It looks like they discovered some gold in California. There are reports that for the first year prospectors easily found and removed gold nuggets from streams. By 1850 gold was more difficult to find and with ever increasing numbers of prospectors crowding the streams, tensions and problems arose in the mining communities. Back in Missouri the Carter land purchases were usually forty acres parcels, only a few were eighty acres. Lemuel moved up to Daviess County after their stint in California, but he had gold fever and returned to California circa 1856. Salathiel moved his family to Davies County and continued buying up land. In a letter to Leroy, Salathiel asked about taxes on a piece of land they had purchased jointly. He didn't want the land to be forfeited for taxes not being paid. There could have been other purchases from individuals not recorded by the Bureau of Land Management. Washington accumulated over four hundred fifty acres in Jasper County. Leroy and his sons acquired over seven hundred acres in Jasper County, Missouri.

Chapter 9 – Leroy and Mary Carter Family

James Gilbert Leroy Carter was born on April 22, 1826, in Hamilton Township of Franklin County, Ohio Country. He was called Leroy by his family and neighbors. Genealogists usually refer to him as JGL. Websites variously list his place of birth as the town of Hamilton in Butler County or in Hamilton County. Both Butler and Hamilton Counties are on the western edge of Ohio. Leroy was born in Hamilton Township of Franklin County about nine years after his parents moved to Ohio. Hamilton Township lies to the south of the city of Columbus. Leroy was four when the family moved from Ohio to Indianapolis, Indiana. He was thirteen when the family moved to Jasper County, Missouri. When he was about nineteen, Leroy contracted infantile paralysis commonly referred to as polio. The disease weakened his leg muscles, and he became dependent on crutches or a cane for the rest of his life. Polio was the reason that he could not join his brothers in their quest for gold in California. He simply could not ride horseback for long distances, and he needed crutches to move about.

Leroy married Mary Means Cooley on July 22, 1849 in Jasper County, Missouri. Mary moved in with her new husband and his mother. They lived in the original one room cabin. Leroy seems to have inherited the homestead and family bible by default. The other brothers moved away while Leroy stayed. Mary Means Cooley was the second daughter of Samuel Means Cooley and Margaret Rusk Cooley. She was the younger sister of Washington's wife Julia Ann. Mary had been born on November 16, 1827 in Crawfordsville, Indiana. After their parents died, Mary and Julia looked after their younger siblings. The 1850 and 1860 US Census records list Cooley children living with each of the Carter families.

Children of Leroy and Mary:

1. Sarah Margaret Carter	b. April 13, 1850,	d. April 21, 1858.
2. Julina Isabelle Carter	b. March 12, 1852,	d. February 15, 1936.
3. **Marion Columbus Carter**	b. September 11, 1854,	d. June 28, 1934.
4. Thomas Alfred Carter	b. February 17, 1857,	d. April 2, 1945.
5. Julyet Amanday Carter	b. July 23, 1859,	d. October 21, 1875
6. William Harvey Carter	b. July 23, 1859,	d. August 7, 1860.
7. Nancy Corine Carter	b. April 23, 1861,	d. August 14, 1938
8. Ardora Florence Carter	b. March 8, 1864,	d. January 21, 1920
9. James Walter Carter	b. November 14, 1866,	d. August 5, 1964
10. Harriet Athelene Carter	b. April 11, 1869,	d. September 23, 1965

After his older brothers Lemuel, Salathiel, and Washington returned from their year long quest for gold in California, Leroy built a new multi-room house for Mary in 1850. Most of Leroy and Mary's children were born in the new house. It is unclear how much gold the brothers had found, but they shared the profits with Leroy. The brothers also made additional land purchases through the Bureau of Land Management.

Before railroads traversed the state, stagecoaches plied routes north and south, and east and west across the territory. In 1850 John Warren Butterfield, a Connecticut businessman partnered with Henry Wells and William Fargo to create a freight transport company which became American Express. In 1852 Mr. Wells and Mr. Fargo founded the Wells Fargo Company to extend service into California. Later Mr. Butterfield received the lucrative contract from the US Post Office to provide mail delivery to California. The Post Office wanted the stagecoach to take a southern route through Texas. Rail lines from the east had been completed to the town of Tipton just west of Jefferson City, Missouri. The Butterfield stagecoach picked up the mail pouch from the railroad terminus at Tipton. The route went south through Polk County, proceeded to Fort Smith, Arkansas, across Texas to El Paso, across Sonora, Mexico, to San Diego, California and up to San Francisco. There were 139 livery stables situated about twenty miles apart to supply fresh horses and drivers. A passenger ticket cost $200 to travel the full route. The mail was expected to be delivered to Sacramento within twenty five days of being picked up from the railroad. At the time mail delivery took about five months traveling by ship around Cape Horn in South America. Rival stagecoach lines attacked the Butterfield stagecoaches. The Butterfield mail delivery route only operated for about two and a half years before the outbreak of the Civil War.

OVERLAND MAIL COACHES

On Wednesday last, we noticed on the freight train from Tipton, a dozen overland mail coaches, designed for the Fort Smith route and upon inquiry, learned that other lots have proceeded at other times during the last few weeks. They were made in Concord, N.H. and are not only decidedly comfortable, but genteel conveyances. Two carloads of very fine horses were also along, and we learned that the company already have one thousand horses designed for this service. The company commence operations the 15th of this month and expect to make the trip through to San Francisco in twenty five days. A semiweekly overland mail, and mail coach conveyance for passengers, across the continent of America, is a new thing under the sun. Its effect will be to cause a line of settlements to be made at an early day along the entire route to California.
Jefferson City *Missouri State Times* Saturday September 4, 1858 page 2

Arrival of the Overland Mail Train – The Quickest Trip on Record – Twenty-three days from San Francisco, and Twenty-four hours ahead of time. A dispatch was received from Jefferson City yesterday afternoon, announcing that the first overland mail train from San Francisco had arrived in that city one day ahead of the time required by law.
Columbia, Missouri *Columbia Herald Statesman* Friday October 15, 1858 page 3

Indians Examining the "Swift Wagon" – A correspondent who has recently crossed from the Pacific on the overland route says: The Indians of the Cherokee nation are very anxious to have the route through their territory. They call the mail coach the "swift wagon". A deputation from the heads of the nation have waited upon the "Great Chief Butterfield of the swift wagon" as they call him and asked him to run the wagons through their country.

Jefferson City, Missouri *Weekly Jefferson Inquirer* Saturday June 4, 1859 page 1

After the Civil War started it was no longer safe to transport mail through Confederate territory. The railroad line from the east had been completed to St. Joseph, Missouri which is where the Pony Express picked up the mail and a single rider headed off to Durango, Colorado. Passengers who had dared to ride the mail coach would not have called the travel comfortable nor genteel. For most of the time the Butterfield mail route operated, armed riflemen road the stagecoach to fight off attackers. The Pony Express only operated for a few years.

The Civil War – April 12, 1861 to May 26, 1865

After the Civil War started with the attack on Fort Sumter, South Carolina, states had to decide if they would stay in the Union or join the Confederacy. The Governor of Missouri was southern leaning Claiborne Jackson. To prevent Missouri from joining the Confederacy, the US Calvary rode into St. Louis and chased the Governor and the Missouri State Militia out of town. Governor Jackson and the Militia fled to the southwest. The opposing sides met near Dry Fork Creek about nine miles north of Carthage. The Battle of Carthage commenced on July 5, 1861. As the fighting progressed the Union forces retreated into Carthage. The fighting lasted two days. Finally, the US Calvary forces pulled out to regroup, retreating to Sarcoxie, Missouri. The Confederates claimed victory. A lopsided victory.

The Civil War battle of Carthage resulted in about 244 casualties. Only 44 were members of the US Calvary while about 200 were Confederate volunteers. Many of the young Confederate soldiers had no military training and were unprepared for being shot at. Their firearms were mostly hunting rifles and their experience with firearms was to be still and aim carefully. A tactic which made them targets for the fast-moving US Calvary on horseback. The US Calvary used pistols and could get off six shots before needing to reload. The unnamed casualties were likely buried in several unmarked graves in more than one location. A search of Find-A-Grave does not locate any marked graves for the Battle of Carthage's fallen participants.

In the months following the Battle of Carthage, Leroy and Mary's farm was raided twice by Confederates. On the first attack, armed soldiers stole all of the Carter horses and hogs, which went to supply Colonel Anderson's men. Confederate leaning Tom Anderson owned a farm about five miles away and was well known to Leroy, but that did not stop his men for confiscating whatever supplies they could locate. During the second attack a confederate soldier took the coat that Leroy was wearing and a new wool baby banket swaddling infant daughter Nancy. After this second raid Leroy wrapped the Carter Family Bible in buckskin and buried it. The treasured bible had belonged to his father James Carter 2nd. The family also buried anything which they considered to be of any value. In September 1862, Leroy was picked up by Union irregulars under the command of Colonel Ritchie. At the questioning, Leroy claimed to be a Union man and was released. Several weeks later those Union irregulars fought in a skirmish with confederates forces led by Col. Anderson. Months after that battle the confederates began arresting men who had been detained by the Union irregulars. Although they were non-combatants, Leroy and his neighbors ended up at a prison camp in Little Rock, Arkansas. Leroy's imprisonment at Little Rock only lasted a few months.

Leroy was liberated from the prison camp by the Union attack on Little Rock which ended on September 14, 1863. Dressed in rags the prisoners accompanied the Union soldiers back to St Louis, Missouri. Once there, Leroy and his neighbor Judge Stevenson asked for assistance from a young boy who led them to the Women's Aid Society. The men were given some clothes and passage to Boonville, a trading post on the Missouri River. The same trading post from which the family had acquired supplies after first moving to Missouri. At Boonville they met a former neighbor who lent them some cash and somehow Leroy and Judge Stevenson made their way from Boonville to Cave Spring, Missouri. Cave Spring is a small farming community in Green County northeast of Springfield. In 1848 Alfred Staley had started a General Store with staples brought by wagon down from Boonville. Importantly for Leroy and Judge Stevenson there was a US Calvary Garrison stationed at Cave Spring.

In the fall of 1863 it was too dangerous to return to Carthage. The confederates had a strong presence in southwest Missouri. Leroy and Judge Stevenson sent word to their wives that they were still alive and holed up in Cave Spring. The wives dug up some of the buried clothing and by traveling in an oxen pulled wagon, the ladies were able to reunite with their husbands. Later the US Calvary escorted the families back to Carthage to gather a few belongings before heading on to Fort Scott, Kansas. The US Calvary had turned Fort Scott into a supply depot for the Union army. At Fort Scott there were minor incidents with confederate sympathizers but no actual battles. Washington Carter's family also evacuated to Fort Scott, Kansas.

During the Civil War the Confederates seemed to be perpetually short on ammunition. Southwest Missouri has lead deposits. The confederates controlled the area and could easily have manufactured lead shot, a resource they did not exploit. After the Civil War ended the town of Carterville started as a lead mining operation.

When the Carters were able to return to Jasper County they found that all of their buildings except the original cabin had been burnt to the ground. The Carters began rebuilding. Leroy designed a two-story house which might have been patterned off houses he had seen in Little Rock or St. Louis. The two story stone house had a wide front porch. Two staircases led from the living room to the upper floor. Local limestone was quarried from the riverbank for the foundation. Brothers Lum and Dick burnt lime to create the mortar. The house took two years to complete, and the resulting house was the talk of the area for some time. The new house had not been completed when Leroy and Mary's youngest son James Walter Carter was born. In later years Jim proudly bragged about having been born in the humble one room cabin. *The History of Jasper County, Missouri* lists Leroy's farm as consisting of 325 acres of which 140 acres were under cultivation in corn and winter wheat. The farm also had black walnut and persimmon trees.

In 1875 Leroy donated land for the creation of the town of Carterville which was named after Leroy. Carterville started as a lead mining operation, but quickly grew into a town. Mary Cooley Carter died on April 8, 1902 and was buried in the Carter-Laxton Memorial Cemetery in Carterville. Leroy died on November 18, 1914 and was buried next to Mary. In the Family Bible Leroy's birth on April 22, 1826 lists his full name – James Gilbert Leroy Carter. His death is also noted in the Bible with his name given as James Gilbreth Leroy Carter. Just above the notation for Leroy's death is the date of marriage for Leroy and Mary, where again Leroy's second name is listed as Gilbreth. Both of these entries appear to be in a different handwriting – probably Jim's since he inherited the homestead and bible. At one time the Carterville, Missouri web page referred to their founder as James George Leroy Carter.

Pioneer Dies

J.G.L. Carter, 88 years old, for whom the city of Carterville, Missouri was named, died at the Carter homestead two miles north of that city recently from paralysis. Mr. Carter homesteaded a quarter section of land adjoining what is now the city, at the close of the Civil War.

The *Missouri Herald* Hayti, MO Thursday, November 19, 1914

Details of the lives of the children of Leroy and Mary:

Julina Isabelle Carter born on March 12, 1852 was nicknamed Issy. She married John Thomas Ferguson. Their son, James Clarence Ferguson used his middle name Clarence. Julina Ferguson died on February 15, 1936 and was buried in Fasken Cemetery in Carthage, Missouri. Find-A-Grave erroneously has her first name as Angelina.

Marion Columbus Carter will be discussed in the next chapter.

Thomas Alfred Carter born on February 17, 1857 was nicknamed Dick. When a housing developer offered to buy his land in Jasper County, he convinced his older brother Lum to try homesteading. They moved their families to Dora, New Mexico Territory in 1906. They soon discovered that dry land farming was not an easy way to make a living. Both families returned to Jasper County. Dick married three times and fathered several children. Dick died on April 2, 1945 and was buried in Fasken Cemetery.

Julyet Amanday Carter was born on July 23, 1859. She died on October 21, 1875 and was buried in the Carter-Laxton Memorial Cemetery. Her grave marker has been broken and is barely legible.

Nancy Corine Carter was born on April 23, 1861 just after the Civil War started. Her family nickname was Corny. She was the infant swaddled in the new wool blanket her mother had made – the blanket that was snatched away by a confederate soldier scavenging for supplies. She married James Franklin Bull. Nancy Bull died on August 14, 1938 and was buried in Fasken Cemetery.

Ardora Florence Carter was born on March 8, 1864 in Fort Scott, Kansas. She was nicknamed Dora. She married Avery A. Foster. Ardora Foster died on January 21, 1920 and was buried in the Carter-Laxton Memorial Cemetery.

James Walter Carter was born on November 14, 1866. His family nickname was Jim. His namesake son was known as Walter. Jim married southern gal Lida Allington James. Her family moved to Jasper County from Kentucky following the Civil War in which her father had served as a Confederate soldier. After Mary passed away Jim's family moved in with Leroy. Two years after Leroy's death, Jim sold the homestead out of the family. Jim purchased the farm where Fasken cemetery is located. After his wife died and losing his eyesight, Jim moved in with his son. James Walter Carter Sr. died on August 5, 1964. In 2006 one of Leroy's descendants purchased the old homestead and extensively refurbished the two story house.

Harriet Athelene Carter born on April 11, 1869 was nicknamed Athey. She married Charles Jefferson McAdoo. Harriet McAdoo died on September 23, 1965.

Chapter 10 – Marion Columbus and Elmeda Carter Family

Marion Columbus Carter was the eldest son of Leroy and Mary. He was born on September 11, 1854. His name comes from Marion County Indiana and Columbus, Ohio. His family called him Lum. He married Elmeda Hester Motley on March 11, 1880 in Webb City, Missouri. Lum was about six feet tall and very strong while his wife was petite. Elmeda was the daughter of William Thomas Motley and Eliza Catherine Ennis Motley. The Motley family claims to be descendants of Rappahannock Indians. The Rappahannock had been an Algonquin speaking tribe living along the Rappahannock River on the Northern Neck of Virginia when the English first arrived at Jamestown. The Motley family can be traced from colonial Essex County, Virginia in the early 1700's through North Carolina and Kentucky to Jasper County, Missouri. Making a connection earlier in Virginia is problematic with several names proposed for spouses.

According to Nell Nugent in *Cavaliers and Pioneers,* John Motley patented 600 acres in Northumberland County on the Northern Neck in the mid 1600's. He was a Wicomico carpenter who had paid for twelve individuals to migrate to Virginia. John Motley claimed each of their 50 acre headrights. John Motley or his son John might have been married to a Rappahannock. The English forced most of the native people to migrate away from Virginia. Only the Pamunkey and Mattaponi managed to hold onto reservation land. The State of Virginia has recognized some tribes including the Rappahannock. The Federal Government has only recently recognized tribes in Virginia.

Children of Lum and Elmeda:

1. James William Carter   b. July 9, 1880,   d. October 2, 1881.
2. Charlie Marion Carter   b. July 28, 1882,   d. April 4, 1950.
3. Walter Columbus Carter   b. October 25, 1883,   d. June 4, 1968.
4. Mary Francis Carter   b. February 10, 1885,   d. February 24, 1980.
5. **Oscar Thomas Carter**   b. October 3, 1888,   d. April 7, 1966.
6. Nannie Isabelle Carter   b. April 10, 1893,   d. July 21, 1946.

As labeled on Jasper County, Missouri Plat Maps, Lum owned the land to the west of the original homestead on Center Creek. This was the same land that had at one time belonged to his uncle Salathiel Carter. After Dick convinced Lum to try homesteading, Lum sold the land to a mining operation in 1906. The 40 acres had a deposit of Galena lead. It does not appear that the lead was ever mined. Later his youngest brother James Walter Carter Sr. ended up owning that piece of land. Elmeda and her youngest daughter Nannie remained in Carthage while the rest of her family moved to Dora, New Mexico Territory. Elmeda was waiting for Lum to build a suitable house before moving.

The Carters soon realized that dry land farming was not a very good way to earn a living. Alfalfa used for livestock feed was their primary crop. Dick was the first to move back to Jasper County, Missouri. Lum's family stayed in Dora until they owned their homestead lands. Lum returned to Jasper County briefly in 1912 to purchase one hundred sixty acres along Dry Fork Creek about nine miles north of Carthage. Note – the description matches the location where the Civil War Battle of Carthage began. The purchase was an investment, and a place to move back to. After the disappointing stint at homesteading, Lum returned to Missouri and started a dairy farm. The farm also raised corn, sugar beets and soybeans.

When the escalating World War I drew the United States into the European conflict, men were required to register for the draft. Charlie and Oscar registered in Dora, New Mexico territory. On his draft registration, Oscar tried to claim a disability, but it was erased and written over. Walter registered for the draft in Springfield, Missouri. None of the brothers were called up to serve.

In the February 26, 1920 edition of *The Jasper News*, it was noted that Lum and his nephew Clarence Ferguson each bought houses in Carterville. They had the houses deconstructed and moved to their respective farms to be rebuilt. The rebuilt house is the same one the author knew as her grandparents dairy farm. The farmhouse had two potbellied cast iron stoves, one in the living room and one in the kitchen. A large enamelware coffee pot was kept warm on the kitchen stove. The house had two front bedrooms and two smaller back bedrooms. There was a cast iron water pump in the back yard. No indoor plumbing – only an outhouse.

When railroad spur lines were constructed in Jasper County, Lum joined one work crew setting ties. Usually, two men alternated swinging a hammer to drive a spike into the tie holding the rail in place. Eleven-year-old grandson Marion later remembered seeing his grandfather working alone set the spike with only three strikes of the hammer. The first strike merely drove the spike down about one third of the way. The second swing took the spike almost down to the rail and finally the third strike would cause the entire length of the rail to vibrate. Lum was muscularly very strong. In May 1933 Lum suffered a stroke which left him disabled and bedridden. He passed away on June 28, 1934. Lum was buried in Fasken Cemetery. When Elmeda passed away on June 22, 1938 she was laid to rest next to her husband.

Details of the lives of the children of Lum and Elmeda:

James William Carter was born on July 9, 1880, in Carterville, Missouri. He died on October 2, 1881 and was interred in Carter-Laxton cemetery.

Charlie Marion Carter was born on July 28, 1882. Charlie never married. After the family moved to Dora, New Mexico, Charlie was caught outside in a blizzard and suffered frostbite on his feet in November 1906. During part of his stay in New Mexico, Charlie worked for the Calumet Cattle Ranch. When the rest of the family moved back to southwest Missouri, Charlie remained in Dora with his youngest brother so that Oscar would be able to own his homestead. After the extra year living in Dora, the brothers worked their way back to Missouri performing odd jobs such as installing electric wiring in buildings. Back in Missouri, Charlie went to work for a silo elevator company. In a few surviving photographs Charlie is seen sporting a thin blond mustache.

Charlie was living with his sister Mary Francis Newcom in Polytechnic, Terrance County, Texas when he died on April 4, 1950. Charlie was buried next to his parents in Fasken Cemetery. His Certificate of Death and his grave marker spell his first name 'Charley'. He had signed his name as 'Charlie' on his draft registration.

Several genealogy websites confuse Charlie Marion Carter with Charles Monroe Carter. Charles Monroe Carter seems to have been the son of John William Carter and Mary Ellen Carter of Joplin, Missouri. Charles Monroe Carter married Bertha Pertuch on December 28, 1897, fathered children, and seems to have lived his entire life in Joplin. Some family trees link Charles Monroe Carter back to Robert 'King' Carter of the Corotoman Plantation through his son Charles Carter of Cleves. Definitely not a descendent of the Cartars from quaker Pennsylvania. Other family trees have Charles Monroe Carter identified as the son of John Clinton Carter and Maggie Gano Carter who were also Joplin, Missouri residents. Charlie Marion Carter and Charles Monroe Carter were two distinctly different individuals.

Walter Columbus Carter was born on October 25, 1883. He married Chloe Turner on June 29, 1921 at the Courthouse in Carthage. Later they had a big community celebration. As reported in the very gossipy *Jasper News*, Walter and his cousin Clarence Ferguson traveled to Kansas City in November 1921 to attend classes at the Sweeney School of Aeronautics and Engineering. Also in January 1922, Walter and Oscar attended a class at the Sweeney School. They wanted to learn about the new internal combustion engine. A newspaper article states that Walter Carter was the first person to own an automobile in Jasper County. This might have been Walter Columbus Carter or possibly his cousin James Walter Carter Jr. who used his middle name to distinguish himself from his father.

Automobiles were soon very popular in spite of the lack of paved roads. Everyone seemed to enjoy the springy ride, and motoring faster than horse drawn wagons usually traveled. One of the early problems of car ownership was frequent flat tires. The road between Leroy's farm and Washington's farm was at one time part of US Highway 66. The US Highway system provided paved roads connecting towns across the continent. To promote car sales and the fun of motoring, advertising agencies created catchy slogans. One of the most memorable slogans – *"Get your kicks on route 66".* Dinah Shore sang the jingle *"See the USA in your Chevrolet.."* Clarence Ferguson purchased a Regal Car.

Cousins Clarence, Walter and Oscar had dreams of starting their own business, possibly an automotive manufacturing company. Clarence had the more outgoing personality. Five years older than Walter, he was married with three children when he made the decision to quit his job, sell his farm and move his family to the big city of Cape Girardeau. For several years Clarence had been president of the school board, from which he resigned on November 10, 1921. By March 1922 the Ferguson family moved across the state. The farm boys had no financing and Cape Girardeau was not the most desirable place for young families. A foggy river boat town with a long history in the cotton trade, Cape Girardeau had too many saloons and gambling, plus the overt politics of the 'Jim Crow' south.

Walter and Chloe's son Harold Franklin Carter was born on April 16, 1922 in Cape Girardeau, Missouri. Chloe died of pneumonia about a week after Harold's birth. Walter returned to Jasper County and asked Chloes' mother and sisters to care for his son. *The Jasper News* reported that Walter's little boy was doing well. Walter and Oscar soon returned to Jasper County permanently and spent the rest of their lives working the dairy farm started by their father. Walter never remarried although at one time he invited a Mrs. Venable and her four daughters to visit the dairy farm. The Venable's had been neighbors in Dora, New Mexico. The small farmhouse might have been quite crowded for a time, before the Venables returned to New Mexico.

Mary Francis Carter was born on February 10, 1885. Mary had her own homestead plot in Dora, New Mexico. She married Jefferson Davis Newcom and had one daughter Maureen. Mary Francis was a school teacher. The Newcom family settled in Polytechnic, Texas which is near Fort Worth. For about a month each summer, Charlie and the Newcoms would visit the dairy farm in Missouri. Maureen got to know her bratty mischievous younger cousins Marion and Harold. Mary Francis Carter Newcom died on February 24, 1980.

Oscar Thomas Carter was born on October 3, 1888. He was an extremely shy person. Like his father, Oscar was muscularly very strong. One family story was of Oscar putting on a new white shirt for church on Sunday only to flex his muscles and split the sleeves. The sleeves were tight and a tad short. Oscar usually wore his flannel shirts with the cuffs folded back.

When the family first moved to Dora, New Mexico territory, Oscar was too young to obtain a homestead. Then when the rest of the family were ready to move back to Missouri, Oscar had not lived on his homestead long enough to own the land. Oscar's older brother Charlie stayed with him in Dora for about a year. The brothers then worked their way back to Missouri. Oscar nearly electrocuted himself on several occasions while installing electric lights in churches at night.

Oscar Carter and Ethel Grace Sims eloped, driving to Neosho, Missouri to get married on April 19, 1921. Ethel was the oldest child of Charley Ceborn Sims and Rozella Ida May Hoffman Sims. Ethel had been born on December 21, 1895 in Webster County, Missouri. Ethel inherited thick black hair and brown eyes from her grandmother Martha Rebecca Box Sims. Martha Sims died from complications of childbirth when her only child Charley Ceborn Sims was born.

Martha was the first wife of Billy Sims. Billy had been orphaned at a young age and didn't know anything about his biological family. Billy was small boned with very narrow shoulders, a long neck and blue eyes. He might have looked young but he had an oversized cocky personality. Billy made up many stories including his name – William Albert Sims and birthdate. His last name probably came from the owner of a livery stable with whom he had lived as a child. From his early teens Billy was on his own to survive. Every ten years when the US census taker asked which state(s) his parents were from he gave a different answer.

After Martha passed away her older sister Sarah Box took care of infant Charley. Five years later Sarah finally consented to marry Billy. Later when Charley was courting Ida May, Billy wished the kid would hurry up and get hitched. Billy thought the courtship was taking way too long. As his third wife Billy married Anna Claretta Hoffman on June 26, 1895. Anna was the younger sister of his future daughter-in-law Ida May. A year later Charley and Ida May married on July 8, 1896 in Buffalo, Missouri. Ida May and Anna Claretta's parents were Noah and Sarah Hoffman. Billy spent most of his life near Goodson in Polk County, Missouri. He worked as a farmer and as a blacksmith. He had learned blacksmithing skills from the owner of the livery stable. The blacksmith had probably spent most of his time crafting horseshoes and caring for the horses of a stagecoach line.

While perusing DNA cousin matches on ancestry.com, the author came across two family trees filled with the last name McCandless. Not finding any names which matched known ancestors, the author suspects that Billy may have been a McCandless. The McCandless family originated in Scotland, then traveled to Ireland before migrating to Scranton, Pennsylvania. The McCandless family had lived in Scranton for more than a century before Billy was orphaned. Billy's birthdate is certain, but it is possible that his parents were traveling to California following notices of Gold being discovered. They could have taken the train to Missouri and then switched to a stagecoach for the remainder of the trip. Unfortunately the stagecoach was probably attacked with the adults being killed. When the stagecoach did not arrive, the blacksmith running the livery stable would have gone looking for the missing stagecoach. He took the toddler back to the livery stable and raised the child until the stagecoach line went out of business. After the Golden Spike was driven at Promontory Point, Utah in 1866, the railroad became the preferred means of travel and stagecoach lines closed. Travel by rail was faster and more comfortable. The blacksmith running the livery stable moved away, but Billy stayed at the only home he could remember. Family members never came looking for him. An image of Charles Robert McCandless looks similar to the poor quality images the author has of Billy. Both men were of small stature, with narrow shoulders, long necks and pale eyes.

Before marrying, Ethel Sims had been a school teacher in Carytown, Missouri. Her younger sister Ola Sims was a correspondent for *The Jasper News*, which helps to account for some of the family gossip in the newspaper. Ethel, Ola and Chloe became good friends. On February 7, 1922, Ethel's son Marion Ceborn Carter was born. Marion inherited his mother's thick black hair and brown eyes.

Oscar broke his wrist when his car backfired and the starter crank spun backwards. After his wrist healed Oscar and family set out to join Walter and Clarence in Cape Girardeau. Following Chloe's sudden death, the Carter brothers soon returned to Jasper County and went back to working on their father's dairy farm.

Daughter Hester May Carter was born on January 5, 1931. Oscar sold his homestead in Dora, New Mexico in the 1930's and used the money to install electricity. This allowed for an electric oven and a refrigerator plus an electric milking machine in the barn. The root cellar continued to be used for storing produce. Ethel did home canning using original *Ball* jars, rubber seals and lids.

The farmhouse had a large wooden telephone that was on a party line. To make a phone call, you first lifted the receiver to be sure no one else was using the line, then you jiggled the receiver to get the operator's attention. The operator would place your call. When the phone rang, you needed to listen and count the number of rings to know if the call was for you or for a neighbor sharing the party line.

Another family story was of Marion bringing a young lady out to the farm to meet his parents. While Ethel entertained the young lady, Oscar and Marion pulled the engine out of Marion's car. When the young lady saw the engine spread out on the ground she nearly freaked out, she was sure that she would be stuck at the farm forever. After the engine was reassembled, the young lady wasn't sure it would be safe to ride in the car. After all what could dairy farmers possibly know about auto mechanics? She didn't know that Oscar had been repairing engines for decades – a necessity to keep tractors running. As for Marion, he had served in the Air Force as an airplane mechanic during World War II.

Ethel died on November 25, 1957 and was buried in Fasken Cemetery. Brothers Oscar and Walter continued to live on and work the dairy farm. For several years the brothers sold their milk in cans to an Amish cheese factory. When the state of Missouri required that milk be stored in insulated tanks, the brothers got out of the dairy business. They continued to grow corn and soybeans. About one year before Oscar died, his son-in-law Tuffy Poulson built a bathroom into a corner of one bedroom. Oscar complained *"he had managed his whole life without porcelain, he didn't need no porcelain."* His daughter Hester told him to 'hush' the bathroom was his Christmas present from her.

Oscar passed away on April 7, 1966. He was buried next to Ethel in Fasken Cemetery, only a short distance from his parents and his brother Charlie. The year after Oscar's death the barn had disappeared. The following year the house was also gone and a field of corn was growing where the house once stood. After Oscar died, Walter did not want to continue living alone at the farm. He moved into town, at first staying with his son Harold and his family. Later he moved in with his cousin Hiram Rusk. Walter and Hiram were killed in a car crash on June 4, 1968. Walter Columbus Carter was buried next to his father in Fasken Cemetery.

Sunglasses to darken the light and then polarized sunglasses to reduce glare were not available until *Ray-Ban* introduced sunglasses to help pilots who complained of being blinded by sunlight. Marketing of sunglasses to the general public began in 1937. By the age of seventy many individuals who had not known sunglasses suffered from blindness. The author does not remember seeing either Oscar or Walter ever wear a pair of sunglasses.

Nannie Isabelle Carter was born on April 10, 1893. She and her mother remained in Carthage for about a year while the rest of the family moved to Dora to try homesteading. She married William Carlton. The youngest child of Lum and Elmeda was the first to marry and the first to have children. The Carlton's three children were: Nadine, William Marion, and Zelfter. Nannie died on July 21, 1946.

When World War II started in Europe, the United States hoped to stay out of the conflict. Then Japan bombed Pearl Harbor – *"the day that would live in infamy"* per the speech by President Franklin Delano Roosevelt. Young men rushed to enlist including many of Leroy's great grandsons. None of them were aware of their quaker ancestry.

Chapter 11 – Appendix – Document Abstracts

1683 Certificate of Friends – Cuthbert Hayhurst

From Settle monthly meeting 4th mos. 7th 1683. These are to certify all whom it may concern that it is made manifest to us that a necessity laid upon several friends belonging to this meeting to remove into Pennsylvania and particular by our dear friends Cuthbert Hayhurst, his wife and four children who has been and is a laborer in the truth for whose welfare and prosperity we are unanimously concerned and also for our friends Nicholas Walne, his wife and three children, Thomas Wrigglesworth and Alice his wife. Thomas Walmsley, Elizabeth his wife and children. Thomas Croasdale, Agnes his wife and six children. Thomas Stackhouse and his wife. Ellen Cowgill widow and her children, William Hayhurst all who we believe are faithful friends in their measure and single in their intentions to remove into the aforesaid province in America, therefore if the Lord permits we do certify our unity with their said intentions and desire their prosperity in the Lord and hope what is done by them do tend to the advancement of the truth in which we are unanimously concerned with them.

Samuel Watson	*John Moore Jr.*	*Christopher Johnson*
George Atkinson	*Anthony Averind*	*Nicholas Frankton*
Thomas Rudd	*George Blande*	*John Driver*
James Tennant	*John Hall*	

1683 Certificate of Friends – Robert Heaton

From Settle monthly meeting 4th month 7th 1683. These are to certify all whom it may concern that whereas Robert Heaton and Alice his wife have acquainted us with their intentions of removing themselves and their family into Pennsylvania in America, there to inhabit if the Lord permits. Now it is the sense of this meeting that they be left to their own liberty in the matter we knowing nothing but that they are honest and faithful friends according to their nature and single in their intentions to remove as aforesaid and hoping they would not take such a weighty course but upon due consideration we can but desire their welfare and prosperity every way being unanimous with them herein so far as we understand their service see after Gods Glory and Honor of his blessed truth. This we thought good to signify the behalf of our friends above said hoping that what is written shall be sufficient for satisfaction concerning their clearness upon truths account. Signed on behalf of the monthly meeting by:

Samuel Watson	*Anthony Averind*	*John Hills*
Christopher Johnson	*Thomas Skirnice*	*Peter B----*
Thomas Rudd	*George Bland*	*John S-----*
George Atkinson	*James Tennant*	*John ------*
John Hall	*Stephen Carr*	

1691 Certificate of Friends – Martin Wildman

To Friends in Pennsylvania. Dear Friends and brethren: In the unity of the blessed spirit which distance of place cannot break as in the love which many waters cannot quench do we at this time very dearly salute you heartily desiring that the God of all our mercies may plentifully shower down of his blessing upon you both spiritual and temporal to your abundant satisfaction where by your hearts may be engaged forever to walk faithfully before him and to return him the praise and the glory overall who is forever worthy. Now dear friends, the chief occasion of our writing to you at present is to that signify that our friend and brother in the truth, Martin Wildman having laid before us his intentions of removing himself and family if the Lord permits into Pennsylvania in America we found a concern upon us to signify (so far as we judge needful in this account) what we know and believe concerning him and in the first place as to his life and conversation we do believe that he is an honest man and faithful to the truth according to his measure having borne a faithful testimony hereto both in sufferings and other ways as occasion was offered and through his innocent behavior among his neighbors and those he conversed with he so gained their love and respect toward him that diverse of them though unbelievers professed him several kindness if he would stay among them and used diverse arguments to persuade his from going his intended journey. And in the second place as to his outward substance or estate he is but a poor man though through his care and industry with God's blessing upon it he so provided for himself and family that he has not hither to been burdensome to any but has lived of his own after a decent and orderly manner according to his station and degree but when at any time there was occasion for contributing to any who were in necessity either friends or others he was always willing to contribute and lend a helping hand according to his small ability nay sometimes beyond what could in reason have been expected from him. And as to his wife and children we do believe they are honestly minded and faithful to the truth according to their measures so that these things above said being considered with more that might be mentioned we desire all friends where he may come as among whom his lot is concern may fall that they be kind and affectionate toward him and assisting to him whether in advice or other ways as occasion may require which for our parts we could freely and willingly have done if he had staid among us and stood in need and which we hope in the fellowship of the same spirit with us you will be engaged to do which is all we think needful to signify at present; So rests your friends and brethren in the unchangeable truth. From our monthly meeting at Settle the 27th day of the 2nd month 1691. Signed on behalf of said meeting by

		George Bland
Samuel Watson	*Ralph Clark*	*Robert Baley*
John Moore Sr.	*Wm Anderson*	*Thomas Wilson*
John Ridd Sr.	*John Kendall*	*Mathew Frankland*
John Robison	*Wm. Ellis*	*Thomas Waite*

Robert Battleship	Rich Wilkinson	John Moore Jr.
John Dodshion	John Ridd Jr.	James Wildman Jr.
James Conyers	John Hall	Tho. Skirson of Nook
Mathew Wildman	John Frankland	Tho. Skirson of the Cross
James Wildman	Thomas Robison	Tho. Skirson Jr.
Wm. Cumberland	Thomas Rudd	William Skirson of the Cross
Thomas Wild	John Wildman	John Tomlinson

Middleton MM Bucks County, Pennsylvania – starting 1686 – dates written day, month, year - An Account of the Births of Friends Children

Robert Heaton Children
Grace Heaton daughter of Robert and Alis Heaton was borne ye 14 day 1st month 1667
Robert Heaton ye sonne of Robert and Alis Heaton was borne ye 3 day of ye 6th month 1671
James Heaton ye sonne of Robert and Alis Heaton was borne ye 25th day of ye 12 month 1674
Agnes ye daughter of Robert and Alis Heaton was borne ye 12 day of ye 9 month 1677
Ephraim Heaton ye sonne of Robert and Alis Heaton was borne ye 17 day of ye 6th month 1679

Alice Wildman daughter of Martin and Ann Wildman was borne ye 2nd day of ye 6th month 1687

Middleton MM Bucks County, Pennsylvania – starting 1686 – dates written month, day, year - An Account of the Births of Friends Children

Cuthbert and Mary Hayhurst children
Margery Hayhurst daughter of Cuthbert & Mary Hayhurst was borne in England 1st month 29 1671
John Hayhurst son of Cuthbert & Mary Hayhurst was borne in England 4th month 7th 1673
Cuthbert Hayhurst son of Cuthbert and May Hayhurst was borne in England 2nd month 29th 1678
Alice Hayhurst daughter of Cuthbert and Mary Hayhurst was borne in England 1st month 29th 1679
Jonathan and Anne Scaife's Children
Mary Scaife was borne in England 6th month 10th 1678
Jonathan Scaife was borne in England 2nd month 16th 1686
Jeremiah Scaife was borne in England 1st month 11th 1679

Robert and Alice Heaton's Children – (ie. Robert Heaton Sr.)
Grace Heaton was borne in England 1st month 14th 1667
Robert Heaton was borne in England 6th month 3rd 1671
James Heaton was borne in England 12 month 25th 1674
Agnes Heaton was born in England 9th month 12th 1677
Ephrain Heaton was borne in England 6th month 17th 1679

Martin and Ann Wildman's Children
Mathew Wildman was born in England 12th month 11th 1678
John Wildman was born in England 2nd month 2nd 1681
Joseph Wildman was born in England 1st month 23rd 1683
James Wildman was born in England 1st month 20th 1685
Alice Wildman was born in England 6th month 2nd 1687
Elizabeth Wildman was born in England 9th month 19th 1689

Robert and Grace Heaton's Children – (ie. Robert Heaton Jr.)
Sarah Heaton was born 7th month 28th 1701
Elizabeth Heaton was born 6th month 15th 1705
Alice Heaton was born 8th month 30th 1708

John and Grace Carter's Children – (? Family link- possible cousin to James Cartar 'blacksmith'?)
Mary Carter was born 1st month 1703

John and Mary Plumly's Children
Joseph Plumly was born 6th month 29th 1709
Charlie Plumly was born 2nd month 26th 1711
Sarah Plumly was born 9th month 22nd 1713
John Plumly was born 11th month 28th 1716 – (ie. John Plumly Jr.)
William Plumly was born 7th month 10th 1719
Edmond Plumly was born 4th month 14th 1722

Henry and Alice Nelson's Children – (ie. Alice Wildman Nelson)
Mary Nelson was born 9th month 6th 1709 – (daughter of Alice Hayhurst)
Alice Nelson was born 6th month 31st 1713 – (daughter of Alice Hayhurst)
Ann Nelson was born 8th month 6th 1720
Letitia Nelson was born 12th month 19th 1721
Jeremiah Nelson was born 1st month 23rd 1724
Thomas Nelson was born 4th month 27th 1726

William and Ann Hibbs Children - James and Susannah Cartar's grandchildren
Susannah Hibbs daughter of William and Ann Hibbs was born 11th month 22nd 1728
Hannah Hibbs daughter of Willaim and Ann Hibbs was born 4th month 6th 1730
Phebe Hibbs daughter of William and Ann Hibbs was born 2nd month 14th 1732
Sarah Hibbs daughter of William and Ann Hibbs was born 1st month 4th 1734
William Hibbs son of William and Ann Hibbs was born 10th month 27th 1735
James Hibbs son of William and Ann Hibbs was born 10th month 7th 1737
Ann Hibbs daughter of William and Ann Hibbs was born 9th month 12 1739

Robert Heaton III and second wife Ann – Susannah Griffith Cartar Heaton's grandchildren
Isabel Heaton daughter of Robert and Ann Heaton was born 5th month 24th 1748
Susanna Heaton daughter of Robert ad Ann Heaton was born 5th month 11th 1750
John Heaton son of Robert and Ann Heaton was born 6th month 20th 1752

William and Mary Carter's children – Susannah Heaton's great grandchildren
Joseph Carter was born   10th month 12th 1772
William Carter was born   3rd month 16th 1774
Rebecca Carter was born   1st month 30th 1777
James Carter was born   11th month 27th 1778
John Carter was born   1st month 22nd 1781

Middleton MM Bucks County, Pennsylvania – starting 1686 Record of Burials

Mary daughter of Henry and Alice Nelson buried 9th month 11th 1711 – (2 years old)

Alice wife of Henry Nelson was buried 7th month 4th 1714 – (1st wife Alice Hayhurst Nelson)

Grace wife of Robert Heaton was buried 2nd month 1719 – (1st wife of Robert Heaton Jr.)
Robert and Mary, son and daughter of Robert Heaton were buried 9th month 23rd 1719
Thomas and Alice, son and daughter of Robert Heaton were buried 9th month 28th 1719
Isaac, son of Robert Heaton was buried 10th month 21st 1719

Henry Paxson died 5th month 19th 1723. Henry Paxon at the time of his death was not in unity with Friends but at the request of his son-in-law John Plumly, friends consented to record it as

Philadelphia MM- Arch Street – Burials of Such as are not Friends

William Carter	*1 – 2 – 1714*	*... hatter*
Katherine Carter	*7 – 2 – 1720*	*wife of William*
William Carter	*12 – 21 – 1738*	*(Probably William Carter of Wapping - ancestry.com date Feb 21, 1739)*

Marriage Records of Christ Church, Philadelphia

9 October 1711	John Carter & Mary Ripley
2 June 1722	John Carter & Sarah Baker
15 June 1726	John Carter & Mary Lawrence
14 October 1731	John Carter & Alice Nelson

Catherine Carter, w Wm.,	*bur*	*7-2-1720*
Frances Carter	*d*	*12-5-1694*
John Carter	*bur*	*3-16-1698*
William Carter	*bur*	*1-2-1714*
Daniel Carter	*d*	*10-8-1761*
Henry Carter	*d*	*3-21-1709*
John Carter, s Elizabeth	*d*	*5-12-1751*
John Carter, s Daniel	*d*	*3-29-1755*
John Carter, s Margaret	*d*	*4-3-1759*
John Carter	*bur*	*8-21-1799 age 23*
Mary Carter	*d*	*11-2-1748*
Rebecca Carter	*d*	*11-7-1819 age 44*
Thomas Carter	*d*	*7-17-1689*
Thomas Carter	*d*	*5-3-1710*
William Carter, s William & Mary	*d*	*6-27-1729*
William Carter	*d*	*12-21-1738*
William Carter	*bur*	*9-19-1783 age 9 m*
William Carter	*bur*	*11-29-1785 age 47*
Susannah Myers, dt Benjamin	*bur*	*4-27-1783 age 2*

Middletown Monthly Meeting – Marriage Certificates

Henry Nelson & Alice Hayhurst

First Intention	6th day 11th month 1708
Second Intention	3rd day 12th month 1708
Marriage	16th day 12th month 1708

Whereas Henry Nelson and Alice Hayhurst both of the County of Bucks and Province of Pennsylvania having declared their intentions of marriage with each other before several publick monthly meetings of the people called Quakers according to the good order used amongst them. Whose proceedings therein (after deliberate consideration thereof, with consent of friends and relations concurred, they being found clear of all others) were approved of by the said meeting. Now these are to certify to all whom it may concern, that for the full accomplishment of their said intentions the sixteenth day of the twelfth month in the year (according to English account) one thousand seven hundred and eight. They the said Henry Nelson and Alice Hayhurst appeared in a solemn and publick assembly of the aforesaid people and others met together for that purpose in their publick meetinghouse in Middletown in the County aforesaid. And in a solemn manner according to the examples of the holy men of God recorded in the Scriptures of Truth, he the said Henry Nelson taking the said Alice Hayhurst by the hand did openly declare, that he did take her to be his wife, promising to be unto her a faithful and loving husband until it please God by death to separate them, And then in the said assembly the said Alice Hayhurst did likewise declare, that she did take the said Henry Nelson to be her husband, promising to be unto him a loving and faithful wife until God by death separate them, And the said Henry Nelson and Alice (assuming the name of her husband now Alice Nelson) as a further confirmation thereof did then and there to those present set their hands. And wee whose names are hereunto subscribed being present at the solemnizing of their marriage and subscription in manner aforesaid, as witnesses have also subscribed our names the day and year above written.

Jane Allin	*John Hayhurst*	*Henry Nelson*
Samuel Allin	*Cuthbert Hayhurst*	*Alice Nelson*
John Wallis	*John Cutler*	
Sarah Wallis	*Margery Cutler*	*William Hayhurst*
Sarah Scott	*Agnes Croasdale*	*Rachel Hayhurst*
William Paxon	*Mathew Wildman*	*Alice Heaton*
Ezra Croasdale	*John Doubigon*	*Grace Harker*
Robert Heaton	*Joseph Chapman*	*Rachel Cowgill*
John Wildman	*William Stockdale Jr.*	*Agnes Penquito*
John Cowgill	*Stephen Twining Jr.*	*Grace Langhorn*
Stephen Twining	*Eleanor Twining*	*Grace Heaton*

John Penquito
John Griffith
Thomas Baynes
Thomas Harding
Adam Harker
Thomas Stackhouse
Aaron Pearson
Henry Couper
Samuel Hilborn
Samuel Hough
Thomas Harding Jr.
William Stockdale
William Atkinson
Henry Comly

Daniel Doans
Hendrick Johnson
John Stackhouse
William Paxon Jr.
William Buckmate Jr.
Samuel Pickring
Abaraham Chapman
John Twining
James Bond
Joseph Tomlinson
Bartholomew Langstrath
Robert Heaton Jr.
William Croasdale

Janet Baynes
Isabel Cutler
Ann Chapman
Mara Croasdale
Elizabeth Hilborn
Mary Doubigon
Agnes Yates
Mercy Twining
Margaret Mitchell
Sarah Bond
Elizabeth Wildman
Alice Wildman

Henry Nelson & Alice Wildman

First Intention	5th day 9th month 1719
Second Intention	3rd day 10th month 1719
Marriage	23rd day 10th month 1719

Whereas Henry Nelson of Middletown in the County of Burks in the Province of Pennsylvania, and Alice Wildman of the place aforesaid, having declared their intentions of taking each other in marriage before several publick meetings of the people called Quakers in their publick Meetinghouse in Middletown aforesaid according to the good order used amongst them. Whose proceedings therein (after deliberate consideration thereof, with regard to the righteous law of God and example of his people recorded in the Scriptures of truth in that case) were approved of by the said meetings. They appearing clear of all others and having consent of friend and relations concurred. Now these may certify to all whom it may concern that, for a full accomplishment of their said intentions this twenty third day of the tenth month in the year (according to English account) one thousand seven hundred and nineteen they the said Henry Nelson and Alice Wildman appeared in a solemn and publick assembly of the aforesaid people met together for purpose in their usual Meetinghouse in Middletown aforesaid. And in a solemn manner he the said Henry Nelson taking the said Alice Wildman by the hand did openly declare that he did take her the said Alice Wildman to be his wife, promising (through God's assistance) to be unto her a faithful and loving husband until death separate them (or words to that purpose). And then in the said assembly the said Alice Wildman did likewise declare that she did take him the said Henry Nelson to be her husband promising in like manner to be unto him faithful and loving wife until death separate them (or words to that effect). And the said Henry Nelson and Alice (assuming the name of her husband now Alice Nelson) as a further confirmation thereof did then and there to those presents set their hands. And wee whose names are hereunto subscribed being present amongst others at the solemnizing of their said marriage and subscription in manner aforesaid as witnesses thereunto have also subscribed our names the day and year aforesaid.

John Routledge	*Thomas Stackhous*	*Henry Nelson*
Ezra Croasdill	*Thomas Thwaits*	*Alice Nelson*
Joseph Bond	*John Laycock*	
Adam Harker	*John Stackhous*	

Index of Bucks County, PA Wills 1684 - 1850

1714	CARTER, James	Southampton	Will	160
1749	CARTER, William	Southampton	Will	680
1749	CARTER, John	Newtown	Adm.	715
1781	CARTER, Joseph	Northampton	Will	1704
1783	CARTER, Christopher		Will	1818
1784	CARTER, William	Northampton	Will	1902
1787	CARTER, John	Lower Makefield	Adm.	2026
1793	CARTER, John	Bensalem	Adm.	2441
1795	CARTER, Ann	Buckingham	Will	2592
1810	CARTER, Benjamin	Buckingham	Adm.	3714
1815	CARTER, Charles	Buckingham	Adm.	4186

'Adm.' Probably stands for Letter of Administration – whereby the Court allowed relatives to settle the estate of an individual for whom no will has been located (ie. Intestate). The 1749 Letter of Administration concerning John Carter was probably given to John Plumly Jr. and Robert Heaton III to settle the estate of Alice Nelson Cartar's first husband – the second son of James and Susannah Griffith Cartar. William Carter's Will also in 1749 was probably John's older brother, the first child of James and Susannah. The 1714 Will for James Carter was for Susannah Griffith's first husband – the father of William and John.

Abstract of Wills for Philadelphia County, Pennsylvania

20 Mar 1709/1710
17 May 1710

John Carter of Bucks Co. Yeoman.
March 20, 1709/1710. Children Robert,
William, Mary and Martha. Kinsman
William Carter of Philadelphia.
Executors: Wife Grace and friends
Jeremiah Langhorne and Francis
White.

This John Carter appears to be related to James Carter 'blacksmith' – possibly a cousin. The William Carter of Philadelphia was probably William Carter of Wapping. This abstract was probably part of the early twentieth Century compilation of records. The child William Carter seems to be the second possibility for Sarah Plumly's spouse.

1714 Will of James Cartar of Southampton, Bucks County, PA

     I James Carter of Southamton in the County of Bucks in the province of Pensilvania being well in health of body & of a sound disposing mind & memory, Praised be the Lord for the same but considering the uncertainty of time here Do make and ordain this my (P...?) Last Will and Testament in manner and forme following viz:

     First my will and mind is that all my just debts and funeral expenses be paid and discharged –

Item I give and bequeath unto my well beloved wife Susannah Carter one feather bed of her own choice with furniture suitable to it, and also one young docile horse with saddle and bridle, and also one third part of all the residue of my personal estate or moot able goods and chattel whatsoever except one Geld with (...?...) and one white mare here after mentioned. And also one third part of all my Land & Accruements during her natural life ----

     Item I give unto my eldest son William Carter all that two hundred acres of land now in my possession bought of my father in law John Griffith, with all the buildings and improvements there upon and all other the privileges & appurtenance there unto belonging. Except the one third part before given to my wife during her natural life, to hold to him his heirs and assignees forever. And I do also give unto my son William one white mare before excepted.

     Item I give unto my son John Carter all that fifty acres of land which I lately purchased from Samuel Griffith with all the buildings fences and improvements there upon and all ye appurtenance there unto belonging to hold to him his heirs & assignees forever. (Except (...?...) one third part given to my wife during her natural life).

     Item I give unto my daughter Ann Carter one feather bed & furniture there unto belonging before here in excepted. And it is my will & mind that my Executors here after named shall build another dwelling house upon my plantation such (...?...) one as they shall see fit. And that they do discharge the cost thereof out of the two third parts of my personal estate and that the residue thereof be equally divided among my five youngest children James Carter, Richard Carter, Joseph Carter & Benjamin Carter and my said daughter Ann Carter.

     And that my said son William shall pay unto my said five youngest children each of them fifteen pounds current silver money of America (...?...) they shall respectively attain to the age of twenty one years. And that all there unto & profits or (...?...) of my whole estate both real & personal shall be disposed of to the maintaining of my family and the education of my children until my said son William shall attain to the age of twenty, and that he shall then enter to the said two hundred acres of land & benefit there unto belonging giving security for the payment of the said fifteen pounds apiece to my said five youngest children.

     And that my son John shall enter to the said fifty acres so soon as he shall attain to ye age of twenty one years and not before.

     And lastly I do here by nominate constitute ordain and appoint my truest friends Jeremiah Langhorne & John Cutter both of Middletown in the said County of Bucks Joynt executors of this my said Last Will and Testament and do hereby give unto my said executors full power to sell or let all or any part of my said lands or accruements for any time or term until my said son William shall attain to age as aforesaid.

In Witness where of is the said James Cartar to this my present Last Will and Testament have set my hand and seal the first day of December in the first year of the reign of King George over Great Britain er Anno Domini 1714.

James Cartar (seal) Sealed Signed published and declared by the said James Cartar to be his last will & Testament in the sight & presence of Robert Cobbert (his mark) I of Jeremiah Bartholomew Baelish March the fifteenth one thousand seven hundred & fourteen. Then personably appeared.

Proved March 15, 1714

1743 Will of Robert Heaton Jr. in Northampton Township, Bucks Co., PA

    In the name of God Amen the seventeenth day of March in the year of our Lord one Thousand seven hundred forty three I Robert Heaton Senior of the township of Northampton in the County of Bucks & province of Pensilvania Yeoman, being very sick & weak in body but of perfect mind & memory thanks be given unto God therefore calling unto mind the mortality of my body & knowing that it is appointed for all men once to die, do make & ordain this my last will and Testament (that is to say) Principally & first of all I give & recommend my soul into the hands of God that gave it; & for my body I commend it to the earth, to be buried in a Christian like & decent manner, at the discretion of my Executor herein after named, Nothing doubting but at the general resurrection I shall receive the same again by the mighty power of God; And as touching such worldly estates wherewith it hath pleased God to bless me in this life, after all my just debts, & funeral expenses are paid. I give devise bequeath and dispose of the same in the following manner & form. (that is to say)

    Imprimis I give & bequeath to my beloved wife Susannah Heaton all my household goods forever, and I also will her the east end of my dwelling house to live, and also twenty pounds a year during her natural life, and likewise keeping for a cow & horse, together with the privilege to take apples at her own discretion to use either green or dried, & likewise the garden belonging to the said house as well as convenient firewood, & all those to be allowed of & paid out of my Estate by my Executor herein after named or by his heirs & assigns for & during her natural life.

    Item I give and bequeath to my eldest daughter Sarah Walker one Bond for fifty pounds of good & lawful money of Pensilvania, Signed by William Noble & dated the twelfth day of March anno domini 1742/3.

    Item I give & bequeath to my daughter Grace Croasdale one bond for fifty pounds of good & lawful money of Pensilvania, signed by William Noble & dated the twelfth of March anno domini 1742/3 & no more.

    Item I do give & bequeath to my daughter Elizabeth Noble the sum of five shillings of good and lawful money of Pensilvania to be paid her on demand & no more.

    Item I do give & bequeath to my daughter Alice Plumley the sum of five shillings to be on demand & no more.

    Item I give & bequeath to my youngest daughter Anna Heaton the sum of one hundred & seventy pounds of good & lawful money of Pensilvania the sum of one hundred pounds to be paid her by my Executor herein after named or by his heirs or assigns in the space of two years after the date of these presents & the other seventy pounds to in four years from the date hereof, & in case of her decease before it becomes due & payable, or if she should die without issue, I do order & will & appoint the Legacy of hers to dying to return into the hands of my son & heir Robert Heaton, or his heirs or assigns forever.

    Lastly I give & bequeath the remainder part of my estate both real & personal to my son & heir Robert Heaton & his heirs & assigns forever, & for what moneys, bonds, stocks or personal estate which should happen undisposed of, after the within legacies are paid, I leave to my son & heir Robert Heaton & his heirs forever. And I do hereby nominate & appoint my said son & heir Robert Heaton whole & sole Executor of this my last will & testament, desiring he will take upon him the Execution thereof & see it carefully performed. In witness whereof I have hereunto this my Last Will & Testament contained in one sheet of paper set my hand and seal the day & year above written, & I do hereby revoke all former & other wills by me made heretofore & declare this to be my only last Will & Testament. Signed Sealed Published & Declared by the Testator to be his last Will & Testament in the presence of us, who have subscribed our names in his presence.

Robert Heaton

Tho*s*. Cooch, W*m* Cartar, Henry Nodon

Whereas I have made my will in this sheet of paper bearing date the seventeenth day of March on thousand seven hundred & forty three and therein having given to my youngest daughter Anna Heaton the sum of one hundred & seventy pounds of good & lawful money of Pensilvania (as therein expressed) the sum of one hundred pounds to be paid her in the space of two years after the date of these presents & the other seventy pounds to be paid her in four years from the date hereof & in case of her decease before it becomes due & payable, or if she should die without issue I do order will & appoint the legacy of her so dying to return into the hands of my son & heir Robert Heaton, or his heirs or assigns forever, This part hereof I do utterly revoke & do leave it as in manner & form following that is I do give unto my youngest daughter Anna Heaton as aforesaid to be left her in this manner & form following, that is the sum of one hundred & seventy pounds of good & lawful money of Pensilvania to be paid her by my Executor & son & heir Robert Heaton or by his heirs or assigns in manner & form following, that is the sum of one hundred pounds to be paid her in the space of two years after the date of these presents, & the other seventy pounds to be paid in four years from the date hereof, & in case of her decease without issue before it becomes due & payable, I do order will & appoint the legacy of her so dying to return into the hands of my Executor & son & heir Robert Heaton or to his heirs forever. I desire & order this codicil may be added to my will & be deemed & taken as a part thereof. In witness whereof I have set my hand & seal this twentieth day of March one thousand seven hundred & forty three. Signed Sealed Published & Declared by the Testator to be his last will & testament in the presence of us who have subscribed our names in his presence.

Robert Heaton

Tho*s*. Cooch, W*m*. Cartar, Henry Nodon

Proved July 23, 1743

1744 Will of Henry Nelson of Middletown, Bucks County, PA

To all to whom this may come greeting, I Henry Nelson of Middletown in the County of Bucks and Province of Pensilvania being weak and indisposed of body but of a sound and disposing mind and memory Thanks be to Almighty God for the same And calling to mind the uncertainty of my time in this world and the mortality of my body do make this my Last Will and Testament, in manner and form following

First and principally I bequeath my soul into the hands of Almighty God that gave it. And my body to be buried in a Christian like manner at the discretion of my Executors hear after named.

Secondly whereas Almighty God has blessed me with some of this worlds substances and also blessed me with children my will and mind is to bequeath and divide it amongst them as foloweth (sic)

First I give and bequeath unto my daughter Alice Cartar all that my plantation situated in or near Wrightstown where on she now lives containing seventy and six akors (sic). I give and bequeath the said plantation to her during her natural life and after her death I give and bequeath the said plantation to my grandson Henry Cartar to him and his heirs and assigns forever.

Secondly, I give and bequeath unto my son Thomas Nelson all this my plantation where on I now live situate in Middletown containing four hundred and fifty akors after my wife decease my will is that my wife Alice Nelson is to have the enjoyment and profits of the said plantation during her natural life and after her death I give and bequeath the said plantation to my son Thomas Nelson to him and his heirs and assigns forever.

Thirdly, I give and bequeath to my daughter Ann Wilson fifty akors of my land in Brighton township joyning (sic) Thomas Dowdneys and the River Delaware. I give and bequeath the said fifty akors of land to her and her heirs and assigns forever. Also I give and bequeath to my daughter Ann Wilson my two lots of land Lying in the Borrough of Brighton. I give and bequeath the said my two lots of land to her my said daughter Ann Wilson to her and her heirs and assigns forever.

Fourthly, I give and bequeath unto my daughter Letitiah Joly all that my plantation in Newtown, situate between Amos Stricklands and William Buckmans containing sixty one akors I give and bequeath the said plantation to her my said daughter Letitiah during her natural life and after her death I give and bequeath the said plantation to my grandson Nelson Joly him and his heirs and assigns forever.

Fifthly, I give and bequeath unto my son Thomas Nelson all that my land in Newtown ajoyning(sic) the mill together with the mill and all the appurtenances there unto belonging containing about thirteen akors. I give the said land and mill and appurtenances to my son Thomas Nelson to him and his heirs and assigns forever.

Sixthly, I give and bequeath unto my daughter Alice Cartar's children namely Henry Carter, John Cartar and James Cartar to each of them I give the sum of ten pounds current money of Pensilvania to be paid them by my Executors hereafter named when they shall arrive or attain to the age of twenty one years and if in case any of the three children to wit Henry Cartar John Cartar and James Cartar do dye before they do arrive *to the age aforesaid that then it is my will that the survivors or survivor of them shall have the legacies of the deceased.*

Seventhly, I give and bequeath unto my daughter Ann Wilson's children Henry Wilson and Elizabeth Wilson to my grandson Henry Wilson the sum of twenty pounds and to my granddaughter Elizabeth Wilson the sum of ten pounds current money of Pensilvania to be paid them when they shall arrive to the age of twenty one years by my Executors hereafter named.

Eighthly, I give and bequeath unto my daughter Letitiah Joly's children namely Nelson Joly and Alice Joly to my grandson Nelson Joly the sum of twenty pounds and to my granddaughter Alice Joly the sum of ten pounds current money of Pensilvania to be paid them when they shall arrive to the age of twenty one years by my Executors hereafter named

Ninthly, I give and bequeath unto my grandchildren descended from my daughter Gemimah Heaton namely Robert Heaton and Thomas Heaton the sum of ten pounds to each of them current money of Pensilvania to be paid them when they shall arrive to the age twenty one years by my Executors hereafter named.

Tenthly, I give and bequeath unto my nephew Edward Worstill the sum ten pounds currant money of Pensilvania to be paid him when shall arrive to the age of twenty one years by my Executors hereafter named.

It is my will and mind that my negro man called Cofe be set free and fully discharged from his servitude and be well clothed by my Executors twelve months after my death and in case my son Thomas Nelson shall not live till he arrives to the age of twenty one years, then and in such case my will and mind that all that I have given or bequeathed to him my said son Thomas Nelson shall be equally divided between the survivors of my children then living.

I do also hereby authorize and fully impower my Executors hereafter named to sell and convey and make be good lawfully settle to all the residue or remaining of that land in Brighton township that will be left remaining when the fifty akors already bequeathed to Ann Wilson is taken of in order to enable them to pay my just debts and legacies herein bequeathed and if anything to remain after my just debts be fully paid and discharged and the legacies herein bequeathed be secured to be paid that then it is my will and mind that my well beloved wife Alice Nelson shall have the remaining of all that shall remain of my personal estate.

And Lastly, I do hereby nominate and appoint my well beloved wife Alice Nelson and my well beloved son Thomas Nelson and my trusty friend Evelydous Longshore to be my Executors of this my Last Will and Testament and I do hereby revoke disanull and make void all wills and testaments by me heretofore made ratifying and confirming this to be my Last Will and Testament in witness whereof I have hear unto set my hand and seal this eleventh day of the month called April and in the year of our Lord one Thousand seven hundred forty and four. 1744

Henry Nelson

Signed & Sealed Pronounced and Declared by me the said
Henry Nelson to be my Last Will and Testament in the presence
Of us the subscribers John Watson, John Woolston, Edward Worstell

May ye 14th 1745 Then came John Watson and John Woolston two of the witnesses to the within written will and on their solemn affirmation according to law did declare they were personally present and also the Testator Henry Nelson sign seal publish and declare the above writing to be his last will and testament, and that at the doing there of he was of sound mind and memory and understanding to the best of their knowledge.

Coram J^n. Hall Dep. Reg.

1761 Will of Joseph Yates in Loudoun County, VA

Be it remembered that this 29th day of the 8th month called August in the year of our Lord one thousand and sixty one I Joseph Yates of Loudoun County and Colony of Virginia being sick and weak of body but of sound mind and memory and having to consider the uncertainty of this transitory life do make this my Last Will and Testament touching the disposal of what temporal estate I have hereby revoking and disannulling all former Will or Wills heretofore made by me and this only to be taken for my last Will and Testament and none other.

Imprimis I will that my body be decently buried at the discretion of my Executors hereafter mentioned.

Secondly that all my debts be fully paid and satisfied.

Item I give and bequeath unto my beloved wife Alice all the profits arising from this my plantation whereon I now dwell for the space of twelve years provided she continue my widow and after that time is expired my will is that she have the thirds of the profits of said plantation also I give her my grey mare and best featherbed also her new riding saddle

Fourthly I give and bequeath unto my son Robert the above mentioned plantation or lot of land containing one hundred and sixty five acres and that after the expiration of the above said term of twelve years this only. Reserved unto his brother Benjamin which is my will and I do hereby direct that my said son Benjamin shall have for the use and profits of half the cleared lands and meadows as also half the orchard for the space of seven years next after the end of said twelve years in which time he may clear land and meadows and plant orchards for himself on a certain lot of land joining this my aforementioned lot and it is my desire that my Executors may get the said adjoining lot surveyed for him and then my son Robert to have the above said plantation to himself only paying unto his mother her thirds as above reserved to her.

Fifthly I give and bequeath unto my daughter Alice one featherbed as also four milk cows.

Sixthly it is my will that my son Isaac have learning at school to fit for a trade and then bound to learn such trade as he may choose I likewise will unto my son Isaac ten pounds of my personal estate to be paid at the age of twenty one.

Seventhly I give and bequeath unto my son Benjamin ten pounds to be paid unto him at the age of twenty one.

Eighthly I give and bequeath unto my daughter Jane five pounds to be paid unto her eighteen months after my decease.

Ninthly I give and bequeath unto my daughter Providences children five shillings to be equally divided among them.

Tenthly I give unto my son Joseph five shillings.

Eleventhly I give unto my daughter Hannah five shillings.

Twelfthly I give unto my son William five shillings.

Thirteenthly it is my will and desire that after all my just debts be paid and all the above legacies discharged if there shall be any personal estate left that the remainder be *equally divided between my wife and our four last children namely Alice, Robert, Benjamin and Isaac but if there should not be sufficient to pay and discharge as above directed that then there be an equal deduction out of every legacy according to the sum thereof.*

Lastly I constitute and appoint my said wife and Israel Thompson Executors of this my Will and Testament. In witness whereof I have hereunto set my hand and seal the day and year as above written.

Signed Sealed Published and Declared to be	
the Last Will and Testament of the said Joseph	*his*
Yates in the presence of us	*Joseph X Yates (..)*
Francis Hague	*mark*
Thomas X Lamb	
William Wildman	

1764 Indentures - Loudoun Couty, Virginia – Thomas Dodd to James Carter

This Indenture made the Sixteenth day of November AD one thousand Seven hundred and Sixty four Between Thomas Dodd of the County of Loudoun and Colony of Virginia of the one part and James Carter of the same County and Colony aforesaid of the other part, Witnesseth that the said Thomas Dodd for and in consideration of the Sum of five Shillings sterling to him in hand paid the receipt whereof is hereby acknowledged Hath Granted Bargained and Sold and by these presents Doth Bargain and Sell unto the said all and Singular that Tract or parcel of Land Situate in the County of Loudoun aforesaid Bounded as followeth. Beginning at a Large white Oak marked **IC** corner to John Carlyle and in a line of Amos Janney Locust Tract thence with his line N°15 Et. two hundred and ten poles to a white Oak his Corner with another of his lines N°30 Et. two hundred and thirty poles to a Black Oak S°73 Et. Eighty Eight poles N°40 Et. one hundred poles to a Chestnut Oak and white Oak corner to Col. Richard Blackburn N°10 Et. Sixty poles to a line of William Cox with said lines S°75 Wt. two hundred and twenty poles to a white hiccory and lpine his Corner and Corner to Col. Grayson with his line S°9 Et. two hundred and fifty poles to white Oak his Corner N°78 Wt. Sixty poles to a white Oak his Corner by Branch then with his line S°25 Wt. two hundred and ten poles to his Corner South twenty five poles to a Line of said Carlyles with said Line East Ninety poles to the first Station Containing two hundred and ninety acres of Land Together with all. Houses Orchards Edifices and all other Appurtenances to the same belonging and Reversion and Reversions Remainder and Remainder Rents Issues and profits of the same To have and to hold the said Land with and Appurtenances unto the said James Carter his Est. And Adm. from the date hereof for one year from thence next ensuing fully to be Complete and ended yielding and paying therefore the Rent of one pepper Corn on the Feast of Saint Michael if demanded to the Intent that by virtue hereof and of the Statute for Transferring Use unto possession the said James Carter may be in Actual possession of the premises and to Enabled to Accept Grant of the Reversion and Inheritance thereof to him his heirs and assigns forever. In Witness whereof the said Thomas Dodd hath hereunto set his hand and Seal the day and year first above written.

Thomas Dodd (LS)

Sealed and Delivered
In presence of
Henry Carter, John Eblen
Peter Eblen, John Hough
Jo. Hough, William Keyers

At a Court continued and held for Loudoun County February the 13th 1765. This Indenture was proved by the Oaths of Henry Carter and Peter Eblen and by the

Affirmation of John Eblen (a Quaker) Witnesses thereto and Ordered to be Recorded.
Teste Cha^l Binns Ct. Cur.

*This Indenture made the Seventeenth Day of November in the year of our Lord one thousand Seven hundred and Sixty four. Between Thomas Dodd and Sarah his wife of the County of Loudoun and Colony of Virginia of the one part and James Carter of the said County and Colony of the other part Witnesseth that the said Thomas Dodd for and in Consideration of the Sum of Forty pounds Current Money of Virginia the receipt whereof the said Thoms Dodd doth hereby acknowledge Hath Granted Bargained sold Aliened Released and Confirmed and by these presents Doth fully freely and absolutely Grant Bargain an sell Alien Release and Confirm unto the said James Carter in his Actual possession now being by virtue of one Bargain and Sale to him thereof made for one year by Indenture bearing Date the day before the Date of these and by force of the Statute for Transferring these into Possession and to his heirs and Assigns forever All that Tract or parcel of Land Containing two hundred and ninety two acres situate Lying and being in the County of Loudoun on and about the Branches of Beaver Dam Branch of Goose Creek Bounded as followeth Beginning a Large white Oak marked **IC** Corner to John Carlyle and in a Line of Amos Janney's Locust. Tract then with his Line N°15 Et. 210 poles to a white Oak Janney's Corner then with another of his lines N°30 Et. 230 poles to a Black Oak S°73 Et. 88 poles N°40 Et. 100 poles to a Chestnut Oak and white Oak Corner to Col. Richard Blackburn N°10 Et. Sixty poles to a Line of William Cox with his Line S°75 Wt. 220 poles to white Hiccory and Ipine his corner and Col. Grayson with his Lines S°9 Et. 250 poles to white Oak his corner by Branch S°25 Wt. 210 poles to another of his Corners S°25 poles to a line of said Carlyles with said Line East ninety poles to Beginning being a Tract Granted to said Thomas Dodd by paten from proprietors Office Dated the Eighteenth Day of September AD 1757 and Recorded in said Office Book **E** Fol. 16 Together with all members and Appurtenances thereunto belonging and the Reversion and Reversions Remainder and Remainder Rents Issues and Profits thereof and all the Estate Right Title and Interest whatsoever both in Law and Equity of him the said Thomas Dodd of in and to the said Premises abovementioned with the Appurtenances To Have and to hold the said the two hundred and ninety two acres of Land with the Appurtenances unto the said James Carter his heirs and Assigns forever and the said Thomas Dodd doth Covenant and Grant to and with the said James Carter his heirs and Assigns that he the said Thomas Dodd hath rightful power and Lawful Authority to Grant Bargain and Sell the said Land Hereditaments all and Singular the premises abovementioned with the Appurtenances unto the said James Carter to the only proper use and Behoof of him the said James Carter his heirs and Assigns forever according to the true Intent and meaning of these presents and also that the said James Carter his heirs and Assigns shall and may at all times hereafter peaceably and quietly have hold occupy possess and enjoy all and Singular the said Land Hereditaments and premises*

123

abovementioned without the Lawful Set Trouble or interruption of him the said Thomas
Dodd his Heirs or Assigns and all and every other person and persons whatsoever
Claiming or Claim by from or under him, them or any of them and that freed and
Discharged well and Sufficiently saved and kept Harmless from former and other
Bargains Sales Gifts Grants Domain Wills Entails Rents or arranges of rents (the Quit
Rents and Land Tax only Excepted) Lastly that the said Thomas Dodd and his heirs
anything having or Claiming in the said premises abovementioned by from or under him
shall and will from time to time upon the reasonable request Cost and Charge in the Law
of him the said James Carter his heirs or Assigns make do Execute and acknowledge or
cause or procure or cause or procure to be made every such further and other Lawful and
reasonable Act and Act thing and things Conveyance and Conveyances in the law for the
better and more perfect Granting all and singular the Land and premises above
mentioned with the Appurtenances unto the said James Carter his Heirs or Assigns as by
the said James Carter his Heirs or Assigns or their Council Learned in the law shall be
reasonably Advised Revised and Required In Witness whereof the said Thomas Dodd and
Sarah his wife hath hereunto set their hands and Seals the Day and year first above
written.   Thomas Dodd (LS)
                                                               Sarah P. Dodd (LS) her mark

Sealed and delivered
In the presence of us
John Hough, Jo. Hough
William Keyes, Henry Carter
John Eblen, Peter Eblen

    Received of James Carter the Sum of Forty pounds Current Money of Virginia being
the Consideration mentioned to be paid me on the perfection of this Deed Witnesses my
hand this 17th day of November 1764.   Thomas Dodd
Testes / L40
John Hough, Jo. Hough
William Keyes, Henry Carter
John Eblen, Peter Eblen

    At a Court continued and held for Loudoun County February the 13th 1765. This
Indenture and the Receipt endorsed were proved by the Oaths of Henry Carter and Peter
Eblen and by the Affirmation of John Eblen (a Quaker) Witness thereto and ordered to be
Recorded.   Teste Chal Binns Ct. Cur.

1766 Will of Susannah Griffith Cartar Heaton of Northampton, Bucks County, PA

N.B. The Legacy given to Mary Plumly Entertained in final ---- Before the Signing and Sealing of this Will.

I Susanna Heaton of Northampton in the County of Bucks and Province of Pennsilvania, being weak of Body but of Sound Mind and Memory. Blessed be God Almighty. I now being Antient (sic) and do in a little Time according to the Common Course of Nature Expect to depart this Life. Do make and Ordain this my last Will in the manner and form following. Principaly (sic) and first of all I Commit my Soul to the hand of God that gave it, and my Body I desire may be buried in a Decent and Christian like manner by my Executor hereafter Named.

Item I Will that all my Funeral Expenses and just Debts be first paid and discharged.

Item I give and Bequeath unto Ann Hibbs my Daughter all my wearing Apparel.

Item I give and Bequeath unto my Grand Daughter Susanna Hibbs one feather Bed and all that thereunto belongeth.

And whereas I (ascription.?.) I have a Right to a Certain Annuity During my Natural life and is now Several Years in Arrears as appeareth (sic) by one Bond or Obligation duly Executed by my Son William Cartar Deceased to my Husband Robert Heaton Deceased bearing Date the Second day of March Anno Domini 1731/2. Relution (sic) being had thereto may more fully appear. It is my Will that all my Right, Title, Interest, Property, Claim or Demand whatsoever arising from the said Rented Bond or Obligation I give and Bequeath unto my Son in Law John Plumly Both what's now Due and to becomes due During my Natural life to be paid to the said John Plumly when Recovered of my Son Robert Heaton Jr. Executor and not before, According to the Said Intent and meaning of the Condition of the said Rented Obligation.

Item I give and Bequeath unto my Grand Son William Cartar Son of Joseph Cartar the sum of five Pounds to be paid by my Executor in one Year after my Decease.

Item I give and Bequeath unto my Grand Son Richard Cartar Son of my aforesaid Son Joseph Cartar the like sum of Five Pounds Current money to be paid as last mentioned.

Item I give and Bequeath the sum of Five Pounds Current money toward the support and maintenance of Katherine Hayhurst the Daughter of Sarah Hayhurst to be paid out at the Discretion of my Executor.

Item I give and Bequeath unto Mary Plumly my Grand Daughter the sum of five Pounds lawful money to be paid as the legacy next mentioned.

Item I give and Bequeath unto Ann Cartar Daughter of Rachael and Joseph Cartar the like sum of Five Pounds lawful money to be paid when she arrives to the age of Twenty one Years or when she shall marry by my Executor or whom he shall appoint.

Item I give and Bequeath the Residue and Remaining part of my Estate unto Isabel Heaton, Susanna Heaton and John Heaton my Three Grand Children to be Equally Divided Between them to be paid by my said Executor to the said Isabel and Susanna when they arrive to the Age of Twenty One years or when they shall marry. To the son John at the Age of Twenty One Years. And if it should happen that any of the four last mentioned Legatees should Dye (sic) under the Ages Expressly set forth it is my Will that the Deceased Share should be Equally Divided Amongst the Survivors of them. And further it is my Will and mind that my Executor Shall not pay or be Accountable for any Interest money on any part of my Estate for any Cause whatsoever.

And Lastly I Do hereby Constitute and appoint my Son Joseph Cartar my Sole Executor of this my last Will Revoking all voiding Every other Will and Wills by me at any time heretofore made and this Will only Remaining my last Will. In Witness where of I have here unto set my Hand and Seal the fifteenth Day of January Anno Domini 1766.

Susanna Heaton (seal)

Signed Sealed Published and Declared by the above named Susanna Heaton to be her last Will in the presence of us. Ezra Croasdale, James Cooper, Sarah Hayhurst.

January the 24, 1771. Then personally appeared Ezra Croasdale and James Cooper, who upon their solemn Affirmation Empaeticaly (sic) did declare that they subscribed their Names as Witnesses to the within written Instrument of Writing and that they were personally present and Saw the Testatrix Susanna Heaton Sign, Seal, and Publish the same as and for her Last Will and Testament. And that at the Time of so doing She was of sound Mind and Memory and of a disposing Mind (standing ?) to the best of their Knowledge and Belief. And the said Ezra Croasdale upon his solemn Affirmation did declare that the words "Mary Plumly" were written upon a Prized Place, and the words "grand" and "to be paid as the Legacy next mentioned" were written and interlined with the Knowledge of the Testatrix before the sealing and Publication of the same. Before me.

Wm Hicks Depy. Reg.

Bucks County Seat

Be it Remembered That on the 24th Day of January Anno Domini 1771. This Last Will and Testament of Susannah Heaton Widow Deceased was Duly Proved According to Law and Probate and Letters of Testamentary were granted to Joseph Cartar Executor in the said Will named. He being first solemnly Affirmed well and faithfully to Administer the Goods and Chattels, Payables and Credits of the said Deceased and to Exhibit in just and time Inventory thereof by Appraisers first Sworn or Affirmed into the Registers Office for the said County of Bucks in one Month after the date hereof and in just and Time Account of his Administration when thereto Required to Render Witness. My Hand and seal of the Office the Day and Year aforesaid.   Wm. Hicks Depy. Reg.

Fairfax Monthly Meeting, Loudoun, Virginia - 25th day of 10th month 1777

At our Monthly meeting of Fairfax held 25th of 10th Month 1777 the Representatives being called appeared. The friends appointed to attend the marriage of Isaiah Mires and Alice Yates report it was orderly accomplished and returned this certificate.

The marriage of Isaiah Myers and Alice Yates the daughter of Alice Nelson Carter Yates and Joseph Webster Yates.

1795 Will of John Eblin in Loudoun County, Virginia

I John Eblin of Loudoun County in the State of Virginia being weak in body but of sound disposing mind & memory do this thirteenth day of the eighth month in the year of our Lord one thousand seven hundred & ninety five make and ordain this my last Will and Testament in manner and form as follows,

First my will is that all my funeral expenses and just debts be fully satisfied and paid by my Executors herein after named.

Secondly, I give and bequeath unto my daughter Eliza Parker during her life eight acres of land in the north corner of my Plantation.

Thirdly my will is that my son-in-law Thomas Chapman have for himself his heirs and assigns forever twenty five acres of land of that land my plantation adjoining to Braden and Pierpoint, laid of by and at the discretion of my Executors so as not to extend further up the run than the head of the mill Pond, and so as not to interfere with the Dwelling house which I live in. Inconsideration whereof he is to assist in the maintenance of my wife during her life in manner as hereafter mentioned.

Fourthly, my will is that my son John Eblin his heirs and assigns have forever all the remaining part of my plantation (including the eight acres after my daughter Liza's decease. Inconsideration whereof he is to pay to my wife Mary Eblin during her life yearly and every year the sum of ten pounds Virginia Currency.

Fifthly, my will is that my wife remain with my son-in-law Thomas Chapman after my decease (if it be agreeable to her) and that he furnish her with every necessary for her support over and above and which may be wanting more than the ten pounds already mentioned will furnish her with, and further, that if either my son John, or son-in-law Thomas Chapman should refuse, or in any wise neglect to administer to the support of my wife as above mentioned, that then my Executors shall have full power to seize upon by way of distress as for a Common Rent, so much of the land as will satisfy the Demand upon him in whom the land is demised, as it is my intent that my wife shall have her support & maintenance from the land.

Sixthly, my will is that my son Samuel Eblin have five pounds paid to him his heirs or assigns out of my personal estate.

Seventhly, my will is that my son Isaac Eblin have the sum of five shillings, having before given him what I thought right.

Eighthly, my will is that my daughter Hannah Carter her heirs and assigns have three sevenths of my personal estate which shall remain over and above paying what is above mentioned

Ninthly, my will is that my daughter Mary Pyott her heirs and assigns have and equal share with my daughter Hannah Carter, and that my daughter Rachel Sloan her heirs and assigns have one third part as (m...?...) and Lastly I do hereby nominate, constitute and appoint my son-in-law James Carter and Jonathan Lovell Executors of this my Last Will and Testament, hereby Revoking all other and former wills by me made. In witness whereof I have hereunto set my hand & Seal the day and year above written.

The written will was Signed Sealed,
Published and declared by the above   John Eblin   Seal
Named John Eblin to be his last
Will & testament in the presence of us
Hopewell Powell
John Oliham
Usual Liffotell
Jeremiah Liffotell

At a court held for Loudoun County February the 13th 1797. This last Will and
Testament of John Eblin deceased was proved by the oaths of Hopewell Powell & John
Oliham and ordered to be Recorded and on the motion of Jonathan Lovell one of the
Executors therein named who made oath there to according to Law and together with
Joshua Gore and Edward Connard his Securities entered into and acknowledged their
Bond in the penalty of five hundred pounds with condition as the law directs certificate is
granted him for obtaining a probate thereof in due form --- and liberty is reserved to the
other Executor therein named to join in the probate thereof when he shall think fit.

Teste Charles Binns At. Law

1804 Will of William Myers of Loudoun County, Virginia

In the name of God Amen. I William Myers of the County of Loudoun and Commonwealth of Virginia, being weak of body but of perfect mind and memory, do make and ordain this my Last Will and Testament in manner and form as follows.

First – To my beloved wife Sarah, I give and bequeath her bed and bedding, and the room where she now lives during her life.

Second – I give and bequeath to my son Lambert Myers the plantation whereon I now live to him his heirs & assigns forever he the said Lambert shall find his Mother Sarah a good and comfortable living during her life but if my wife Sarah shall see proper to remove from where she now resides the said Lambert shall pay to his mother ten pounds in cash yearly and every year during her life.

And Jonathan my son I give one Mare known by the name of Gin.

And to my Daughter Sally I give and bequeath twenty five pounds to be paid her in cash out of my personal Estate likewise to have forever (ledge?) of the aforesaid (Resen?) which her Mother has in possession as long as she remains single and unmarried – my personal Estate to be sold and after deducting the aforesaid twenty five pounds the remainder to be equally divided between my wife these children and likewise is to be understood that my son Lambert is to pay all my Lawful Debts out of the Land and I do constitute and appoint my Trusty friends James Moore, Joseph Braden and my son Lambert Myers Executors of this my Last Will and Testament.-

Signed and Acknowledged   *William Myers Seal*
In the presence of
William Fox
Samuel Wright
Asa Harriss

At a Court held for Loudoun County February 9th 1804
This last Will and Testament of William Myers dec'd was proved by the oaths of William Fox, Samuel Wright and Asa Harris the subscribing witnesses thereto, and is ordered to be recorded and on the motion of James Moore, Joseph Braden and Lambert Myers the Executors therein named who made oath according to Law and Together with Asa Harris and Patterson Wright their (Le curilais?) who entered into and acknowledged their Bond in the penalty of one thousand Dollars Conditioned according to Law Certificates granted them for obtaining a probate thereof in due form.

Teste C Binns Jr. CLC

1810 Loudoun County, Virginia – Indenture – William Vickers to James Carter Sr.

*This Indenture made this Sixteenth day of February in the year of our Lord one thousand Eight Hundred and ten Between William Vickers and Anne his Wife of the County of Loudoun and State of Virginia of the one part and James Carter of the County of Loudoun and State aforesaid of the other part, Witnesseth that the said William Vickers and Anne his Wife for and in Consideration of the sum of Five Hundred Pounds lawful money of the Commonwealth to them in hand paid by the said James Carter Before the unsealing and delivery of these presents the Receipt whereof is hereby acknowledged have Bargained and Sold and by these presents do and each of them doth bargain and sell unto the said James Carter his Heirs and assigns a Certain Tract of Land lying being & situated in the County of Loudoun and State of Virginia and Bounded as follows Beginning at a walnut Stump on the bank of Goose Creek and in line of Monteith (Glance?) with the line of Monteith Nº 44 1/2 Et Et. 182 poles to a Box white oak on a ridge thence Sº11 Wt. 132 poles to the edge of Goose Creek & a small dogwood bush & Stone marked **RP** thence up the said Creek the Several meanders Thereof to the beginning containing Fifty acres be the same more or less also the residue of another survey beginning at the forked Hickory near a branch of Goose Creek thence Nº 102 poles to two white oak near said branch thence Sº 18 Et. 20 poles To a white oaks thence Sº 71 3/4 Et. 137th poles to a stone one pole northward to a Scrubby box oak thence to the beginning supposed to be 50 acres be the same more or less together with all and Singular the appurtenances and The Reversion and reversions remainder and remainders Yearly and other rents issues and profits the tenements Hereditaments and all and singular other the premises herein before mentioned or extended to be Bargained and Sold and every part or parcel thereof with every of their rights members and appurtenances unto the said James Carter his heirs and assigns forever and the said William Vickers and Anne his wife for themselves and their Heirs the said Tract or parcel of Land with all and Singular the premises and appurtenances unto said James Carter his heirs and assigns free from the claim or Claims of the said William Vickers and Anne his Wife or other of them their or either of their Heirs and of all and every person or persons whatsoever shall do warrant and forever defend by these presents To witness whereof the said William Vickers and Anne his wife have hereunto Set their hands and Seals the Day and Year first above written.*

William Vickers   Seal
Anne Vickers   Seal

Signed Sealed and delivered
In presence of

(Men..?) the words "for and" between the 13th ... 14th lines from the top and the words
supposed to be 50 acres be the same more or less between the 13th & 14th lines from the
top enter lines before signing.
Jesse McHugh Burr Powel
(Agibson?) Hugh Smith

At a Court held for Loudoun County the 10th day of Sept 1810. This Indenture from
William Vickers and Anne his Wife to James Carter as acknowledged by the said William
Vickers and Anne wife. (rest of document was not copied)

Examined & delivered to Eden Carter for James Carter August 27th 1811.   William Elgin

1812 Will of James Carter Senior of Loudoun County, Virginia

Be it remembered that I, James Carter, Senior, of Loudoun County, Virginia, being attacked with a pain in my breast, and considering the uncertainty of time, but still blessed with a sound and disposing mind and memory and desirous that the Goods of this life, with which it hath pleased Heaven to bless me, may at my death be rightly distributed among my offspring, do this twenty-fourth day of the seventh month, in the year of our Lord one thousand eight hundred and twelve make, publish and declare the following to be my last Will and Testament.

First, it is my will and desire that my Wife Hannah shall continue to live on the Farm which I now occupy, with the right of using as her own all the personal property which I leave there on, and that she shall have the whole profits of the said farm during her natural life excepting as here in after excepted, cc. I will that my son Dempsey shall continue with his mother, provided they can agree to stay together with the right of keeping his choice of the horses which I leave which I hereby give him, and as a reward for his services to his mother, such parts of the profits of the said farm as she may not want for her own use which shall be at least one hundred dollars yearly.

Secondly, I give to my son John a tract of land in Hampshire County containing one hundred and fifty-four acres or there abouts.

Thirdly, I give to my son Henry that part of my land in Loudoun County which he has heretofore occupied & subject, however to such conditions as shall hereafter be mentioned.

Fourthly, I bequeath to my son Dempsey the remainder of that part of my land in Loudoun County, which I now occupy, of which he shall come into full possession at his mother's death.

Fifthly, I bequeath to my son Asa that part of my land in Loudoun County which he now occupies.

Sixthly, I bequeath to my son Edon the tract of land which is now occupied by my son Mahlon in Loudoun County subject to such incumbrances as herein after mentioned.

Seventhly, I bequeath to my son Mahlon that part of my land in Loudoun County which is now occupied by my son Eden, subject to no incumbrance excepting as herein after mentioned.

All the grants which I have herein made to them are to be considered to them and their Heirs forever, and the Boundaries of the lots which I have assigned to Asa and Mahlon are to be determined as follows:

Asa's lot begins at or a little south of the stump of a large chestnut oak in William Carter's line, thence in a straight line over a large rock near the stone fence to a point in Drake's line near a Black oak, two chestnuts and a white oak, and includes all lying northeast of said line. Mahlon's begins at a point in Drakes line on the east bank of the south fork of Beaverdam, thence with the present meanders of the said Stream to a white oak and ash on its west bank near the house in which my son Edon now lives, thence in a straight line to a corner of the meadow fence about two poles west of a persimmon tree, thence in a straight line to a small black oak at the intersection of a

133

stone fence with the meadow fence. Thence with the said stone fence to a point in Grayson's line and includes all lying northwest of these boundaries.

Eighthly, I wish to leave my son, James what will make use, with what he already had one thousand dollars that is the sum of eight hundred and forty dollars. My daughter Sarah Yates 40 dollars, and my daughter Ruth Newton three hundred and twenty dollars and it is my will and desire that my son Henry shall pay two hundred dollars in two equal payments for the use of the said Ruth Newton within two years of my death, that within the term of one year of my death each of my sons, Edon and Mahlon shall pay for the use of my son James, the sum of two hundred dollars, and within the term of two years of my death the additional sum of two hundred dollars toward paying the Legacies herein bequeathed and that the Balance of said Legacies shall be raised from the sale of my personal property as soon as it can conveniently be done after the death of my beloved wife. The balance of the proceeds of said sale I leave to her disposal.

Lastly, I nominate and appoint my sons, John Carter and Mahlon Carter, the Executors of my last Will and Testament, and it is my request that they will have my body decently buried in Friends Burying Ground at Southfork, the expenses of such interment, together with such small debts as I may owe at my death to be paid out of any money which I may have on hand at my death, or otherwise raised from the sale of some part of my personal property. --- As my last and best Legacy to all of my children, I request that they may carefully suppress any emotions of discontent with respect to the division of my estate and endeavor to live in love and harmony with each other.

Signed, Sealed and delivered   his
In presence of us the date   James X Carter   Seal
Above written   mark

Abner Humphrey
Thomas Barton
Issac Cowell
Seth Smith

At a court held for Loudoun County, Sept, 11, 1812, this last Will and Testament of James Carter, deceased, proved by Abner Humphrey, Thomas Barton, and Seth Smith, three of the subscribing witnesses thereto and ordered to be recorded and on the motion of Mahlon Carter one of the Executors there in named who made oath there to and together with --- Vickers, Isaac Drake and James --- his securities entered into and acknowledged & their bond in the --- office five thousand dollars conditioned as the law directs, certificate is granted him for obtaining a probate there of in due form. The other Executor in writing from under his bond refused to qualify.

Teste C. Binns
CLC

1814 Probate for Estate of James Carter Senior – Loudoun County, VA

Account of sales of the property of James Carter deceased by Mahlon Carter his Executor

Names	Property	$ Cents
William Powell	2 Swingle trees & Shovel	00.35
Mahlon Carter	3 horse tree & Shovel plow	00.50
Jacob Silcott	1 Axe	00.25
Ditto	1 Collar & hams	00.60
John Neal	1 Rick of hay	16.25
Peter Rust	1 Mow of hay	2.00
Joseph Lane	1 White back steer	20.50
Jacob Silcott	1 Red Heffer	15.00
Mahlon Batey	1 Brindle cow	15.00
Robert Patterson	1 Black Bull	7.00
Jacob Silcott	3 Colors	10.25
Peter Rust	2 Shoats first choice	3.45
Ditto	3 Shoats second choice	5.00
Ditto	1 Small black Shoat	00.50
Mahlon Carter	1 Dark gray colt	60.80
Ditto	1 Small gray Do	22.00
Henry Carter	1 Iron Kettle	3.00
Do	1 Sledge	00.75
William Powell	Mall rings	00.13
John … Johnston	Scythe & Cradle	00.55
Mahlon Carter	1 Case Drawers	13.35
Ditto	1 Table	6.50
Peter Rust	1 Grid iron	00.70
Thomas Barton	4 Sheep 1 Choice	8.41
Gabrel Starkey	4 Do 2 choice	8.80
Thomas Barton	4 Do 3 choice	6.00
Jacob Silcott	1 Slide	00.10
Joseph Fored	1 Mow of hay	6.50
Andy Dormal	1 (siden ?) Cannel	00.50
Mahlon Carter	8 Bushel of wheat	66.00
Ditto	1 Rick of wheat	80.00
Ditto	2 stacks of rye	30.00
Ditto	Corn in field	10.50
Isaac Cowgill	1 Cyder Barrel	00.50
Mahlon Carter	1 Cag	00.30
Jacob Silcott	1 Scythe & tackling	00.50
Johnathan Gibson	1 Small wheel	2.60
John Patterson	1 Check reel	00.50
Busey Triplett	1 Wooling wheel	00.53
Mahlon Carter	1 Small Table	2.55
James McDonald	1 Pewter pot & Bail	1.50
Mahlon Carter	1 Small Do	1.00
Eden Carter	1 Small Do	00.36
Mahlon Carter	3 old chairs	1.25
Do	3 Do	1.10
Jonathan Gibson	1 Bake Iron	1.80

Eden Carter	1 Mattock	1.25
Do	2 old casks	00.31
Mahlon Carter	2 Gumbs	00.30
Do	2 old Barrels	00.25
Do	1 Dutch oven	00.87
Abner Humphreys	2 Collars 2 Blind Bridles	00.65
Wm Garrison	1 Chest	00.70
Mahlon Carter	1 Armchair	00.80
James McDonald	2 Pewter Dishes	3.70
Amos Hibbs	5 Pewter Plates	00.20
James McDonald	6 Pewter Plates	3.20
Mahlon Carter	1 frying pan	1.50
Do	2 tin pans	00.75
Joseph Gourley	1 Pewter Bason	00.81
Do	fire shovel & Tongs	1.50
Eden Carter	1 Pot enamel	0.80
James McDonald	1 Trammel	1.76
Mahlon Carter	2 fat Irons	1.00
Isaac Cowgill	1 Small Ladle	00.13
Reuben Triplett	2 jugs	00.31
Joseph Gourley	1 Sifter	1.15
Michael Plaster	1 Pair (Stilbards ?)	1.75
Mahlon Carter	1 Cullender	00.50
Do	4 knives & forks	1.01
Lusey Triplett	1 Dough Trough	00.26
Joseph Gourley	1 watering pot	1.26
Eden Carter	1 ...	00.50
Do	Bed & furniture Bedstead	17.50
Hannah Carter	1 Do with Do	19.00
Eden Carter	2 candlesticks	00.15
Thomas Popkins	1 Bed & furniture	9.25
Jacob Silcott	1 Looking glass	1.75
John Walker	1 weeding hoe	00.51
David Galleham	1 Sugar box tin kettle mug	00.41
Jonathan Gibson	1 water bucket	00.35
Mahlon Carter	2 Earthen pots	00.25
Reuben Triplett	2 Coverlids	00.25
Do	2 Trays	00.06
Benjamin Brooks	2 hogs first choice	9.00
Do	1 Do Second choice	4.61
Mahlon Carter	1 (tea...?)	00.75
Do	half of the (..ing ?) of a wagon gears	17.50
David Galleham	1 Mow of hay	8.00
Mahlon Carter	1 Pair hames & chains	2.54
Do	1 Pair Do	2.12
Benjamin Brooks	1 Gray mare	37.50
Mahlon Carter	1 Bay horse	85.00
Joseph Gourley	2 (..uiln)	00.50
Mahlon Carter	2 rakes pitchfork & Shovel	00.25
Wm Hart	1 Collar	00.16
Mahlon Carter	1 Dutch pan	24.00
Wm Hart	1 Cutting box & knife	2.10
Do	1 gum	00.06

Jacob Silcott	3 Sheep	7.50
Mahlon Carter	2 Cloves 3 swing trees	00.45
Joseph Lovett	1 washing tub	00.36
David Galleham	1 Black cow	18.00
Jonathan Gibson	1 Black heifer	12.05
Hannah Carter	1 Red cow short tail	10.00
Do	6 Pewter Plates	3.20
Do	1 trench	1.50
Wm Hart	1 shear (...crues ?)	1.25
Mahlon Carter	1 Collar	00.25
Hannah Carter	2 (Cittles ?)	4.00

At a Court held for Loudoun County Oct 10th 1814 This a/e Sales of James Carter deceased was returned & ordered to be Recorded.

Teste C Binns CLC

1814 Probate for Estate of James Carter Senior – Loudoun County, VA

The Estate of James Carter deceased in a/c with Mahlon Carter the Executor

			$ Cents
To Mahlon Beadly's proved account	No.	1	38.67
To paid Jacob Silcott for attendance		2	1.59
To do ditto attendance ... Clerk		3	1.00
To pd Stephen McPherson his account		4	5.37 ½
To pd Wm Powell for (...ing ?) the sale		5	5.00
To pd Thomas M Smith his account		6	3.31 ½
To pd Abner Gibson do		7	10.00
To pd Owen Thomas for a coffin		8	10.00
To cash pd Sm Balance in part of fees		9	10.00
To cash pd Ditto in part of fees		10	5.00
To cash pd Do Do Do		11	3.00
To cash pd 1 Clerks note		12	0.88
To cash pd Sm Balance in part of fees		13	5.50
To cash pd ditto do do		14	3.00
To cash pd do Do do		15	9.00
To cash pd 1 Loudoun Clerks note		16	10.91
To cash pd A Rec'd 2 fee bills		17	1.26
To cash pd ... note of fees		18	0.18
To cash pd A Rec'd Eden Carter Cost		19	22.00
To cash pd James Rust costs and damages		20	32.27
To cash pd for digging grave		21	1.50
To cash pd George Scoto his a/c 4 Bushels Plaster @7/6			5.00
To cash pd Wm Nickers Judge ... Execution	No.	22	10.83
To cash for ¾ gallons whiskey for the Sale			3.00
To my commission 7 ½ ... on $765.08			57.37 ½
Sum			$255.15 ½

November 1812 by Amt of Sales of the Personal Estate	$765.08
To Amt debts brought up to be deducted	$255.15 ½
Amt due from Executor	$509.82 ½

Loudoun County Set Pursuant to an Order of the worshipful Court of Loudoun County to us directed date the 10 day of October 1814 we have this day Examined the vouchers and accounts produced us by the Executor of James Carter deceased and find them as above stated and after allowing him a commission of seven and a half cent on the account sales do find a balance remaining in his hands do due the Estate of $509.82 ½ Given under our hands the 17 day of May 1815.

Abner Humphrey
Benj Grayson
Daniel Paches

At a Court held for Loudoun County the 14 day of August 1815 This Estate Account of James Carter deceased was returned and Ordered to be Recorded.

Teste C. Binns CLC

1841 Letter of Administration for Estate of John Carter, Hampshire Co.

__Know all men by these presents__, that we Albert Carter, John Carter & Robert Carter, William Monroe & Benjamin Corbin are held and firmly bound unto John Ioner, David Gibson, Narcisse Fore & Elisha Thompson. Gentlemen Justices of the County Court of Hampshire, now sitting, in the sum of Four Thousand dollars to be paid to the said Justices, and their successors; for which payment, well and truly to be made, we bind ourselves, and each of our heirs, executors and administrators, jointly and severely, firmly by these Presents.

Sealed with our seals, and dated this 25 day of October 1841

__The condition of this obligation is such__, That if the said Albert Carter administrator of the goods, chattels and credits of John Carter deceased, do make a true and perfect inventory of all and singular the goods, chattels and credits of the said deceased, which have or shall come to the hands, possession or knowledge of him the said Albert Carter or into the hands or possession of any other person or persons for him and the same so made do exhibit into the County Court of Hampshire, when he shall be thereto required by the said Court; and such goods, chattels and credits, do well and truly administer according to law; __and further__, do make a just and true account of all his actings and doings therein, when thereto required by the said Court, and all the rest of the said goods, chattels and credits, which shall be found remaining upon the account of the said administrator (the same being first examined and allowed by the Justices of the said Court for the time being) shall deliver and pay unto such persons respectively as are entitled to the same by law; and if it shall hereafter appear that any last will and testament was made by the deceased, and the same be proved in Court, and the executor obtain a certificate of the Probate thereof, and the said Albert Carter do in such case, being required, render and deliver up his letters of administration, - then this obligation to be void; else to remain in full force.

Signed, Sealed and Delivered
In the Presence of

Albert Carter	*Seal*
Robert Carter	*Seal*
John Carter	*Seal*
William Monroe	*Seal*
Benjamin Corbin	*Seal*

1846 Settlement of Estate of John Carter dec'd

1843 Estate of John Carter		$ Cent	1844 Albert Carter Administrator		$ Cents
Jun 43	Cash paid John Sloan Surveyor	2.06	Jun 44	balance due – interest	121.96
Feb 44	Cash paid AP White atty fees	7.50			
Jun 45	balances due	823.84	Jun 45	Balance due – interest	170.82
Jun 46	balances due	833.39			
Nov 46	Clerks fee	1.00	Jun 46	Balance due – int to Nov	191.42
	Commission fee	1.50			
	Balances due	823,84	Nov 46	Balance due per debit	821.34
				Deduct Sarah Bradfield	37.04
Nov 46	To Henry Bilbes & Hannah	463.02		not paid	784.30
	Widows distribution	325.24		add interest	191.42
	Hannah's distribution	130.09 ½			975.72
	Overpaid	7.68 ½		Widows share	325.24
Nov 46	To Robert Carter	137.09 ½			650.48
	Overpaid	7.68 ½			
	To James Carter	130.09 ½		5 heirs each	130.09 ½
	To John Carter	136.10			
	Overpaid	6.00 ½			

Commissioners Office Romney
Dec 5, 1846

In obedience to an order of the County Court of Hampshire I have examined estate & settled the accounts of Albert Carter upon the estate of John Carter dec'd and respectfully submit the foregoing as my report.

John Kern

... ...

At a Court held for Hampshire County the 28th day of December 1846 This settlement of the estate account of John Carter dec'd was returned and ordered to lie until the next term. And at a Court held for Hampshire County the 25th day of January 1847 the same was ordered to be recorded there being no exceptions thereto.

Teste J.B. White
CHC

Replevin – restoration of property

Trespass – recover damages for the harm done

Trover & Conversion – recover value of property but not the actual property

Capias Warrant – arrest for contempt of court – detain or bring to court

Tavern License
Cover Sheet
To Grand Jury March Term 1833

List of Licensed Store, Grocery and Tavern Keepers in the County of Marion at the March Term 1833 of the Marion Circuit Court. (Two pages of names and license expiration date – including).

James Carter   Tavern   Expiration   December 12, 1833

                            Teste Joseph M. Moore
                            Clerk pro tem of the Marion Circuit Court

I. 1834 State of Indiana – Marion County – James Carter vs. Abraham Bowen, Jacob Scott & James Kimberlin - Trespass

1 – September 19, 1833 - State of Indiana vs John Blackburn - Vagrancy

State of Indiana

vs

John Blackburn

Be it remembered that on the oath of James Carter, filed on the 14th day of September 1833 A Warrant issued & handed to Jacob Roberts Constable who Returned the same Executed with the body of John Blackburn issued subpoena in behalf of the complaint for James Carter, Willis Atkins, John Angle, Joseph Coats – all appeared but James Carter also issued a subpoena in behalf of – the Defendant for John Harrison, Wiley Wright, John Wright, John Reagan & William Branson which appeared & the Defendant ordered his trial & after hearing the proofs & allegations of the above Cause & all things touching the same it is considered that the Defendant is Not guilty of the above charge; & be acquitted & go hence without Day this 19th of September 1833. Be it further Remembered that in consequence of the complainant failing to prosecute his Complaint it is considered that the Defendant recover the Cost of suit by the complainant Expended.   A. Bowen Justice of Peace

I certify this to be a true Transcript - Drawn from my Docket this first Day of February 1834.

Abraham Bowen Justice of Peace

Justice Costs

Taking complaint	$ 0.50
Issue warrant	$ 0.25
Issue 2 subpoenas	$ 0.50
Summary & writ	$ 0.25
Judgement	$ 0.25
	$ 1.75

Witness fees 8 $ 2.00

Constable Costs

One warrant	$ 0.71
On 2 subpoenas	$ 2.13 ½
	$ 2.84 ½

Total $ 6.59 ½

First Writ – December 11, 1833

State of Indiana Marion County J^s.

      To Jacob Scott Constable of Washington township greetings; whereas John Blackburn obtained a judgement before me Abraham Bowen Justice of Peace in said township on the 19th of September 1833 against James Carter for $ 6.59 ½ cents Costs by said Carter Expended - these are therefore to Command you of goods & Chattels of said Defendant to cause to be made the said Costs & accruing Costs by Distress & sale thereof return the overplus if any to said Defendant & of this Return in thirty Days given under my hand & seal this 11th December 1833.

                                    Abraham Bowen Justice of Peace

Second Writ – February 6, 1834

State of Indiana, Marion County greetings:

      To Jacob R. Scott Constable of Washington Township greetings; Whereas John Blackburn obtained a judgement before me A. Bowen Justice of Peace in said township on the 19th of September 1833 against James Carter for $ 6.59 ½ cents Cost by the said Carter Expended since that has accrued on Execution $ 1._7 ½ cents more & 20 cents made on Execution with 12 ½ cents more for this Execution. These are therefore to Command you of the goods & Chattels of said Defendant Carter to cause to be made the said Costs & accruing Costs, after Deducting 20 cents which has been made – by Distress & sale thereof return the overplus if any to said Defendant & of this return in 30 Days given under my hand and seal this 6th of February 1834.

                                      A. Bowen Justice of Peace

Declaration – March 8, 1834

James Carter
vs
Abraham Bowen
Jacob Scott
James Kimberlin

Declaration

The clerk of the Marion Circuit Court will please to issue a Capias ad respondendum on the written declaration and endorse "This is an action of trespass with force & arms – Damages $500.00 as Bail required.   Fletcher for the plaintiff

Filed in the Clerk's office of the Marion Circuit Court on March 8 AD 1834 and Capias issued.

                                I.M. Mone clerk pro tem

 # 2 – Marion Circuit Court March term 1834

James Carter plaintiff complains of Abraham Bowen, Jacob Scott and James Kimberlin defendants of a plea of trespass.

For that heretofore to wit on the fifth day of February in the year 1834 at Marion County and State of Indiana with force and arms the said defendants broke and entered the close of the said James Carter situate and being in the County and State aforesaid and then and there took and drove away one yoke of oxen of the proper goods & chattels of the said Plaintiff of great value to wit of the value of Forty dollars there then found and being and converted and disposed thereof of the same to their own proper use and benefit & other wrongs then and there did to the said Plaintiff against the peace of the State of Indiana.

And for that also on the 1st day of March in the year aforesaid at the County and State aforesaid the said defendants broke and entered a certain other close of said Plaintiff lying and being in the County and State of aforesaid and with force and arms took and seized one wagon of the proper goods and chattels of said plaintiff of great value to wit of the value of seventy five dollars and converted and disposed thereof of the same to their own use and benefit, and other wrongs then and there did of the said law and against the peace of the State of Indiana to the damage of the said Plaintiff five hundred dollars wherefore he sues.   Fletcher for plaintiff

3 – Abraham Bowen – Trespass

Abraham Bowen, impleaded in trespass
a of
James Carter

And the said Abraham Bowen, who is impleaded with Jacob Scott & James Kimberlin and who swears his plea, by J. Morrison his Attorney, comes and defends the force and injury when J^c, and says that he is not guilty of the said several trespasses in manner and form as the said plaintiff hath above thereof complained against him: and of this he puts himself upon the Country.

J. Morrison Atty for defendant Bowen

Plaintiff doth the like.

Nick Fletcher for plaintiff

And for further plea in this behalf as to the breaking and entering the said plaintiff's close and then seizing and taking the said wagon & oxen as in the first and second counts in said plaintiff's declaration mentioned, and converting and disposing of the same to the use of said defendants; above supposed to have been done by them, he the said defendant Bowen says action non J^c, because he says that before the said time when J^c in said declaration mentioned, the plaintiff appeared before said defendant, who was then and still is an acting justice of the peace in the said County, and made complaint on oath, that one John Blackburn of said County, was an idle, vagrant dissolute person, rambling about without any visible means of substance and did not belittle himself to labour to procure a livelihood, and that said Blackburn was an able bodied man and had a wife and three children, and that he the plaintiff verily believed that said Blackburn and his family were likely to suffer without being supported by the neighborhood or county: when which complaint the said plaintiff prays a warrant against said Blackburn, under and in perseverance of the Act concerning vagrants: and on which complaint and prayer, Court on the fourteenth day of September AD 1833. The said defendant as justice of the peace as aforesaid issued his warrant in due form of law to Roberts a Constable of said County, commanding him to have the body of said Blackburn forthwith before said defendant justice as aforesaid, to answer said complaint which was thence upon returned by said Constable, with the body of said Blackburn in custody, and such proceedings were thereupon had before said defendant, justice as aforesaid that said Blackburn was found not guilty by said defendant. Justice as aforesaid and it was considered by the defendant, justice as aforesaid and judgment was so then & there rendered that the said Blackburn should be acquitted did go thence without day and recover of the said plaintiff the cost of said suit, in consequence of the said plaintiff failing to prosecute his said complaint: and afterwards viz; on the 7th day of January 1834, at J^c aforesaid, the said defendant contriving to be a justice of the peace as aforesaid by the license & request of the plaintiff a writ of execution was duly issued by the said defendant, justice J^c as aforesaid, and which was directed & delivered to said Jacob Scott, one of the defendants in this suit, a constable of said county, commanding him that of the goods and chattel of said plaintiff, he said defendant constable J^c should cause to made the said costs, amounting to $ 6.59 ½ cents, and the accruing costs by distress and sale thereof returning the overplus if any to said plaintiff. And of the said writ to make return in thirty days; and which writ was under the hand and seal of said defendant, justice as aforesaid.

By virtue of which execution, the said Scott, constable as aforesaid, afterwards and before the return thereof, to wit at the said time when J^c peaceable and quietly entered into the said close in order to seize and take, and did then and there seize and take in execution the said oxen in the said first count and introductory part of this plea mentioned, and did then & there by sale thereof levy a certain sum of money, to wit, the sum of twenty cents, and there upon returned said execution to the defendant justice as aforesaid with his doings thereon; and afterwards, to wit, on the sixth day of February AD 1834, an alias execution was issued by said defendant, justice J^c the ordinance of office as aforesaid, on said judgement of said plaintiff license & request & delivered to said constable to be executed by which said constable was commanded that of the goods and chattels of said plaintiff he should cause to be made the said costs amounting to $6.59 ½ cents and $1.07 ½ cents more afterwards accrued (accruing costs) deducting 20 cents, made on said first writ of execution, by distress and sale thereof, returning the overplus if any to said plaintiff, and of said writ to make return in 30 days, which writ was & is under the hand & seal of said defendant justice J^c, as aforesaid.

By virtue of which last named execution the said constable, afterwards and before the return thereof, at the said term when J^c in the said second count of said declaration mentioned, peacefully and quietly entered into the said close and did then & there seize and take in execution the said wagon in the said count, and introductory part of this plea mentioned, and did then & there by sale thereof levy a certain further sum of one dollar and 31 cents and thence for returned said last named execution to said defendant, justice J^c as aforesaid with his doings thereon, which are the said several supposed trespasses in the introductory part of this plea mentioned, and whereof the said plaintiff hath above thereof complained against the said defendant. And this he is ready to verify; wherefore he prays judgement. J^c

J. Morrison for defendant.

4 – Jacob Scott - Trespass

Jacob Scott, impleaded in Trespass
a of
James Carter

And the said Jacob Scott, who is impleaded with Abraham Bowen & James Kimberlin and who swears In his plea, by J. Morrison his Attorney, comes and defends the force and injury when J^c, and says that he is not guilty of the said several trespasses, in manner and form as the said plaintiff hath above thereof complained against him, and of this he puts himself upon the country.   J. Morrison Atty, for Scott
Plaintiff doth like wise.   Nick Fletcher for plaintiff

And for further plea in this behalf as to the breaking and entering the plaintiff's close, and there seizing and taking the said oxen and wagon in the first and second counts in said declaration mentioned, and converting and disposing of the same to his own use, he the said defendant says acted non J^c because he says that before the time when J^c viz on the 19th day of September AD 1833 judgement had been rendered by Abraham Bowen Esq; A justice of the peace in and for said county, on the trial and determination of a complaint made by said plaintiff on behalf of the said State against one John Blackburn, who was charged in said complaint on the oath of said plaintiff, with being an idle, vagrant & desolate person, J^c - and it was on the trial and determination of said complaint, adjudged and considered by said Justice of the peace that said Blackburn was not guilty of the charge, and was therefore discharged by said justice; And it was then & there further considered and adjudged by said justice, who had full form & authority to inquire of, try & determine said complaint that in consequence of the said plaintiff then & there failing to prosecute his said complaint, the said Blackburn should recover of the complainant the cost of said suit by him defended J^c; And afterwards viz: on the 7th day of January 1834, at J^c aforesaid by the license & request of said plaintiff an execution was duly issued, by said justice on said judgement, who still was a justice of the peace as aforesaid, and which came to the hands of the defendant as a constable of said county, in due form of law to be executed, who was then and now is a constable as aforesaid, by which the said defendant, constable J^c as aforesaid was commanded – that of the goods and chattels of said plaintiff he should cause to be made the said costs (amounting to $6.59 ½) and accruing costs by distress and sale thereof, returning the overplus if any to said plaintiff and of said execution to make return in thirty days, which execution was and is under the hand and seal of the said justice.

And the said defendant, constable J^c as aforesaid, at J^c in virtue of said execution, on J^c then next ensuing peaceably and quietly entered unto the said close, in order to seize and did then & there levy and seize in execution the said oxen in the said first count of said declaration mentioned, as the property of said plaintiff to satisfy said execution, and after having posted notices, notifying the time and place of the sale thereof according to law before the Day of sale, the said defendant at J^c aforesaid, did again quietly and peaceably enter the said close on the day of sale, and sold the said oxen at public vendue to one James Kimberlin he being the highest & best bidder, for the sum of twenty cents, and there afterwards and J^c aforesaid made return of said execution to the said justice, with his doings thereon, - and afterwards to wit on the _ day of February AD 1834, an alias execution issued by said justice and said judgement; which came to the hand of said defendant, by which the said constable was commanded that of the goods & chattels of said plaintiff he the defendant, constable & sheriff cause to be made the said costs viz the said sum of $6.59 ½ and $1.07 ½ cents afterwards accrued and accruing costs, after deducting twenty cents, which has been made, by distress and sale thereof, returning the overplus, if any to said plaintiff; which writ was and is under the hand & seal of said justice.

By virtue of which last named execution the said defendant, as constable as aforesaid, at the said time when he J^c issued declaration mentioned, peaceably and quietly entered into the said close, and then & there seized and took in Execution the said Wagon in the said second count mentioned, and after having posted notices of the time and place of sale thereof, according to law, the said defendant did again quietly and peaceably enter the said close on the day of sale, and sold the said wagon at public auction, to one James Kimberlin he being the biggest and last bidder, at the sum of $1.31 cents and thereof afterwards to wit in the first day of March 1834, made return at said last mention execution to said justice, with his doings therein, which are the same trespasses in said declaration and in the introductory part of that plea mentioned, and this he is ready to verify: where upon he prays judgement. J^c

J. Morrison for defendant

And the said defendant for further plea in this behalf says action was J^c, because he says that at the said times when J^c in said declaration mentioned, he was a constable of Washington Township in said County, and that on J^c at J^c aforesaid on execution in due form of Law was issued by one Abraham Bowen a justice of the peace in & for said County by the license & request of said plaintiff and delivered to said defendant constable as aforesaid, in due form of law to be executed, by which he the defendant, constable J^c as aforesaid was commanded that of the goods & chattels of said plaintiff, the said defendant, constable J^c should cause to be made the sum of $6.59 ½ cents the costs which by & in the said writ of execution it was & is certified had been recovered, and for which judgement had been rendered before the said justice in favour of one John Blackburn against the said plaintiff, on the 19th September 1833 and accruing costs, by distress & sale thereof, returning the overplus if any to said plaintiff, and of said writ to make due return in thirty days, which writ was J^c under the hand & seal of said justice and the said defendant, constable J^c and as aforesaid at J^c in virtue of said execution, on J^c next ensuing peaceably and quietly entered unto the said close, in order to, and did then & there seize and take in execution the said oxen in the said first count in said declaration mentioned as the property of said plaintiff to satisfy said execution, and after having posted notices notifying the time and place of the sale thereof according to law. The said defendant did again peaceably enter the said close on the day of sale, and sold the said oxen at public vendue to one James Kimberlin at the sum of twenty cents he being the best bidder; and there afterwards on J^c, made return of said execution to said justice with his doings thereon; and afterwards went on J^c at J^c on alias writ of execution was issued by the said justice by the license & request of said plaintiff and delivered to said defendant in due form appears to be executed, as constable as aforesaid, by which he was commanded that the goods and chattels of said plaintiff, he should cause to be made the sum of $6.59 ½ cents of costs which (...?...) was and is certified in said writ had been on this 19th September 1833 recovered & judgement thereof rendered by said justice in favour of one John Blackburn against said plaintiff and $1.07 ½ cents that has afterwards accrued with 12 cents more for said last execution, and accruing costs, after deducting 20 cents which has been made, - by distress and sale thereof, returning the overplus if any to said Carter the plaintiff and that of said writ the defendant should make return in 30 days, which event was and is under the hand & seal of said justice by virtue of which said last named execution the said defendant, constable Jᶜ as aforesaid at Jᶜ on Jᶜ peaceably and quietly entered into the said close, and did then & there seize & take in execution the said wagon in the said second count of said declaration mentioned, and after having given due notice of the time & place of sale, by notifications posted according to law, the said defendant constable as aforesaid did again peaceably and quietly enter the said close on the day of sale; and sold the said wagon – at public vendue to one James Kimberlin for the sum of one dollar 30 cents (he being the best bidder). And there upon afterwards to wit, in Jᶜ at Jᶜ made return of said execution to the said justice, with his doings thereon, - which are the said several supposed trespasses in the introductory said plaintiff declaration mentioned, And this he is ready to verify: wherefore he prays judgement Jᶜ   J. Morrison for defendant

5 - 1834 - James Carter vs. Abraham Bowen & others

James Carter

vs.

Abraham Bowen & others

     And the said Carter for replication to the second plea of the defendant Bowen as amended comes and saith that by reason of any (True..?) therein construed he ought not to be barred or precluded of hearing or maintaining said action because he saith that said plea is insufficient in Law for said plaintiff to have or preclude said plaintiffs action here in he the said plaintiff bound by the law of the land to answer the same _ and this he is ready to verify & therefore he prays judgement.

     And for special cause of dismisses to each plea the plaintiff (...?...) the following. Said plea is double & attempts to set out two distinct defenses to wit a justification under a judgement & execution and also under a license of the plaintiff. Said plea sets forth a judgement liken judicial perversity which was (...?...). Said plea is also in other respects deficient & insufficient.   Fletcher for plaintiff

     And the said defendant Bowen, as to the plea of said defendant secondly above pleaded says action was Jᶜ because he says that the said second plea of said defendant above pleaded in manner & form is sufficient in law to bar said plaintiff's action Jᶜ, and that he is bound by law to answer the same, and this he is ready to verify. Wherefore he prays judgement .
                                                     J. Morrison for defendant

6 – 1834 - James Carter vs. Jacob Scott & others

James Carter

vs.

Jacob Scott & others

And for replication to his plea of this defendant Scott (...?...) above pleaded as amended this said plaintiff saith (precluded now) because he saith that said last named plea and the matters & things therein set forth are insufficient in law to bar or preclude said action and this the plaintiff is ready to verify & herein prays judgement. And for especial cause of dismisses to said plea said plaintiff sets Down the following.

1st said plea is double in this. By said plea it is attempted to justify the trespass complained of under an execution issued by a justice of the peace. And also under a license each of which would constitute a separate dismiss.

2nd said plea is also in making other aspects insufficient. And there is much of (implusey?) in said plea for of the lesson is which affirm them & much as sets forth the (...?...) (implusey?) & of their execution is which appears a justification then to much as sum the (...?...) is (Implusey?).   Fletcher

And the defendant Scott says that his said plea secondly whom pleaded as amended is sufficient & good to bar said plaintiff of his said action / (...?...) prays judgement.

                                                                    J. Morrison for defendant

II. September 16, 1834 - State of Indiana – Marion Circuit Court – S. H. Cunningham vs. James Carter - Summons

The State of Indiana to the Sheriff of Marion County, Greetings: You are hereby commanded to summon Soloman George, David Allison, John Allison and Leven T. McCabe to personally be and appear before the Judges of Marion Circuit Court, on the seventh day of their next term, to be holden at the Court House in Indianapolis, on the fourth Monday in September instant to testify on behalf of the plaintiff in a certain case pending in said court between S. H. Cummingham plaintiff and James Carter defendant an herein they may not fail at their peril; have you then there this writ. Witness Robert B. Duncan, Clerk of said Court, this Sixteenth day of September AD 1834   Robert B. Duncan

This Subpoena issued in place of one here before issued, which has been lost.

                                                                    R. B. Duncan clerk

III. March 25, 1835 – State of Indiana – Marion County – Marion Circuit Court vs James Carter – 2 cases of Replevin & Trover

February 1835 – Cover Sheet

Henry Nevill and
James Nevill part.
vs
James Carter
Writ of Replevin
Damages $1,000.00
To March Term 1835

February 23, 1835 – Plaintiff Allegations

The State of Indiana SS
Marion County
The State of Indiana to the Sheriff of Marion County Greetings.

      Whereas Henry Nevill and James Nevill merchants, partners trading under the firm of H. & J. Nevill, have on the day of the date hereafter filed in the Clerk's Office of the Marion Circuit Court, the affidavit of Henry Nevill one of the firm of Henry Nevill and James Nevill aforesaid, of lawful age, shewing among other things that James Carter heretofore, to wit, on the 21st day of February instant (1835) at his dwelling and residence in Washington Township in Marion County having lawfully acquired did then & there unjustly and unlawfully detain from the said H. & J. Nevill certain personal goods and chattels of said H. & J. Nevill of the following description and weights, to wit, three bags of coffee 488 lbs., 1/3 chests of tea 12 lbs.; 14 kegs of merchandise 725 lbs.; ½ barrel of sugar 120 lbs.; 1 barrel of merchandise 7 lbs.; 1 bale of merchandise 103 lbs.; 2 bags of shot 50 lbs.; 9 bundles of lead 108 lbs.; 1 box of tea 18 lbs.; 1 crate of merchandise 548 lbs.; 3 boxes of merchandise 174 lbs.; 1 other box of merchandise 37 lbs.; 1 cask of merchandise 380 lbs.; the whole thereof being of the value of seven hundred dollars at least.

      Therefore you are hereby commanded to take into your custody the goods and chattels above particularly described, and them safely keep until said plaintiffs Henry Nevill and James Nevill partners as aforesaid, shall well and truly satisfy you by good and sufficient pledges that they will well and truly prosecute said writ to effect, and return such goods and chattels provided a return on the final bearing of the cause should be adjudged by the Marion Circuit Court to this said Defendant James Carter and you are also hereby commanded to summon the said James Carter to appear before the judges of the Marion Circuit Court, on the first day of their next term to be holden at the Court House in Indianapolis on the fourth Monday in March next, to answer unto the said Henry Nevill and James Nevill merchants, partners trading under the firm of H. & J. Nevill, in an action of Replevin of and concerning the unjust and unlawful detention aforesaid to the damage of the said plaintiffs one thousand dollars, and have you then there this writ.

Witness Robert B. Duncan Clerk of the Circuit Court aforesaid and the seal thereof, hereunto affixed at Indianapolis this February 23rd 1835   Robert B. Duncan

February 23, 1835 – Sheriff Actions

Came to Hand, February 23, 1835

By virtue of the writ, to me directed & delivered, I did on the 24th day of February 1835, take into my custody, the following goods & chattels, part of those within described, delivered the same to the within named plaintiff H & J Nevill. They having first satisfied me, by good and sufficient pledge, to wit, by bond & approved securities as required by law, J^c, being of the value, & description & weights, respectively as follows viz. One bag of coffee 144 lbs., $21.00; one keg of brimstone, 57 lbs., $6.46; three bundles of lead, 34 ½ lbs., $2.25; one bag of shot, 25 lbs., $1.87; and one box of axes, $20.00; the whole thereof of the value of $51.58 cents; Ascribed not found in my county, but (...?...) to parts unknown. Also same day (February 24, 1835), summoned Defendant (Carter) to appear & answer, J^c as within required J^c. So amends Israel Phillips, Sheriff Marion /county, By (...?...) Deputy A.W. Nooe February 24, 1835

Sheriff's fees herein: serving writ 50 cents; mileage 11 ½ miles, 69 cents - $1.10; returning writ, 10 cents – Amt. $1.20
The Sheriff asks the court to make him the following additional allowance for services, J^c in this case, for which there does not appear to be any fee fixed by cause or compensation, viz. 2 Assistants in taking & delivering goods, J^c 1 day each $2.00

March 6, 1835

State of Indiana, Marion County J^s
In the Marion Circuit Court, to March term 1835
Henry Nevill & James Nevill, Merchants, partners in trade under firm of H. & J. Nevill
vs
James Carter - Case for Trover & Conversion, Damages $1,000
Amount of damages proved to by one of Jolffs $650.00
Official bail ordered by a judge in sum of $1,000
Marion County, J^s

John H. Scott, one of the Attorneys for the plaintiffs in the above named suit, being duly sworn by & before me, Wilks Reagin, a Justice of peace of Center township, in said County & at my office therein, on his oath saith, that he is informed & believes that the above named defendant James Carter, who was, at the time of the commencement of said suit, on the 24th day of February last part, a resident of Marion County aforesaid, hath, since that time fled from said county, to avoid the service of process therein, & hath been lurking in Hamilton County in said State & may probably be found either in the County of Hamilton or the County of Madison or the County of Henrich, in said state: And further saith not. Subscribed & sworn to, this 6th March 1835, before me.   John H. Scott
Wilks Reagin, J.P.

A. W. Nooe, Deputy for Israel Jobilliss, Sheriff of Marion County, in the state of Indiana, being duly sworn, on his oath states, that he hath gone four several times, the last of which was the 5th instant to the house & residence of the above named defendant, James Carter, in the county aforesaid with the writ of Capias and respondendum originally issued on the 24th February last in the above case of H. & J. Nevill against said Carter, & for the purpose of executing the same, & came from his said house & residence this morning, but hath not been able, even after diligently searching & watching for him (Carter), with the aid & assistance of others, to take or find him, & that he (this Affiant) hath been credibly informed & verily believes, that said Carter both, knows the issuing & date of said writ, fled from said County of Marion to Hamilton County in said state to avoid the service of said writ, & is now probably lurking in the latter county, for the purpose aforesaid: and further saith not.   A. W. Nooe
Subscribed & sworn to, March 6, 1835 before me, a Justice of said Marion County & at my office therein.   Wilks Reagin J. P

March 6, 1835 - Cover sheet

Marion Cir. Court
H. &. J. Nevill - Affidavit
vs
James Carter
For Capias to adjoining county, Jc.

Issue a Capias, in this within case, directed to the Sheriff of Hamilton County. Merrill & Scott J.q
R. B. Duncan, Esq. clerk Marion Circuit Court March 6, 1835

Filed March 6, 1835 in the Clerk's office of the Marion Circuit Court
Robert B. Duncan clerk
Scott & Merrill Jo.q.

Subpoenas

H & J Nevill – 2 cases of Replevin & Trover

vs

James Carter

       Issue subpoenas on behalf of Jolffs, for the following witnesses to the following counties viz: To the Sheriff of Marion County for Alexander Culbertson, Levin T, McCabe, William West, Charles Allison, William Deford, John West, S.H. Cunningham, John McDowell

       To the Sheriff of Hancock County for Peter J. Newland & Amos Dickerson

       Also make out two commissions of *dedimus potestatem* in each case, to take depositions of witnesses for Jolffs residing without the state of Indiana dictate as follows: one in each case,

       To James Glenn, Justice, Isaiah (Uling?) Justice, Johan Fobes, Justice, or John A. Mocuran, Justice or either of them, or some other Justice of peace or other competent officer of Hamilton County in the state if Ohio, to take the depositions of John W. Ryan, J. McGregor, Keith McGregor, McClellan, York, H.H. Hill, & others, at such time & place in said county as may be specified in the Notices of Jolffs, to defendant touching the same J^c. one in each case & to Levi Osborne, Justice or Benjamin Blackburn, Justice or some other Justice of peace or other competent officer in the state of Ohio to take the deposition of Matthew Minten & others at such time & place as enclosed be specified.

March 11, 1835 - Depositions

The State of Indiana LS

Marion County

       The State of Indiana to Lewis Osborne Justice of the peace, or Benjamin Blackburn Justice of the peace, or some other Justice of the peace or other competent officer of Warren County in the State of Ohio Greetings:

       You or either of you are hereby authorized to take the Deposition of Mathew Minten and others, at such time and place as may be specified in the notice of plaintiffs to Defendant, herein enclosed, touching the matters on controversy in a certain action of Trespass on the case for Trover and Conversion pending in the Marion Circuit Court, of Marion County State of Indiana, wherein Henry Nevill and James Nevill, merchants, partners, trading under the firm of H. & J. Nevill are plaintiffs and James Carter is Defendant; to be read in evidence on the trial of said cause on behalf of said plaintiffs (allowing the said defendant to ask questions on cross examination) and the Depositions by you so taken, you will carefully certify under your hand and seal, adding your costs therein, and the same carefully seal up and transmit to our said Court enclosed with this writ and the notice above mentioned.

       In testimony whereof I Robert B. Duncan Clerk of the Circuit Court of the County aforesaid, hereunto set my hand and office the seal of said Court at Indianapolis this eleventh day of March 1835   Robert B. Duncan

March 25, 1835 – H & J Nevill vs James Carter – Marion County Circuit Court

H & J Nevill

vs

James Carter

James Carter the above named defendant being duly sworn saith that Henry & James Nevill the plaintiffs in a suit in Replevin and one in Trover now pending against him in the Marion Circuit Court, are and each of them is now residents of the State of Illinois as the defendant is informed and verily believes and further saith not.

Sworn to in open Court on March 25, 1835   Robert B. Duncan   clerk

March 1835 - Henry & James Nevill vs. James Carter – 2 Cases – Replevin & Trover

State of Indiana, Marion County, Marion Circuit Court, March term AD 1835

Marion County ss: James Carter, defendant, was sworn moved to answer Henry Nevill & James Nevill, merchants, Partners trading under the firm of H. & J. Nevill, plaintiffs of a plea wherefore he lawfully acquired and unjustly & unlawfully detained, from the said plaintiffs, their goods, chattels, wares, & merchandise, (...?...) sureties & pledges until, J^c: And therefore the said plaintiffs, by Samuel Merrill & John H. Scott their Attorneys, complain for that the said defendant on the 22nd day of February A.D. 1835 at the dwelling house of said defendant in Washington township in Marion County aforesaid, lawfully acquired the personal goods, & chattels, wares & merchandise to wit, one bag of coffee, weighing 144 lbs., one keg of brimstone, of the weight of 57 lbs., three bundles of lead of the weight of 34 ½ lbs., one bag of shot, of the weight of 25 lbs., & one box of axes, that is to say one box containing twelve axes, of them, the said plaintiffs, of great value, to wit, of the value of fifty-one dollars & fifty eight cents lawful money, and unjustly & unlawfully detained the same, from said plaintiffs, against sureties & pledges until J^c. Wherefore the said plaintiffs say that they are injured & have sustained damage to the value of one thousand dollars, therefore they bring their suit. J^c.   Merrill & Scott Jo.q.

March 25, 1835 State of Indiana – Marion Circuit Court – James Carter vs. Henry Nevill & James Nevill - Replevin

James Carter - Replevin

At.

Henry Nevill & James Nevill

And the said Defendant Carter comes & defends the wrong & injury where J^c prays (..?..) of the *scire facias* writ, & affidavit which (...?..) to him in their words (here inset them) & there upon prays judgement of the *scire facias* writ because he says that the *scire facias* writ of replevin herein issued on the 23rd day of February 1835 - discloses & sets forth is a different cause of action & is altogether variant from the Declaration filed in the cause on the 18th day of March 1835 in this to wit – the *scire facias* writ does not allege the tortious taking or the wrongful detention by the defendant, of one Keg of Brimstone of the weight of thirty four & one half pounds and one box of axes; nor are the saws named in *scire facias* writ, nor is the Sheriff commanded by *scire facias* writ, to take said brimstone or axes into his custody & keeping, but that the *scire facias* Declaration sets forth against the said defendant & alleges, that the said defendant having lawfully acquired & did unjustly & unlawfully detained the said Brimstone and axes from the said plaintiffs as will more fully appear from the Writ of replevin and declaration now pending & remaining in the honorable Court, therefore he prays judgement of the *scire facias* writ and that the same may be granted.   James Carter by Morrison & Fletcher

Now Comes James Carter the defendant in the above, entered suit & being duly sworn in open Court upon his oath says that the plea hereto amended is true in substance & fact. Sworn to in open Court on March 25th 1835.   Robert B. Duncan clerk

IV. 1837 – State of Indiana vs James Carter – Dueling

January 19, 1837 - Affidavit

State of Indiana

Marion County

Sc. 1

       Before me Daniel R. Smith A justice of the peace of said County aforesaid this day personally came James C. Kimberlin of lawful age. Who being by me duly sworn saith that on the fourth Day of January in the year 1837 at and in the County of Marion aforesaid James Carter Late of said County Did Challenge him the said James C. Kimberlin to fight a duel with him the said James Carter and then and there intending to instigate and provoke him the said James C. Kimberlin to fight a duel with him the said James Carter and to brake the peace he the said James Carter with force and arms, out of his malice aforethought in the presence and hearing of him the said James C. Kimberlin, and others. Then and there spoke and uttered to him the said James C. Kimberlin these hostile threating and challenging words following that is to say. If you swear that, you will swear a lie, & if you will take rifles, we will decide it, or we will take pistols, and you may load them and we will Decide it, that way, which words he the said James Carter then and there spoke and uttered with the intention to instigate and provoke him the said James C. Kimberlin to fight a Duel with him the said James Carter in order to kill and murder him the said James C. Kimberlin and against the statute in such peace made & provided and further saith Not

James C. Kimberlin his mark

Sworn to & submitted to

Before me this 19th Day of January 1837

Daniel R. Smith

Justice of the Peace   Seal

I certify the above to be a true copy of an affidavit filed before Daniel R. Smith J.P. by James C. Kimberlin

Cover Sheet – March 1837 Term

No. 21

State of Indiana

vs

James Carter

Giving Challenge to fight a duel

A (trice?) Bill

Charles J. Hand

Foreman of the Grand Jury

Filed in Open Court March 27, 1837

R. B. Duncan Clk.

Witnesses

James Kimberlin &

Charles Allison

.... State April 10, 1837

State of Indiana Marion County Marion Circuit Court March Term Eighteen Hundred and thirty Seven

      The Grand jury for the said State of Indiana (..?..) Sworn in the Marion Circuit Court to inquire in and for the body of the same County of Marion where their oath present that James Carter late of said County. Gentlemen on the fourth day of January in the year of our Lord one thousand Eight hundred and thirty seven with force and anus at the County of Marion aforesaid did then and there unlawfully and knowingly verbally challenge one James Kimberlin to fight a duel with him the said James Carter with deadly weapons to wit with pistols.

      Contrary to the form of the Statute in such case made and (..?..) and against the peace and dignity of said State of Indiana.   N. Nicarles for the State

Cover Sheet - Capias

State

vs

James Carter

Capias

To July term 1837

Came to hand April 15th 1837

The Sheriff will take Bail of the defendant with one or more Securities in the sum of three hundred dollars By order of the Court.   April 14th 1837   R.B. Duncan Co. Clerk

State of Indiana, Marion County, Sct.

THE STATE OF INDIANA, TO THE SHERIFF OF MARION COUNTY – Greetings: You are hereby commanded to take James Carter if he may be found in your bailiwick, and him safely keep, so that you have his body before the Judges of the Marion Circuit Court, on the first day of their next term, to be holden at the court house in Indianapolis on the third Monday in July next then and there to answer unto The State of Indiana on an Indictment for Giving Challenge to fight a duel. And have you then there this writ.

Witness, Robert B. Duncan, clerk of said court, and the seal thereof, hereunto affixed, at Indianapolis, the fourteenth day of April 1837

R. B. Duncan

Cover Sheet

State of Indiana

vs

James Carter

Bill of Execution

Filed November 25, 1837

R. B. Duncan clerk

State of Indiana

vs

James Carter

Challenging duel

Be it remembered that on the trial of the above cause this indictment offered to prove the giving of the challenge as charged on the indictment was as follows. Kimberlin named in the Indictment stated on oath that at this time & place named in the indictment the defendant speaking in reference to the meeting which he (...?...) & should state on oath as an untruth in a matter affecting the defendant said. If you swear to that you will swear to a lie – the defendant then invited the said Kimberlin to fight him which being declined as not assented to by Kimberlin the defendant said – If you will take rifles we will decide it or we will take pistols and you may load them & we well decide it that Way, which words the witness imposed were uttered in an angry & threatening manner, and there were all this words proved to have been spoken by this defendant on so force to fighting with this witness. Charles Allison another witness fully corroborated said Kimberlin as to the substance of the words spoken by this defendant as aforesaid. And on the part of the Defendant the following copy of an affidavit made by said Kimberlin against the Defendant, say first Defendant proved by the oath of parties Bow in succession to Smith Justice before whom the (...?...) was made.

And on said trial the defendant moved to instruct the jury as follows to wit 1st That the indictment should contain the language used in jury the supposed challenge whether written or verbal. 2nd That afore the trial the prosecution should prove the giving of the challenge in substance in the form & language used in the indictment or the defendant must be acquitted. 4th That the jury in order to convict the Defendant must believe from the testimony beyond a reasonable Doubt that the defendant unlawfully intended to fight Kimberlin with pistols in deadly combat – and in Determining that intention the jury should take into consideration all the Circumstances of the case, and the Character standing and habits of the defendant – which instructions and each of them separately the Court refused to give, but did instruct the jury that unless the prosecutor has proved the intend of the defendant to Challenge Kimberlin to fight with deadly weapons they ought to acquit the defendant, to which refusal to instruct the jury & to each refusal separately the defendant insists. Be it further remembered that after the reading of said conduct & before judgement rendered thereon the Defendant moved the court to arrest judgement upon said verdict for the insufficiency of said indictment, and also for a new trial because his evidence does not support his indictment & because the court ought to have instructed the jury as requested by the Defendant which motions being considered by the Court are overruled, and to the opinion of the Court in overruling each of said motions this defendant accepts and prays that this his will of exceptions be sealed & made a first of kind (...?...) which is ever daily done.   H. H. Huk   Seal

State of Indiana
vs
James Carter
Challenging to fight
        The defendant asks the Court to instruct the Jury: 1st that the indictment should contain the language used in giving the supposed Challenge whether written or verbal.
        2nd That upon the trial the prosecution should prove the giving of the Challenge in substance in the form and language used in the Indictment or the defendant must be acquitted
        3rd Unless the prosecution has clearly proved the intent of defendant to challenge Kimberlin to fight with deadly weapons – they must acquit
        4th That the Jury in order to convict the defendant must believe from the testimony beyond a reasonable doubt that the defendant feloniously unlawfully intended to fight Kimberlin with pistols in deadly combat – also in determining that intention jury should take into consideration all the circumstances of the case – and the character standing & habits of the defendant

V. 1837 State of Indiana – Marion County – Salathiel Carter vs. Carson Nickers – Replevin

The State of Indiana
Marion County

The State of Indiana to the Coroner of Marion County, Greetings.

Whereas by the affidavit of Salathiel Carter of the County aforesaid, it is shewn among other things therein, that on the eleventh day of July 1837 he was the owner and had been for the term of about one year of one bay Mare six years old also, fifteen hands high, and worth seventy five dollars, and that he was owner of the sucking Colt of said Mare, being a strawberry roan – and being about three months old. That he had said Mare and Colt in his peaceable possession on the said day, and that he is still the legal and equitable owner of said Mare and Colt that on said 11th day of July instant at the County of Marion in aforesaid Washington Township therein, one Carson Nickers with force and arms did tortiously take and unjustly and unlawfully detain, and so continues to detain said Mare and Colt from said Carter.

Therefore you are hereby commanded to take into your custody the said Bay Mare and the Strawberry roan Colt above described, and them safely keep until said Salathiel Carter shall well and truly satisfy you by good and sufficient pledges that he will well and truly prosecute said writ to effect, and return such goods, and chattels, provided a return on the final hearing after cause should be adjudged to said Salathiel Carter by the Marion Circuit Court.

And you are hereby further commanded to summon said Carson Nickers to be and appear before the Judge of the Marion Circuit Court on the first day of the next term to be hold at the Court House in Indianapolis on the Second Monday in November next, then and there to answer unto Salathiel Carter of a plea wherefore he said Nickers on the 11th day of July 1837 did tortiously take with force and arms, and unjustly and unlawfully detain and so continues to detain the Bay Mare worth seventy five dollars and Strawberry roan Colt of said Carter from him said Carter - and herein he may not fail at his peril. Have you then there this writ.
Witness Robert B. Duncan Clerk of said Court and the seal thereof hereunto affixed this July 17, 1837.
                                                                Robert B. Duncan

State of Indiana Marion County Marion Circuit Court July Term 1837

Be it remembered that on the first Judicial day of said Term, personally came into open Court Salathiel Carter, who being by me duly sworn on his oath saith that on the 11th day of July, instant he was the owner, and had been for the term of about one year, of one bay mare six years old, fifteen hands high and worth seventy five dollars, and that he was the owner of the sucking colt of said mare, being a strawberry roan and being about three months old. That he had said mare and colt in his peaceable possession on said day and that he is still the legal and equitable owner of said mare and colt, but that on said 11th day of July instant at the County of Marion Indiana, Washington Township of said County one Carson Vickers, with force and arms did tortiously take and unjustly & unlawfully detain and so continues to detain said mare and colt from said plaintiff Carter. Wherefore he prays that a writ of Replevin may issue according to the form of the statute in such cases made & provided, directed to the coroner of said County. Returnable to the first day of the next Term of said Court.

Sworn to in open Court July 17, 1837.   Robert B Duncan Clerk

Selathiel Carter
Vs.
Carson Nickers
Writ of Replevin
For November Term 1837

Revised the within writ for service July 17, 1838, Executed the within writ as the Law directs July 18, 1837

Mileage	11 miles	$ 0.66
For taking Bond & Delivering Property		$ 0.50
Returning writ		$ 0.10
		$ 1.25 Ahira Wells

Know all men by these presents that we Salathiel Carter and Aaron Gaman are held and firmly bound unto Ahira Wells in the penal sum of two hundred dollars for the payment whereof well and true to be made we find ourselves jointly and (...?.ally) signed, sealed and delivered this 18th July 1837. Now this condition of the above obligation is such that, whereas the said Carter had commenced in the Marion Circuit Court as action Replevin against one Carson Vickers the sheriff of said County for a certain Mare and Colt together worth one hundred dollars, if the said Carter shall well and truly prosecute said action of Replevin to effect, and if said case should be determined against him and a return of said property should be adjudged to said Vickers by the Court, that he will so return the (...?...) there the above obligation to be void, otherwise to be & remain in full force & effect.

Salathiel Carter
Aaron Gaman

State of Indiana, Marion Circuit Court
Marion County SS - November Term eighteen hundred thirty seven

Salathiel Carter plaintiff complained of Carson Vickers defendant, in a plea of Replevin - For that the said defendant heretofore to wit on the eleventh day of July eighteen hundred and thirty seven, in Washington Township of said County, did tortiously take and unjustly and unlawfully detain the personal goods and chattels of said plaintiff, then in his peaceable possession, following to wit one Bay Mare six years old, fifteen hands high, of value of seventy five dollars - one strawberry roan sucking colt of the value of twenty five dollars to the damage of said plaintiff three hundred dollars and hence he sues.   Ketchaw for plaintiff

Said plaintiff further complaining says that on & J^c aforesaid, at & J^c aforesaid, the said defendant having lawfully acquired a certain other bay mare of said plaintiff of the value of seventy five dollars, & a certain other strawberry roan colt of said plaintiff of the value of twenty five dollars, did then and there unjustly and unlawfully detain said mare and colt from said plaintiff to his damage three hundred dollars & hence he sues.   Ketchaw for plaintiff

VI. 1839 – State of Indiana – Arson – Lemuel, Salathiel & James Carter

The State
Vs.
Lemuel Carter & Salatiel Carter
Instruction to jury

Gentlemen of the Jury.

The defendants stand indicted by the Grand Jury of Hamilton County for the crime of Arson, for the burning of a Mill situate in that county, the property of Gilbert Kemp; and the cause comes to this county to be tried on the application of the defendants.

If guilty, the defendants are subject to a fine, not exceeding number the value of the property destroyed, and imprisonment in the State's Prison, at hard labor, for a period not less than two, nor more than ten years.

To convict the defendants it must appear by the evidence that they willfully & maliciously burnt the Mill, and if the jury believe they willfully burnt it, the malice will be inferred.

The case, whether viewed or affecting, as it assuredly does most seriously, the characters and destiny of these defendants, or as affecting the interests of society at large is of great importance, and merits examination by the jury, demands, and will doubtless receive the most careful examination,

The court in this the charge of their peculiar duty, proceeds to give you, as they understand it, a view of the law of evidence so far as it is considered applicable to the case. And in doing so, they have to quote from the law which has been so fully read to you by the counsel on both sides,

Evidence is of two kinds 1st Direct and positive and 2nd presumptive or circumstantiate. It is direct and positive when the facts in dispute are sworn to by those who have had knowledge of them by means of their senses, It is presumptive or circumstantiate, where the evidence is not direct: but where a fact is presumed or inferred from some other facts or circumstances which are known.

The necessity of resorting to presumptive evidence is manifest, It very frequently happens that no direct and positive testimony can be had; and often where such can be had it is necessary to try its accuracy by comparing it with surrounding circumstances.

In criminal cases especially from the secret manner in which guilty actions are generally done it is seldom possible to give direct evidence of the commission of the offense that is, to produce witnesses to saw the guilty deed committed. Hence the necessity of in relying in many cases of acting on presumptions in which must of course be more or less forcible as the circumstances may be stronger or weaker. And the more extensive the view of the jury is of all the minute circumstances of the transaction, the more likely will they be to arrive at a true conclusion,

There has been much said and much written on the comparative excellency and danger of the two kinds of testimony, as if they were antagonist theories in the administration of justice – This is not so. The efficacy and excellency of either mode of proof, (for they are only different modes and not different things) are best tested by the result produced on the mind. It is certain that where positive proof can be had, circumstantial testimony would be but secondary evidence, but they not have as more particularly in civil cases. But in criminal cases, for the reason before suggested circumstantial testimony cannot be viewed in many cases as secondary evidence. Therefore where no nascent doubt exists in either case, comparison is useless,

There is nothing artificial in the rule of law which authorizes arson to circumstantial evidence. The force and reason of the rule are found and acted upon in the commonest transactions of life, in the highest courts and in trials for the bequest exams, The reason & force of the rule is almost intuitively procured by all mankind, and recognized alike by the illiterate and the learned. Presumptions could never have been adopted as the means of proof before a jury, if these nature and force could not be perceived and estimated by men of plain ordinary senses & discretion

This much others (.....?.....) proffers to remark unto you Grant: in regard to the kind of Testimony which has been submitted to you in this important cause. And it is for you exclusively, to consider and censor well and auspiciously, this testimony.

In determining the guilt or innocence of these defendants, the inquiry will very naturally present itself to your mind, as to the motive which could induce the commission of the crime with which they stand charged, for the latent want of are motive, whether of avarice or revenge, or hatred, would afford a strong presumption of innocence and it is because of the admissions of some of testimony given in the cause which was objected to by defendants counsel at the time its introduction; that the court feels bound to explain its legitimacy, and the use which the jury, have a right to make if it.

Several witnesses have testified to the fact of the existence, before the burning of the Mill of a long cherished and bitter feud & mutual hatred between Kemp the owner of the Mill, and James Carter named in the Indictment, the father of these defendants out of which had originated quarrels, & lawsuits; & that at (the time of this hostility and at the time the Mill was burnt, Lemuel Carter, one of the defendants being unmarried resided with his father: and it was stated by other witnesses that Lemuel Carter admitted that on the Day of the burning, he went from his father's house to Noblesville, at and near which place he was seen the same Day, in company with the other defendant Salathiel.

The testimony giving to prove the state of feeling between James Carter and Kemp. Taken in connection with the other facts & circumstances was allowed to go to the jury, for the purpose of enabling of them to determine whether these defendants may not have cherished against Kemp a similar feeling, or may not have been instigated by the father, to perpetuate the crime charged.

Like most of the other Testimony in the case it is a concern and as the admission of this kind of testimony has been so very earnestly objected to, it may not be amiss to say something to the propriety of the reasonableness of its introduction, and properly appeal to your own knowledge of the force of parental authority and of filial affection to say whether it is not in strict accordance with the philosophy of human nature, that the child shows, if not always, yet espouses the quarrels of the parent, at least as far as to share his likes and dislikes, and be imbued at least to some extent with those feelings of hatred & revenge which may be manifested in his sight by a parent, against an enemy, when that child is still under the parental roof, and eats at his board; and believes that his father is suffering grievous wrong at the hand of an enemy. The court in admitting this reason for the testimony alluded to cannot analyze the profanity of this (harms?) but they may try (...?...) of the testimony. Any intention of being understood as nothing the jury that because James Carter & Gilbert Kemp were enemies, that they are bound to believe that these defendants were necessarily or in consequence of that state of feeling, also the enemies of Gilbert Kemp; They only contend to say that the jury are to know that kind of natural inference from these circumstances of relationship & residence, as well as the other connecting circumstances, which they may naturally infer reasonably because those circumstances conduce to prove.

The court with was undertaken to recapitulated the Testimony in this cause. The jury have heard it patently and the arguments of counsel, & their comments on the Testimony. It is deemed only necessary to direct their attention to sound rules of law governing this case, and which may labor the jury the more curiosity to elucidate the main fact; - that is, the guilt or innocence of these defendants.

The goodness of a defendants character in society is a presumption in his favor; but it should never weigh against evidence which is in itself satisfactory of guilt, and ought never to have any weight except in doubtful cases.

If these defendants after they were accused of the crime, made inconsistent and contradictory statements also where they were on the day and night the mill was burnt, it is a circumstance against them.

If they stated falsehoods in regard to the sworn matters; it is a circumstance against them.

If these defendants are being accused stated they were not at or near the mill or in that direction when it was burnt, nor on that day, but were at other places remote and in another direction and had returned to their several homes that evening; at places remote from the burning and if it appears by the testimony that & from their own admission that there must have been persons with whom they were acquainted on their route that day by return they might be proved to have pursued the route designated by them that day and that these members of their several families by whom they might have proved that they were at their homes on the night and at the time the mill was burnt, had they or either of them been so at home, the absence of these witnesses is a circumstance against the defendants.

The production of witnesses to explain suspicious appearances is dictated by the nature of self-preservation - a man is naturally subscribes to explain a circumstance which appears against him. And circumstances which obstinately or in themselves considered would be inconclusive, sequined a conclusive, character and tendency, by the silence of a defendant, or his failure in attempting to explain them.

If after they were traced from Noblesville two miles beyond Kemps mill where they were seen at half past 3 o'clock on the evening the mill was burnt and further traces of them is last mile back and may have shown when they offended went or were that evening and night - it is a circumstance against. If the defendants (...?...) means to prevent detection on the day the mill was burnt, by pretending to go one direction, and actually loitering another, it is a circumstance against them.

These circumstances are merely alluded to – that you may read and review attentively the whole conduct of the defendants as detailed in evidence, so that you consider the moral connexion & coincidences between the circumstances and the hypothesis, and not confine your view to those of a natural or mechanical character only. Those of the latter class, that is, the natural or mechanical kind, consist as has been read to you, in proximity or nearness in point of time or space and all other circumstances which show that the supposed agents had the means and opportunity of doing the particular act, and connect him with it. To apply this rule to the case under consideration, - Is it proved that on the day and evening the mill was burnt, the defendants were near it – in its vicinity? If so, their proximity in point of time & space is established, and the jury will determine from the circumstances detailed whether they had the means and opportunity of doing the act, - In their further inquiries the jury are not limited to the question whether there exists a natural or mechanical link, between the other mechanical connexion and the defendants, so as to connect the defendants with the burning, for if it were necessary to show this by mechanical connexion only, the charge would be imperfect, and the court would be bound to instruct the jury that they ought to acquit. This conclusive would be inescapable if it were necessary to supply the (...?...) link by one of a natural or mechanical kind only. But it must not be overlooked that moral coincidences are often quite as strong & satisfactory as natural ones. The case of the broken pen knife – the pistol, and the patch and the key are all coincidences of the natural kind. The indications which they afforded were objects of sense. They afforded visible means of tracing the act to the agent; - the thing and with the person doing; - and even these indications only afforded probable traceable ground for believing that the persons connected in these cases were really the guilty persons. They can't establish nothing like absolute certainty, for the broken knife affirms the point was found in the cinders might have been picked up in the road; so might the fragment of the letter found in the pocket, as it might have been placed "there" by somebody else, by design, and many persons were pertinent trickers. But they were by jury, and courts trying the causes were satisfied of the guilt of the defendants and they suffered the penalties of the case – as before amended.

Circumstances of a natural kind which are of themselves of an imperfect and inconclusive nature often derive on conclusive testimony from those of a moral kind, as is said in the same book – read by counsel, and which depend upon a knowledge and experience of a man as a natural and moral agent, Experience it is said, ferrets out same laws of human conduct. A truth as general and constant in their oppression as the laws of the natural world themselves. That a man will consult his own preservation and serve his own intuits. The presumption that a man will do that which tends to his obvious advantage, if he possess the means, supplies a most important test for judging of the comparative weight of evidence.

Apply these presumptions to the case in kind. These defendants are indicted for burning Kemp's Mill. Witnesses testify that they were seen near the mill on that day & towards night – having left Noblesville & passed there on return – & next seen on their way up to & beyond the mills. These are natural circumstances or coincidences, but by no means of themselves sufficient to convict – Suspicion from these and other circumstances falls upon the defendants. – They are apprehended & accused – and witnesses swear they made statements as to where they were going that day where they did go as where they stayed that night.

If then they made contradictory & false statements about these matters that falls under the class of moral coincidences against the defendants. And would it cast scorn to be the most natural thing imaginable that the defendants should endeavor to explain away the suspicious appearances & circumstances that are against them. If on the night the Mill was burnt they were at home and there were persons there by whom they might prove the fact why have they not showed it? By that single circumstances they must have (repeated?) all that has been afford to these (pry...?). And if such evidence was within their reach, the omission to produce it is another of these moral coincidences against them the defendants which go to convict the guilty agent whom the act committed. The law lays it down in strongest language such an omission may offer as strong presumptive evidence that the charges is well founded.

Wherever appearances are against an accused person which he regrets or refuses to account for or explain it is a circumstance against him. And the consideration in criminal cases, that it is contrary to every principle of reason and to all experience of human conduct, not to explain such appearances, when it might be done, frequently gives a conclusive character to circumstances which would otherwise be of an imperfect & inconclusive nature.

The rule that "the circumstances should to a moral certainty actually exclude every hypothesis but the one proposed to be proved, is like the one on the subject of the coincidence of circumstances, liable to be misunderstood in its application" - Append to the case, it means, that the facts and circumstances should to a moral certainty, actually exclude every hypothesis but the one that the mill was feloniously burnt. This is what is called the Corpus Delicti and so long as the least doubt remains as to the act, there can be no certainty as to the criminal agent.

The rule that "all the circumstances should be of a conclusive nature and tendency", will be lastly noticed. "Evidence as has been read to you by counsel is always insufficient, where assuming all to be true which the evidence conduces to prove, some other hypothesis may still be true; for it is the actual exclusion of every other hypothesis which invests mere circumstantial evidence, with the force of truth." We cannot suppose that counsel intend you should understand this rule, as requiring you to acquit these defendants, on the mere feasibility that some other hypothesis may be true.

If there is any testimony tending to show that any other person did the act, or that any other person may seem under circumstances calculated to excite suspicion of having done it, so that if by any means the jury are left in doubt whether the one hypothesis or the other be the true one. – or if the evidence leans it in different or uncertain who was the guilty agent, the jury cannot convict.

So too, if it be doubtful whether the mill was burnt by the defendants or from a cigar, or from any other cause – the jury will acquit.

To assume a hypothesis either way would be wrong -

Is there then any probability that the mill was burnt by the cigar or in any other way or by any other persons besides these defendants. If so the defendants must be acquitted. – And the jury will consider well, what other hypothesis seems to agree with the facts and circumstances of this case.

In the language of an authority read to you "what circumstances will amount to proof can never be matter of general definition; The legal test is the sufficiency of the evidence to satisfy the understanding and conscience of the jury. It is sufficient if the circumstances produce moral certainty to the conclusion of every reasonable doubt; even direct & positive testimony does not afford grounds of belief of a higher or superior nature.

The jury must be satisfied from the testimony, whether the evidence be positive or circumstantial, that the mill was burnt feloniously, that is, not by accident, last by some person intentionally, and that these defendants were guilty of the crime. – and if these circumstances detailed in evidence go to point out these defendants as the perpetrators of the crime beyond a reasonable doubt, the jury are bound to convict. – To acquit upon light, trivial and fanciful suppositions and remote conjecture is 'in the language of the authority just quoted' a virtual violation of the juror's oath, and an offense of great magnitude against the interests of society.

VII. 1839 State of Indiana - Marion County – James Carter vs. Gilbert Kemp - Trespass

James Carter Plaintiff complains of Gilbert Kemp Defendant in custody & of a plea of Trespass on the case For that whereas the said plaintiff now is a good true and reputable citizen of the State of Indiana, and as such hath always behaved and conducted himself, and until the time of the committing of the several grievances, by the said defendant hereinafter mentioned, and hath not once been guilty or suspected of having been guilty of felony or any other such crime, by means where of the said plaintiff before his committing of the several grievances hereinafter mentioned had actually obtained the good opinion and credit of all his neighbors. And all others to whom he was any wise known to wit at the County of Marion. Yet the said defendant well knowing the premise, but contriving wickedly and maliciously intending to injure the said plaintiff in his said good name and credits, and to bring him into public infamy scandal and disgrace, and to cause him said plaintiff to be imprisoned for a long space of time, and thereby to impoverish, oppress and wholly ruin the said plaintiff, heretofore to wit on the twenty fourth day of September in the year of our Lord one thousand eight hundred and thirty eight went and appeared before Lepe Wilson Esq. then a Justice of the peace in and for the County of Hamilton in the State of Indiana and then and there before said Justice to wit on the day and year last aforesaid at the County of Hamilton to wit, the County of Marion falsely and maliciously and without any reasonable or probable cause whatsoever. & by his the said defendants affidavit under the oath of said defendant charged the said plaintiff with having on the sixteenth day of September in the year Eighteen hundred and thirty eight, with force and arms, feloniously, willfully, unlawfully and maliciously set fire to and having burnt a certain mill house of the value of four thousand Dollars, of the said Gilbert Kemp, then and there situate in the County of Hamilton and upon such charge he the said defendant falsely and maliciously and without any reasonable or probable cause caused and procured the said Lepe Wilson so hereof (...?...) justice to make and grant him certain warrant under his hand and seal for taking and apprehending the said plaintiff, and for bringing the said plaintiff forthwith before said Lepe Wilson as (...?...) Justice, or some other Justice of the peace and for said County of Hamilton to be dealt with according to law for said supposed offense, and the said defendant under and by virtue of said warrant afterward to wit on the twenty fifth day of September aforesaid at Hamilton County to wit at Marion County wrongfully, unjustly and without any reasonable or probable cause caused and procured the said plaintiff, to be arrested by his body and to be imprisoned and kept and detained in prison for a long space of time to wit for the space of twenty four hours there next following and until he the said defendant afterward to wit on the day and year last aforesaid at the County of Hamilton falsely and maliciously and without any reasonable or probable cause caused and procured the said plaintiff to be carried and conveyed in custody before the said Lepe Wilson so being (...?...) Justice as aforesaid to be examined before the (...?...) Justice touching and concerning the said supposed crime, which said Justice having heard all that the said defendant could say or allege against the said plaintiff touching and concerning the said supposed offense then and there on that day and year aforesaid at Hamilton County to wit of Marion County acquiesced and determined that the said (...?...) plaintiff was not guilty of the said supposed offense & then and there caused the said plaintiff to be discharged out of custody fully acquitted and discharged.

And for that whereas the said Defendant further contriving and maliciously and (...?..) wholly intending as aforesaid heretofore to wit on the 24th day of September in the year 1838 at Hamilton County falsely and maliciously and without any reasonable or probable cause charged the said plaintiff with having committed felony and upon such Court mentioned charges, this the said defendant on the 25th day of September in the year last aforesaid at the Hamilton County to wit at Marion County falsely and maliciously caused and procured the said plaintiff to be arrested by his body and to be imprisoned or the space of twenty four hours, the next following with expiration of which said him the said plaintiff was duly discharged and fully acquitted of the said case mentioned offense at Hamilton County and for that whereof heretofore to wit on the _ Day of April in the year of our Lord 1838 at the April Term of the Hamilton Circuit Court before the Judges thereof he the said defendant falsely and maliciously and without any reasonable or probable cause indicted and caused and procured to be indicted the said plaintiff by the name and description of James Carter late of the County of Hamilton, for this he the said James Carter on the sixteenth day of September in the year of our Lord one thousand and eighteen hundred and thirty eight at Hamilton County with force and arms did unlawfully willfully and maliciously burn a certain mill house of the property of said Gilbert Kemp of the value of one thousand Dollars. Then & there in said County of Hamilton situated contrary to the form of the Statute in such case made and presided and against the peace and dignity of the State of Indiana, which said indictment this Grand Jury of the State of Indiana for the County of Hamilton, to serve for said term of said Court, then and there brought unto the said Courts affidavit by these forenamed a lien bill and the said plaintiff further said that the said defendant afterward falsely and maliciously and without any reasonable or probable cause prosecuted and caused to be prosecuted the said indictment against the said plaintiff until the said plaintiff afterward as the term of said Court aforesaid as the di day of April aforesaid before the Judges of said Court was in due manner and by due course of law acquitted of the said premise in said indictment charged upon him by a Jury of the said County of Hamilton and whereupon it was afterward to wit on the day and year last aforesaid considered and adjudged by the said Court there sitting as the term aforesaid that the said plaintiff should depart thence without day in that behalf and the said plaintiff was and is duly discharged of and from the premise in the said indictment specified as by the (...?...) and proceedings thereof remaining in the said Circuit Court of Hamilton County office. By means whereof the said plaintiff is greatly injured in his said good name and reputation and brought into public scandal infamy and disgrace with and amongst all citizens to whom he was in any wise known, and on another of the personal to wit absence has impacted and do impact who believed and do believe to have been guilty of arson & felony and also the said plaintiff by means these the premises suffered great pain and anxiety of body and mind and hath have forced to lay out and expend large sums of money to wit the sum of three hundred dollars in and about the defending of himself in the proving and the manifestation of his innocence in that behalf and hath been greatly hindered by reason of the premises from following and transacting his lawful and necessary business to wit for the space of four weeks and also by reason of the premise he hath been otherwise greatly injured in his credits and circumstances to wit at Marion County aforesaid. To the Damages of said plaintiff two thousand Dollars.   P. L_____ for plaintiff

Please issue prompt returnable writ in first day this next term.   P. L_____ for plaintiff

171

August 1st 1839.

3rd Day
James Carter
Vs.
Gilbert Kemp
Narr in case
Dam. $2000

This August 2nd 1839
R.B. Duncan Clerk

VIII. State of Indiana – Lemuel & Salathiel Carter – Discharge Forfeiture of Recognizance – Pardon

In the case of the State of Indiana against Lemuel and Salathiel Carter in which the Carters were sentenced to the penitentiary this recognizance given by said defendants was forfeited execution awarded therein, and is now in this (...?...) Sheriff for $500. And costs.

R.B. Duncan Clerk MCC

Cover Sheet
Remission
Issued 20th May 1841

The writ in forfeiture is remitted except five hundred Dollars May 15, 1841
Sam Biggins

Not to issue until the terms specified in the petition are complied with

Errors in the writ in named judgements are remitted this day 20 May 1841.
Philip Liocetes Ally
For Defendants

Whereas at the October Term of the Marion Circuit Court 1839. After the conviction of Lemuel Carter and Salathiel Carter for arson and judgements of this Court against them the said Carters entered into a recognizance to appear at the May Term of the Court in the sum of one thousand Dollars with William Rice and Elijah Brock their securities which recognizance was forfeited and judgement ordered *Fieri facias* has been rendered against said Rice and Brock which judgements have been taken on the Supreme Court on writ of error and is now pending in said Court, which recognizance is for the benefits of Hamilton County Seminary in which County the offense was committed, but trial in Marion County by change of venue. And when by doubts exist by each party as to the validity of said recognizance and five hundred Dollars of the (...?...) can be made of said Carters property. We recommend to the Governor to remit five hundred Dollars of (..?..) recognizance upon condition that the said Lemuel Carter, Salathiel Carter, William Rice and Elijah Brock release all error in the judgement rendered and to be rendered against them and to be rendered against them on said recognizance in the Marion Circuit Court. And request that Judges of the Hamilton Circuit Court, make a dismiss recommendation to the Governor. April 28, 1841   Luel Wylly

We the Judges of the Hamilton Circuit Court concur in the with in reexam and action – proved – the one half to wit $500- be paid as secured to the satisfaction of the Trustee of the County. January 30th AD 1841   J. Morrison
William D. Booker
Thomas A. Emmaus

Judgement against Elijah Brock at November Term for $1000.-
Same against William Rice at same Term.
Judgement against Salathiel Carter for $1000. May Term 1841
Same viz Lemuel Carter at the same Term.

Cover Sheet
Marion County
Petition
To
Governor Whitcomb

For Lemuel & Salathiel Carter

Filed 19th September 1846 Jc
Pardons issued

    To his Excellency James Whitcomb Governor of the State of Indiana:
    We the undersigned very respectfully represent to your Excellency, that at the fall term 1839 there was a judgement rendered in the Marion Circuit Court of Indiana, in the case of the State against Lemuel Carter & Salathiel Carter, that the defendants should each be in prisoned for two years in the State Penitentiary and pay a fine of five dollars & cents in a charge of Arson: That execution of said judgement was respited until the then next term of said Court, and the recognizance taken of the said defendants and their securities severally, on which recognizance judgements have been obtained and the land of the defendants thereby bound: That the evidence on which the defendants was convicted was merely circumstantial: That the undersigned do not consider it right that said defendants should be liable on their said recognizance, & also liable to said judgement first mentioned:
    We, therefore, & for other reasons, pray that said imprisonment in the Penitentiary be remitted, & the defendants as to such injuriousment be pardoned. August 17, 1844
                                           R.B. Duncan
(an additional sixty plus signatures are included below the signature of R. B. Duncan)

    Issue a pardon in favor of Lemuel Carter & Salathiel Carter of the crime of Arson for which they were convicted by a jury on an indictment in the Marion Circuit Court at the fall term thereof in the year 1839, their property having already become liable for a judgement of $500 against them in a recognizance in said case. September 19, 1846
                                         J. W. Whitcomb

Chapter 13 – Images

Bucks County, Pennsylvania Province

An enlarges portion of the Thomas Holmes Map of Bucks County. William Penn's home is labeled the Proprietary's Mannor of Penns berry. Near the top about one inch in from the left edge is a lot labeled 'Widdow Hurst and Chris Taylor'. This is where an earlier researcher has added a star suggesting that this is the lot where John Griffith purchased 290 acres. The Plumly family land is two lots down closer to the Falls on Neshaminy Creek. Wil. Carter's land is near the center of the images just below the land of Hen. Paxton.

Gemimah Nelson name misread by 20th century copyist -
written as Jeremiah using a metal nib pen – Month, Day, Year.

Gemimah Heaton name as it appears on an image of
Henry Nelson Will written with a quill pen.

Middletown Monthly Meeting
Burials of Robert Heaton Jr's first wife and five children
Written with a Quill pen as Day, Month, Year

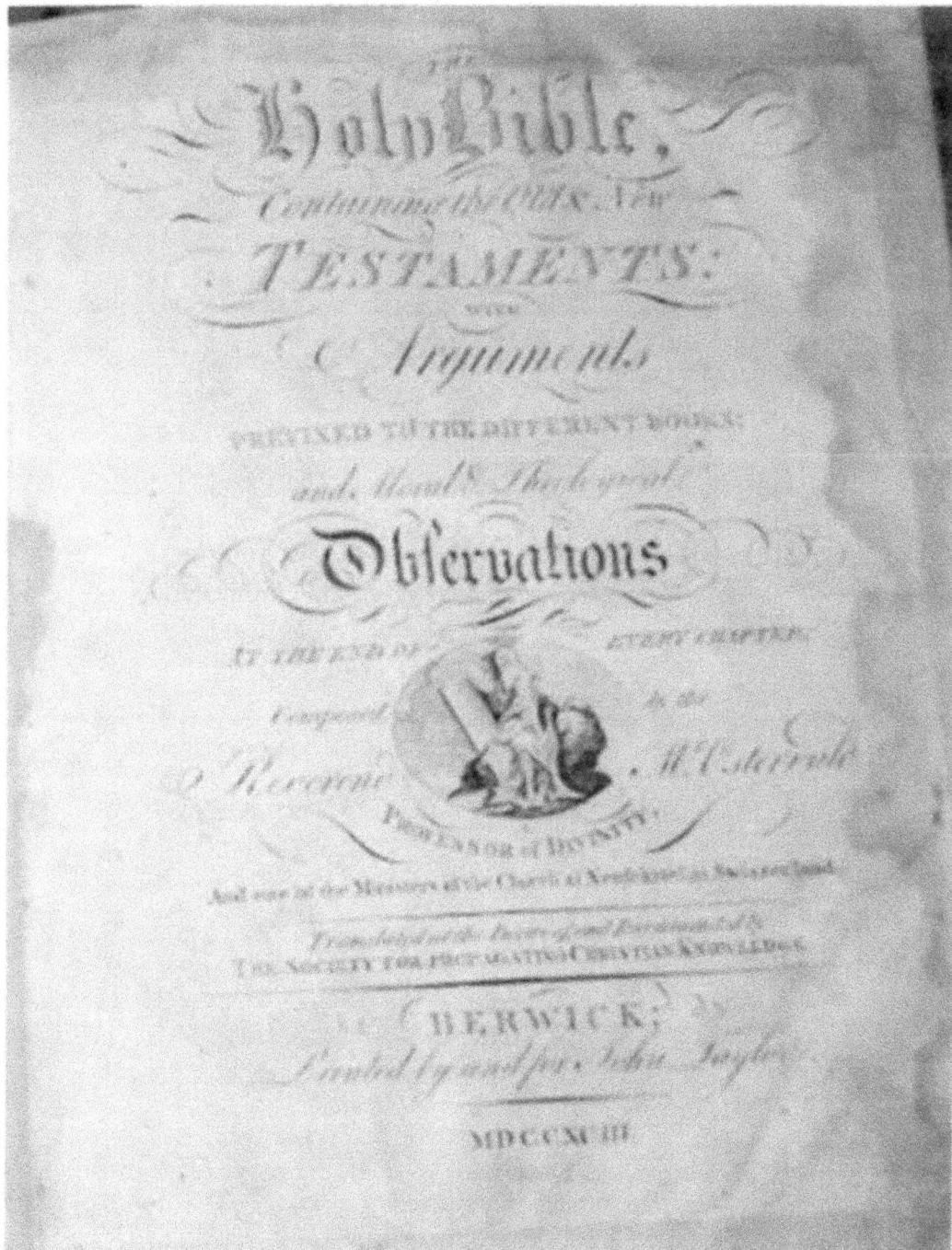

Carter Family Bible

This Bible was given to James Carter 2nd on September 16, 1798.
The Bible contains the names and birthdates of his children,
plus some dates of death.

John Littlejohn – Traveling Methodist Minister
Performed marriage of Asa Carter and Cinthia Parker

Grandsons of Leroy and Mary: Oscar Thomas Carter, James Clarence Ferguson, Walter Columbus Carter and Charlie Marion Carter

Carter / Laxton Memorial Cemetery in Carterville, Missouri

A short distance from the larger and better maintained Carterville Cemetery, the Carter Cemetery has over one hundred fifty grave markers nestled under mature oak and walnut trees. At least thirty of the markers are for Carters, their children and spouses. Many of the limestone markers are no longer legible and several have been broken or toppled. Oak tree roots are one of the destructive forces toppling markers. The grave markers for Mary Means Cooley Carter and James Gilbert Leroy Carter are set to one side surrounded by flat stones. In the center there is a large last name memorial stone which seems to have been a popular feature in the early twentieth century.

Mary Means Cooley Carter   **James Gilbert Leroy Carter**

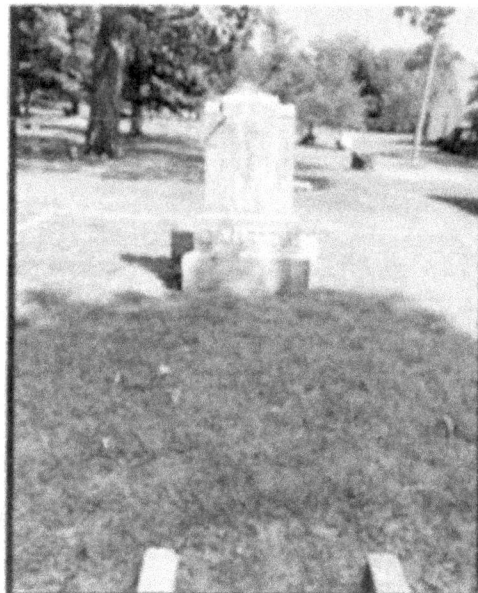

Fasken Cemetery – Carthage, Jasper County, Missouri

Surrounded by fields Fasken Cemetery is out in the country to the north of Carthage. The few small trees provide little shade for the thousand grave markers. After the Civil War this cemetery was were generations of Carters were laid to rest.

Marion Columbus Carter & Elmeda Hester Motley Carter

Charlie Marion Carter – son of Lum & Elmeda is buried next to his mother.

Walter Columbus Carter – son of Lum and Elmeda was buried next to his father.

Oscar Thomas Carter and Ethel Grace Sims Carter – Oscar was the youngest son of Lum and Elmeda. This gravesite is a few feet away from his parents and older brothers.

Forest Park Cemetery Joplin, Jasper County, Missouri

Charles Monroe Carter - Genealogy websites have confused Charles Monroe Carter for Charlie Marion Carter. Two distinctly different individuals.

Billy Sims and Anna Claretta Hoffman Sim

Charles Robert McCandless

"As my last and best Legacy to all of my children, I request that they may carefully suppress any emotions of discontent with respect to the division of my estate and endeavor to live in love and harmony with each other."

James Carter 1812 Will - Loudoun Co., Virginia

Sage words for all of us – we are all part of the family of mankind.

The author sincerely hopes erroneous misleading information has not been included. Researchers make guesses depending on the information they have uncovered. New discoveries can completely change an interpretation of the limited original material. Most original material today is behind pay walls and copies are often blurry and barely legible.

Churning Butter

    This Ole Dinosaur turning a hand crank butter churn at her grandparents dairy farm in rural Jasper County, north of Carthage, Missouri. Grandma knew how to harness toddler energy while keeping the toddler out of mischief. Teaching a work ethic at a young age – slow and steady yields sweet rewards.

www.ingramcontent.com/pod-product-compliance
Lightning Source LLC
Chambersburg PA
CBHW080811280326
41926CB00091B/4307